HARRY WATON

A True
Monistic Philosophy

Comprehending
The Absolute, God, Existence,
Man, Society and History

BY

HARRY WATON

VOLUME ONE

Published by
THE SPINOZA INSTITUTE OF AMERICA

PRINTED IN THE UNITED STATES OF AMERICA
BY J. J. LITTLE & IVES COMPANY, NEW YORK

Contents

Preface

The Spinoza Institute in publishing Mr. Waton's "True Monistic Philosophy" is aware that the province of philosophy today has been so restricted as to make it practically identical with the field of the specific sciences. This absorption of philosophy by the natural sciences has not only impaired the prestige of philosophy by depriving it of any genuine function but has added nothing that science could not furnish itself. The pretensions of science to preempt all domains of existence make the philosophical enterprise wholly superfluous.

The chief assumption of the Monistic Philosophy, as here presented, is the affirmation of an independent rôle for philosophy. True heir of the philosophic tradition, Mr. Waton attaches cardinal importance to the function of philosophy as the clarification of meaning. The basic assumptions of the knowledge of nature and the presuppositions of our thinking are rendered intelligible and meaningful. It is the author's purpose to make us aware of the meaning of such fundamental concepts as: The Absolute, Reason, Cause, Matter, Force, Motion, Space, Time, Freedom, Will, Necessity, Body, Mind, Progress, Society, State, and History. If this work should succeed in making the foundation concepts clear and intelligible, a distinct contribution to philosophic understanding will have been made.

Mr. Waton, however, sees clearly that while the analysis of meaning is crucial for the foundation of philosophy, thinkers must advance beyond clarification to the stage of integrating the fruits of inquiry into a comprehensive theory of man's ultimate position in the cosmic order. Monistic philosophy is concerned, therefore, with the interrelationships existing among the categories involving The Absolute, God, Nature, Man, Society, and History. Can these diverse aspects of existence be comprehended and reconciled as a unified whole by a monistic formulation? The solution of this problem touches on the very validity of a monistic philosophy.

Monism is concerned also with methodology. In presenting the correlative categories the author seeks to find a third element that both reconciles and integrates opposite elements of existence. In dealing with specific correlatives, the influence of the Hegelian dialectics is evident.

Monistic philosophy as presented by Mr. Waton is vitally concerned with process rather than with the mere organization of external elements. All reality is seen as process; creation as a divine process; nature as a process of entropy; man as a process in evolution; and society as a process of historic transformations.

Monistic philosophy is characterized by still another aspect. When we investigate existence scientifically we examine events as the outer structure of reality. It is the essence of history to grasp the inward process. A Monistic philosophy, therefore, reaches its culmination when regarded as an interpretation of the historic process. History becomes the crucial test of a monistic philosophy, not only in the sense that history supplies the evidence for the confirmation of the metaphysical implications of monism but in the sense that that nature of man and society take on meaning only in the context of an historic process.

The value of the monistic philosophy is of transcendent significance at this critical historic period. We live in an epoch in which the social foundations of society have been profoundly shaken. The overwhelming experience of two world wars is symptomatic of a deep seated tension in the very soul of society. A further probing into the crisis of our age reveals the presence of polarities that demand reconciliation and integration. Consider the pressing problems: How can the interests of the State and the Individual be harmonized? How can a planned economy reconcile initiative and democracy with the requirements of social life? How can freedom and order be integrated to make for a more abundant life? What is crucial for us is not the existence of the alternatives but the discordance arising from a failure to synthesize the polarities of our dilemma. Human progress consists in the synthesizing of opposites.

The recognition of opposites as different aspect of the divine nature of the world and that their harmonization is the task of philosophy and history were first perceived at the dawn of philosophy. Heraclitus wrote in his fragments: "God is day and night, winter and summer, war and peace, surfeit and hunger but he takes various shapes." (fragment 36) and "Men do not know how what is at variance agrees with itself. It is an attunement of opposite tensions like that of the bow and the lyre". (fragment 45) Where correlatives are united through the attunement of opposites, the tensions arising from the unresolved conflict disappear.

This philosophic insight has received current recognition in Toynbee's formulation of history in terms of a response to a challenge arising from within or without a civilization. Until a challenge is answered successfully, society is torn by tensions, a condition which Hegel has aptly described as the "unhappy consciousness."

No one has described this process with greater insight than has Hegel: "The unhappy consciousness divided and at variance with itself, must, because this contradiction of its essential nature is felt to be a single consciousness, always have in the one consciousness the other also and this must be straightway driven out of each in turn, when it thinks it has therein attained to victory and rest in unity. . . . It is itself the gazing of one self-consciousness into another and itself in both. . . . Here then there is a struggle against an enemy. . . . Consciousness of life, of its own existence and action is merely pain and sorrow over this existence and activity." (Phenomenology of Mind Vol. 1 Pages 200-219)

The solution to the present state of insecurity and disunity can be achieved, in the first instance, by a clarification of a philosophy of life and existence, a philosophy which not only comprehends the correlatives of existence but effects their unity, and secondly, by a recognition of the nature and destiny of history.

Since the inception of history guiding ideals have exerted a powerful influence in man's spiritual progress; we need mention only the resolutions to establish the ideal of the unity of mankind through a universal government under the reign of law; and the determination to submit to rational control in the ordering of social life. Are these ideals constitutive ideas in the order of existence such that history is bringing them ever nearer to a state of realization? The monistic philosophy seeks to establish the unity of the ideal and the real and to demonstrate the identity of the theoretical formulation in philosophy with the pattern of history. The object of philosophy is to bridge the gap between the insight of our reason and the objective process of history.

Modern science, too, possesses a guiding principle—a belief in the rationality of nature. Science is based on the belief that the constitution of existence will some day be comprehended in its logical simplicity and be confirmed by observation. In an illuminating passage Albert Einstein wrote: "Our experience up to date justifies us in feeling sure that in nature is actualized the idea of mathematical simplicity. It is my contention that pure mathematical construction enables us to discover the concepts and the laws governing them, which gives us the key to the understanding of the phenomena of nature. Experience, can of course, guide us in our choice of serviceable mathematical concepts. It cannot possibly be the source from which they can be derived. . . . In a certain sense, therefore, I hold it to be true that pure thought is competent to comprehend the real as the ancients dreamed." (quoted by Philipp Frank; Einstein, His Life and Times, Page 282)

A striking example of the fruitfulness of a monistic approach is found in the scientific problem dealing with subatomic phenomena. Scientists have been baffled by the strange behavior of an electron. It appears that light, for example, behaves both as a particle and as a wave. This apparent contradiction defied a monistic understanding of the nature of light. Today the complementary nature of light is clearly understood; it depends on the arrangement of the apparatus whether light is to be described as a wave or a particle. The nature of the phenomenon may best be expressed by paraphrasing the language of the author, "Both wave and particle are correlatives; they imply each other. Neither can be conceived without the other, and neither can exist without the other."

Philosophic tradition stemming from the Platonic dualism of Episteme and Doxa perpetuated the sharp separation between rational knowledge and empirical knowledge. Christian tradition extolled the former and deprecated the latter. Modern philosophers ascribe to rational knowledge absolute certainty, although a knowledge that can make no statement about experience, and accord to empiric knowledge the status only of "merely probable" knowledge. It is the task of a monistic philosophy to destroy this dualism; that while monism recognizes that both types of knowledge are distinguishable they are not separable; that both involve and stem from the same source; and that both yield insight into the ultimate nature of existence. A monistic formulation rejects the primacy of the one over the other aspect. There is an equality of status and an essential unity in the rational and the empirical. The monistic viewpoint suggests fruitful possibilities in effecting a reconciliation between Reason and Revelation, Science and Philosophy, and the Real and the Ideal.

The monistic philosophy shares with Spinoza the belief in an intelligible universe because the divine cause communicates its intelligibility to existence; that the human mind is a part of that order and is therefore capable of grasping the fundamental rational nature of existence; that the attributes thought and extension are mutually inseparable, implying each other, and each in its own nature revealing the essential structure of the totality of existence. Monism, moreover, has its metaphysical roots in the Kabbalah where basic categories and such as God, Substance, Destiny are clarified. This aspect has been treated in a former work. On its ethical side there is much in common with the Kantian formulation of the principle of moral autonomy—which for Kant remained a purely subjective norm. The state of moral autonomy becomes in the hands of the author an objective historical category. Finally, monism is deeply influenced by the dialectics as formulated by Hegel. The author accepts the Hegelian description of dialectics as a process in which reality is transformed in a way to conform with a divine purpose. In short, the philosophy of monism has roots in the philosophic speculations of the great intellectual masters and utilizes their contributions in a way that would make philosophy both relevant and adequate to the problems of today. Only in this way can philosophy provide a dependable guide for a perplexed and disillusioned age.

Modern positivist philosophy substitutes the instrumental value of reason for its autonomy; denying the competence of reason to make assertions as to the ultimate nature of existence. Positivism substitutes the logic of probability for that of truth. The monistic philosophy rejects this negativistic and arbitrary emasculation of reason. On the other hand, monism as against idealism, accepts the claim of empiricism in the postulate that there is immediate knowledge of sensuous phenomena. There are, therefore, truths of reason no less than truths of fact. Reason and experience are the two-fold source of the divine manifestation of the nature of things—two aspects of one essential unity. If the two-fold source of the knowledge of reality is severed, there results the impasse previously described as the "unhappy consciousness."

Dualistic thinking like fetishes generally hold a great fascination for mankind. The prospect for thinkers altering their frame of reference even under the compelling tensions of their time is not reassuring. The history of the decay and annihilation of past civilization is a dramatic witness to the failure of intellectual and spiritual readjustment. Will this book change the course or the direction of history or thought? We entertain no such optimism. What is true of a great book is true of any pioneer in a new aspect of thought. One accepts from a seminal thinker the thoughts that have been quietly groping for clarification in one's mind.

The noted historian of political thought, J. W. Allen, expressed this profound and pertinent observation: "Yet it remains true, that in general, a man finds in a book what consciously or unconsciously he is looking for. He accepts its teaching so far as it fits with or clarifies his own thoughts or experience, his own secret tendency or desire. He rejects it so far as it does not conform. A writer may of course, do much to clarify and define the thoughts of others, he may bring order into what was chaotic and give the formless form . . . He may show a man clearly what he wanted to see and could not see unaided. . . ." (J. W. Allen, A History of Political Thought in the Sixteenth Century. Page 489)

I. H. Muraskin

Brooklyn, N. Y.
June, 1947

Introduction

1. An idea is the essence of reality. The destiny of an idea is to realize itself in material form. An idea is true if it can realize itself in material form. A square-circle is a false idea, because it cannot realize itself in material form. Truth is the perception of the correspondence between an idea and its material form. What is true of an idea is true of a system of ideas. A science, a religion or a philosophy is true, if it can realize itself in material form; otherwise, it is an illusion. Likewise, an idea is true if it can realize itself in material form; otherwise, it is a utopia. All this is so because the destiny of existence is to realize itself in material form.

Knowledge implies understanding, they are correlatives; without knowledge there can be no understanding, and without understanding there can be no knowledge. Knowledge without understanding is blind, understanding with knowledge is empty. Since the destiny of an idea is to realize itself in material form, all knowledge must be useful in the material world. Knowledge which is not useful is not worth the effort to acquire it.

The monistic philosophy which is here presented comprehends a knowledge and understanding of the Absolute, God, Existence, Man, Society and History. Unlike other systems of philosophy, which start in the middle of the story and end in the middle of the story, the monistic philosophy starts with the absolute beginning and ends with the absolute beginning. At the outset, the question must be answered: What useful purpose in life can the monistic philosophy serve? An adequate answer to this question can be given only by the monistic philosophy itself. One must first know and understand the monistic philosophy to perceive its usefulness. Nevertheless, some idea of its usefulness can be given at the outset.

2. Existence in all its infinite parts and aspects is absolutely one and indivisible. All realities and processes in existence are organically interconnected, interrelated and interdependent. We are part of existence. To exist and to satisfy the requirements of life, we must conform with the nature of things and the order of existence. This implies a knowledge and understanding of the nature of things and of the order of existence. In proportion as mankind acquired such knowledge and understanding, in that proportion they made progress. Whatever man does, he does to realize some purpose or aim. But the supreme aim of all human endeavors is happiness. All other states of gratification and well-being are limited in scope and duration, but happiness is unlimited in scope and duration. And, while science, art and industry can satisfy the limited and immediate requirements of life, only philosophy can satisfy the supreme aim of human endeavors.

Philosophy does not determine life, it is life that determines philosophy. We do not live according to philosophy, but we philosophize according to the life that is in us. One whose life does not transcend the immediate and limited needs—he does not need a philosophy; but one whose life reaches out beyond the immediate and the limited needs—he needs a philosophy, and his life will endeavor to acquire a philosophy of existence. But to realize the supreme aim in life mere philosophy is not enough, it must be a monistic philosophy comprehending all of existence in all of its infinite aspects. Thus one can at once decide whether this book will serve him a useful purpose or not.

3. Spencer defines life as a continuous adjustment of inner relations to outer relations. Living beings, if they are to exist, must adjust themselves to the outer conditions of existence, which conditions are of a material nature and form. A failure of such

adjustment is inevitably punished with death. This law is infinite and eternal and admits of no exceptions; it operated from the beginning of time, and it will operate to the end of time. This is true of the smallest as well as of the largest being, it is true of the lowest as well as of the highest form of life, it is true of the individual, of the species, of the race and of all orders of life.

If the conditions of existence were of a fixed and permanent nature, given once for all time, then the task for life would be simple and comparatively easy; all that life would have to do would be to adjust itself to the fixed and permanent conditions of existence. But the conditions of existence are not of a fixed and permanent nature, they perpetually change. Change is the eternal and infinite order of existence. Hence, living beings must perpetually readjust themselves to the ever-changing conditions of existence. This adjustment to the ever-changing conditions of existence is not a mere mechanical process; life is not a mere reflex of the conditions of existence. Life must actively adjust itself to the ever-changing conditions of existence. But even this is not enough. Life must anticipate the coming changes in the conditions of existence and beforehand prepare itself to meet the coming changes.

Insects, in anticipation of the coming changes in themselves and in the conditions of existence, deposit their eggs at such places in which, during the coming spring, their offspring may hatch out and find the means of their immediate subsistence. Some insects, like bees, in anticipation of the coming winter, store up food for themselves during the summer. Birds, in anticipation of the coming summer, migrate from the south to the north; and, in anticipation of the coming winter, return to the south. In anticipation of the coming generation, the birds mate themselves and build nests. And so it is in varying degrees and manners with all living beings. The degree of intelligence of any living being is proportionate to its capacity to anticipate the future changes in the conditions of existence.

But even this is not enough. The adjustment to the ever-changing conditions of existence could not bring out higher forms of life. That life may continue to advance from lower forms to higher forms, it must transcend the forms of life already brought out, and must create the conditions of existence fit for the higher form of life. This is especially true of man. Man is destined to rise higher and even higher. Man must not only adjust himself to the ever-changing conditions of existence, he must not only anticipate the future changes in the conditions of existence, he must also create the conditions of existence fit for his higher state of development. For this purpose man was endowed with reason. Reason distinguishes man from all other living beings and realities. Reason raises man above the animals and realities, it emancipates him from the necessity of nature, and makes him to become the master over nature. Reason makes of man a being that looks before and after. In proportion as man attains to reason, in that proportion does he concern himself about the past and the future. It is then that man becomes conscious of history. He then perceives that history is a process, like all other processes in existence, which is independent of the will and consciousness of man. He then perceives that, not men make history, but history that makes men. And then he endeavors to conform with the process of history as he endeavors to conform with all other processes of existence.

4. But men who have not yet attained to reason naively believe that they can make history as they please. They plan, scheme and plot to realize petty aims and vain ambitions, and they endeavor to determine the course of history. In their ignorance, they believe that they can make their history as they please. And, when by destiny they are placed in a position of power, they imagine themselves to be supermen who, with impunity, can disregard reason, defy justice and trample upon morality and humanity. But there is a logic of events, there is a causal relation between conduct and consequence, and, above all, there is a historic destiny which overrides and overrules all plans, schemes and plots of men. What Nebuchadnezzar, what Alexander, what Caesar, what Genghis-Khan, what Napoleon, what Mussolini,

and what Hitler ever realized his aims and ambitions? And what was true of rulers, conquerors and leaders was true of ordinary men. Hegel said: the study of history convinced him that men never learn from history. They do not learn from history, because they do not understand history. Men study history, not for the purpose of finding out the nature, course and destiny of history, so that they may be able to conform with the requirements of history; but they study history to find out how they can cheat history, how they can evade the consequences of their evil and insane deeds, how they can save themselves from the fate that befell others like themselves. Men are like children. Children know that sickness, misfortune and death are the common lot of men; yet children believe that they will never be sick, they will never suffer misfortune, and they will never die. In days of prosperity, men believe that they can make history as they please; but in days of adversity, they blame history; worse still, they deny that there is history. And so it came to pass that until now history was but a record of frustrated aims, ruined ambitions and bitter disappointments. And thus races, nations, peoples, states and empires, after a brief existence, perished and were forgotten. Chronos swallowed its children. Chronos—that is unhistoric time, it was the time when men were not yet conscious of history.

5. What, then, is history? History is a process of human existence that realizes the predetermined destiny of mankind. This destiny was determined by God. Mankind are destined to become rational and morally autonomous, to become united in one human society resting on universal communism, and realize the kingdom of God on earth. The kingdom of God on earth—this is happiness. Mankind are destined to attain to happiness. So long as men are ignorant of the nature, course and destiny of history, history presents itself to them as a process that frustrates their aims, ruins their ambitions and brings them bitter disappointments. But in proportion as men acquire a knowledge and understanding of the nature, course and destiny of history,

in that proportion they conform with the requirements of history, and in that proportion they realize their aims and purposes, because then their aims and purposes conform with the requirements of history. Man must not only conform with the requirements of the conditions of existence, he must also conform with the requirements of history. For this purpose man must know and understand existence and history. This knowledge and understanding are the very essence of the monistic philosophy. Thus the monistic philosophy is essential and most useful in life.

6. Finally, the question presents itself: Can men attain to a monistic philosophy of existence and of history? Many thinkers tried to prove that this is impossible. If these thinkers had learned from past experience, they would not be so certain; for experience abounds in cases in which thinkers declared that certain things were impossible, which in the end proved to be possible. If these thinkers had been modest, they would say that for them a monistic philosophy was impossible, but they would not assert that for mankind it will forever be impossible. Now, whether a monistic philosophy is possible, the monistic philosophy here presented must prove. Whether this monistic philosophy will justify itself, this is for the readers to judge. But this much I can assure at the outset that, if the reader of this book will duly reflect on what it presents, he will learn much about existence and history, and this will be ample compensation for the time and effort that will cost him to read this book.

CHAPTER I

What Is the Monistic Philosophy?

7. Spinoza states as an axiom: Man thinks. The realities and processes in existence present themselves to man, not only as objects for perception, but also objects for thought. By means of the senses man perceives the realities and the processes in existence, and by means of the understanding he thinks of them. The understanding reveals to him that all realities in existence are related to one another. Relation implies an identity, and identity implies unity. The realities and processes in existence appear to the senses to be distinct from one another, but the understanding perceives that, in essence, they are all one. All infinite realities are carved out of one infinite and eternal substance, and all processes in existence are the manifestations of one cause. It is with the human mind as it is with existence. Just as existence manifests itself in infinite realities and processes, so the human mind manifests itself in many faculties that perform distinct functions. But, though the faculties appear to be distinct from one another, yet they are all one mind. Between existence and the human mind there is an identity, because the human mind is part of existence. The oneness of the human mind perceives the oneness of existence and the identity of itself with existence. The perception of the identity of the human mind with existence is the essence of the monistic philosophy. The monistic philosophy is inherent in existence and in the human mind. When the human mind perceived this identity, then the monistic philosophy was born. The monistic philosophy grew and developed as the human mind grew and developed. In due time mighty thinkers came to the fore and crystallized systems of philosophy. Great were their achievements, but thus far

they did not succeed to crystallize a true monistic philosophy. The task before them was very great, and therefore they could not adequately complete it. But we, who are standing on the shoulders of these mighty thinkers, and who are helped by what they had achieved, we are able to complete the task they left incomplete. A great responsibility rests on us, but we assume this responsibility in the confidence that we will justify ourselves.

8. The monistic philosophy starts out with the following postulate: Existence in all its infinite and eternal attributes, aspects, modes, extent, duration, essence, method, plan and destiny—is absolutely one and indivisible, and is in perfect harmony with itself. This postulate is the soul of the monistic philosophy. Every system of thought centers around one idea, which is the soul of the system of thought. To understand a system of thought, we must know and understand the soul of the system of thought; but, in turn, to understand the soul of the system of thought, we must know and understand the system as a whole. A monistic philosophy which comprehends all existence implies a knowledge and understanding of the Absolute, God, existence, man, society and history. Thus the starting point of the monistic philosophy will be the goal to be attained.

Koheleth tells us: What was will be, and what was done will be done; there is nothing new under the sun. Is there a thing whereof it may be said: see, this is new? It was already in the ages which were before us. Yes, there is nothing new under the sun, there is nothing new in existence. Substance, force, matter, light, life, thought, and so on—all were from eternity, and eternally and infinitely remained the same; they never change, and they never become something new, something which did not exist before. And yet, everything in existence perpetually changes and becomes something new, something which did not exist before. Thus existence reveals itself in two aspects; on the one hand, existence eternally and infinitely is and remains the same; on the other hand, existence eternally and infinitely changes and becomes something new. Existence is both old and new. The old and the new are correlatives, they imply each other; neither can exist without the other. Change implies something which is permanent, for only that which is permanent can change; that which is not permanent does not change. Something cannot arise out of nothing and cannot disappear into nothing. The new can arise only out of the old, out of that which already existed. On the other hand, something can become old only by becoming something new. That which does not become something new does not become old. A triangle does not become something new. Eternally and infinitely the triangle is and remains the same. Therefore it does not become old. Thus existence eternally and infinitely is and remains the same—yet, on the other hand, it eternally and infinitely becomes something new. The new is implicit in the old, and the old becomes explicit in the new; the new arises out of the old, and the old realizes itself in the new. What is true of existence universally is true of knowledge and understanding, and is true of the monistic philosophy. The monistic philosophy is both old and new; it was implicit in all systems of thought crystallized by the human mind; and all these systems of thought become explicit in the monistic philosophy. There is nothing new in the monistic philosophy, yet it is altogether new. What one would have to gather from numerous systems of thought—ancient and modern—he will find it in the monistic philosophy.

SCIENCE AND THE MONISTIC PHILOSOPHY

9. Marx tells us: Unlike other builders, science not only erects castles in the air, but constructs separate stories of the building before it has laid the foundation. Science erects castles in the air and constructs separate stories of the building before it has laid the foundation, because science cannot lay the foundation. And, while science builds the separate stories of the building, it cannot complete it. Science deals with time, space, matter, force, light, gravitation, life, thought, and so on. Out of these elements

science constructs a wonderful building, and yet science does not understand the elements out of which it constructs the building. What is time, what is space, what are force, matter, light, gravitation, life, thought, and so on? Science neither knows nor understands; therefore science cannot construct the foundation of the building. Thus, like Einstein's iron chest in his Relativity, the building of science hangs in an absolute vacuum. This is the reason why science begins in the middle of the story and ends in the middle of the story.

What is science? Science is knowledge resting on demonstrated truths. These truths are demonstrated by counting, weighing, measuring and testing. Science concerns itself about realities which can be perceived by the senses, and which can be counted, weighed, measured and tested. But these realities are not the only realities in existence; there are other realities in existence which cannot be perceived by the senses, and which cannot be counted, weighed, measured and tested. Again, counting, weighing, measuring and testing are not the only methods for ascertaining truths; there are other methods for ascertaining truths. Existence presents itself in two aspects: a transcendental aspect and a phenomenal aspect, a transcendental world and a phenomenal world. The phenomenal world consists of realities which can be perceived by the senses, and which can be counted, weighed, measured and tested. The transcendental world consists of realities which cannot be perceived by the senses, and which cannot be counted, weighed, measured and tested. The phenomenal world is not an original world, and it is not an independent world; it is only a material manifestation and realization of the transcendental world.

Science comprehends the phenomenal world, its realities and its truths; but science cannot comprehend the transcendental world, its realities and its truths. All realities are carved out of one infinite and eternal substance, but science cannot comprehend substance. Science can comprehend the manifestations of matter, but science cannot comprehend matter itself. What is matter? Science cannot tell. Light, heat, gravitation, electricity, and the like, are manifestations of force. Science can comprehend the manifestations of force, but it cannot comprehend force itself. What is force? Science cannot tell. All living beings are manifestations of life. Science can comprehend the manifestations of life, but it cannot comprehend life itself. What is life? Science cannot tell. Science can comprehend the manifestations of the mind, such as perceptions, concepts, ideas, and the like; but science cannot comprehend the mind itself. What is the mind? Science cannot tell. All desires, feelings, emotions, aspirations and aims are manifestations of the soul. Science can comprehend the manifestations of the soul, but it cannot comprehend the soul itself. What is the soul? Science cannot tell. Finally, all realities and processes in existence are manifestations of one absolute, infinite and eternal cause. Science can comprehend the realities and processes of existence, but it cannot comprehend the cause of the realities and processes.

Thus we see that science cannot build the foundation; it must therefore begin in the middle of the story and end in the middle of the story. Only the monistic philosophy comprehends both the transcendental and the phenomenal world, the transcendental and the phenomenal realities and processes, and the transcendental and the phenomenal truths. Science is knowledge resting on truths demonstrated by counting, weighing, measuring and testing; but the monistic philosophy rests on truths of both natures; truths which can be demonstrated by counting, weighing, measuring and testing, and truths which are directly perceived by the mind. Spinoza tells us: Truth is its own index, and, like light, makes itself manifest. A truth directly perceived by the human mind is self-evident and infinitely more certain than a truth perceived by the senses and demonstrated by counting, weighing, measuring and testing. The monistic philosophy comprehends existence in all its infinite and eternal aspects; it comprehends a knowledge and understanding of the Absolute, God, Existence, Man, Society and History.

WHERE TO BEGIN?

10. George Eliot tells us: "Man can do nothing without the make-believe of a beginning, and yet no retrospect will take us to the true beginning; and whether our prologue be in heaven or on earth, it is but a fraction of that all presupposing fact with which our story starts." Indeed, no retrospect can take us to the true beginning, because in an eternal and infinite existence there is no beginning. But man must begin somewhere. The point where man begins he regards as the beginning. And so every system of thought crystallized by the human mind starts out with some beginning. The Bible starts out with the statement: In the beginning Elohim created the heaven and the earth. The Kabbalah begins with the Ain-Sof—the absolute, infinite and eternal. St. John tells us: In the beginning was the word. Spinoza begins with the Cause of Itself. Hegel starts out with Being. Spencer starts out with the Unknowable. And so all systems of thought start with some beginning. Now, whether all these beginnings were the true beginnings in existence or not, this is certain, namely, they were not the beginnings for men; for men they were rather the ends, and not the beginnings. Men had to live a long time and acquire sufficient knowledge and understanding to be able to reflect on the beginning of creation, on the Ain-Sof, on the Word, on the Cause of Itself, on Being or on the Unknowable. And even to this day, very few thinkers reached these beginnings: to most men these beginnings never presented themselves for reflection or consideration. The beginning for men was knowledge; man was born with the birth of knowledge. Before man attained some knowledge, he was but an animal. Hence man's starting-point was knowledge. For this reason, the monistic philosophy begins with knowledge.

WHAT IS KNOWLEDGE?

11. Knowledge, which implies understanding, is the comprehension of cause and effect. The perception of cause alone or

effect alone is not knowledge. Knowledge originates in a problem, and the solution of the problem is knowledge. If no problem presented itself to the human mind, man would acquire no knowledge. Existence presents itself to the human mind as an ultimate problem, which is in infinite proximate problems. Inherent in life is the consciousness that whatever takes place or exists was determined to take place or to exist by some cause. Without this consciousness, living beings could not exist. All realities and processes in existence present themselves to the human mind as effects of some causes. Man sees the effects, but he does not see the causes of the effects. When something affects man, consciously or unconsciously the question presents itself to him: what was the cause of this effect? Thus the proximate problem that presents itself to man is: what was the cause of this effect or that effect? The ultimate problem which presents itself to the developed mind is, what is cause itself? A problem implies its solution; they are correlatives, there can be no problem without a solution, and there can be no solution without a problem. The problem is: what was the cause of a given effect? The cause already exists or existed, and because of it we have the effect. When the cause of the effect is discovered, then we know and understand both the cause and the effect. Thus knowledge is born. Knowledge, then, is the comprehension of cause and effect. This is the essence and basis of all knowledge. When we analyze all kinds of knowledge, we perceive that, in essence, they are the comprehension of cause and effect. Even the knowledge which we derive from our endeavors to realize any purpose or aim and to satisfy the requirements of life, even this knowledge is a comprehension of cause and effect. To realize any purpose or aim, we must conform with the nature of things and the order of existence. We act upon the external realities, and through their reactions we realize our purposes or aims. Between our actions and the reactions of the external realities there is a relation of cause and effect. Through our actions and reactions of the external realities we acquire a knowledge of cause and effect. The effect manifests itself to the senses, but the cause remains hidden behind the effect. The effect raises the question: what is the cause of the effect? Through the manifested effect the mind endeavors to discover the cause, and when the mind discovers the cause it perceives the relation between the cause and the effect. If the perception of the cause corresponds with the effect, then the mind acquires a true idea. A true idea is the perception of the correspondence between the cause and its effect, and this true idea constitutes knowledge. Knowledge, then, is the comprehension of cause and effect.

When the human mind comprehends cause and effect, it is satisfied, and for a time the mind rests. But a problem begets another problem. The first problem was: what was the cause of the given effect? This problem was solved. But now the cause itself raises the problem: what was the cause of the cause itself? When the human mind examines the cause just discovered, it perceives that this cause was itself only the effect of a prior cause. Since the cause just discovered was itself but an effect of some prior hidden cause, it was not the cause of the given effect; and, since it was not the cause of the given effect, the original problem arises: what was the cause of the given effect? And thus the problem was not solved and no knowledge was acquired. The human mind is now where it was in the beginning. Hence the human mind starts out again to discover the cause of the given effect. When the human mind discovers the hidden cause, it turns out, upon examination, to be only the effect of some other hidden cause. And so for thousands of years the human mind was searching for a true cause. In the course of time, the human mind discovered infinite causes which, upon examination, turned out to be only effects of some hidden cause. At last, the human mind reached the first cause, and there it stopped, because beyond the first cause no other cause is conceivable. Then the human mind endeavored to comprehend the first cause. For thousands of years the profoundest thinkers endeavored to comprehend the first cause, but they failed. In the end, they reached the conclusion that the first cause is and forever will remain to the human mind unknowable. In the meantime, the human mind constructed many systems of thought—religious, metaphysical, philosophic and scientific. Upon examination, all systems of thought rest upon an Unknowable. All systems of thought begin in the middle of the story and end in the middle of the story. But can knowledge and understanding rest upon an Unknowable?

12. Inherent in the human mind is the postulate: the knowledge and understanding of an effect depend upon and involve the knowledge and understanding of the cause. If we do not know and understand the cause of an effect, we cannot know and understand the effect itself. This is the reason why the human mind endeavors to discover the cause of any effect. All realities and processes in existence present themselves to the human mind as but effects of some causes. To know and understand the realities and processes in existence, the human mind must discover their causes. But what appear to be causes turn out, upon examination, to be only effects of some hidden causes. And this forced the human mind to reach the first cause. The first cause, then, is the cause of all realities and processes in existence. To know and understand the realities and processes in existence, we must know and understand the first cause. Since, however, the first cause is and forever will remain to the human mind unknowable, then the realities and processes in existence are and must remain to the human mind unknowable. Thus knowledge is impossible. And thus it came to pass that, after the human mind crystallized many systems of thought and knowledge, they perceived that they are all without a foundation. To meet this difficulty, they consoled themselves with this: though the first cause is and forever will remain to the human mind unknowable, proximate causes are knowable; absolute knowledge is impossible, but relative knowledge is possible; absolute truth is impossible, but relative truth is possible. Thus upon the basis of proximate causes, relative knowledge and relative truths systems of thought

and knowledge were constructed. But proximate cause implies the first cause; proximate cause is not a cause at all, it is only an effect of the first cause, which is the only cause in existence. Since proximate cause is not a cause at all, it cannot produce any effect. Again, relative knowledge implies absolute knowledge; relative knowledge itself is not knowledge at all; without absolute knowledge there can be no relative knowledge. Since absolute knowledge is impossible, relative knowledge is impossible. Finally, relative truth implies absolute truth; relative truth itself is not truth at all; without absolute truth there can be no relative truth. Since absolute truth is impossible, relative truth is impossible. Thus the problem with which we started, what is knowledge, remained unsolved. Now, for thousands of years profound thinkers struggled to comprehend the first cause, assuming that they knew and understood what cause itself is. They did not realize that they had no idea of cause itself. Before they endeavored to comprehend the first cause, they should have first solved the problem, what is cause itself. Knowledge comprehends cause and effect. Before we can crystallize an adequate idea of knowledge, we must first adequately know and understand what is cause and what is effect. Thus the problem, what is knowledge, resolves itself into the problem, what is cause and what is effect?

CHAPTER II

What Is Cause and What Is Effect?

13. The proximate answer is: cause produces an effect, and an effect is produced by a cause. A cause originates existence, motion and change; an effect is the existence, the motion, the change. Between cause and effect there is an organic relation; a cause produces an effect in accordance with the nature of the cause, there is a correspondence between the cause and the effect. We begin with an effect, and then seek the cause of the effect. To know and understand either the cause or the effect we must know and understand both. This is a general idea of cause and effect. But we must examine cause and effect more closely.

Cause and effect are regarded by philosophers, as well as by ordinary men, as two distinct realities or processes: cause produces the effect, and the effect is produced by the cause. The question was: how can cause produce an effect, how can they relate to each other? For instance, Kant starts out his Critique of Pure Reason with the problem: How are synthetic judgments *a priori* possible. The main purpose of the Critique was to prove how such judgments are possible. I must briefly state what is involved in this problem. Kant draws a distinction between an analytic judgment and a synthetic judgment. Take the proposition: All bodies are extended. This is an analytical judgment, because the concept of extension is already involved in the concept of body. We cannot conceive body as not being extended. Hence in this proposition nothing is added to the concept of body; all that the proposition accomplishes is to make explicit what was already implicit in the concept of body. But if I say: all bodies have weight, this is a synthetical judgment, because the concept weight is not involved in the concept body. Weight is something outside of the body, yet is connected with it. Now in propositions concerning objects of experience there is no difficulty. From experience we learned that all bodies have weight. But a great difficulty presents itself in the case of objects that are not of experience. Take the proposition: All which happens has a cause. This is a synthetic judgment *a priori*. Here the proposition asserts an eternal and infinite fact, and an eternal and infinite fact cannot be learned from experience, because experience is limited in time and in space. The problem, then, is: how did we arrive to this synthetical judgment *a priori?* Since this proposition transcends all experience, how did we come to combine two concepts in one proposition, how did we come to think that all which happens in eternal and infinite existence has a cause? Thus it is clear that Kant regarded cause and effect as two distinct realities or processes. An examination of the works of the philosophers will show that they all regarded cause and effect as two distinct realities or processes. We shall presently see that this was a false idea of cause and effect. And it is clear that upon a false idea of cause and effect no true knowledge and understanding can be crystallized.

Cause and Effect are One

14. Cause and effect appear to be two distinct and opposite realities or processes, but they are one. We cannot conceive a cause without an effect, and we cannot conceive an effect without a cause. If we banish from thought cause, we thereby also banish from thought effect; and, if we banish from thought effect, we thereby also banish from thought cause. Cause and effect are correlatives, they imply each other; neither can exist without the other. If there is no cause, there can be no effect, and if there is no effect there is no cause. The cause becomes a cause only because and when it produces an effect, and the effect becomes an effect only because and when it is produced by a cause. If a cause does not produce an effect, it is not a

cause at all; and, if an effect is not produced by a cause, it is not an effect at all. If cause could speak to us, it would tell us this: I am cause, this is my positive aspect; but my positive aspect implies a negative aspect, the effect is my negative aspect. I cannot be a positive cause without at the same time also be a negative effect. In turn, if effect could speak to us, it would tell us this: I am effect, this is my positive aspect; but my positive aspect implies a negative aspect, the cause is my negative aspect. I cannot be a positive effect without at the same time also be a negative cause. From the viewpoint of cause, cause is positive and effect is negative; but from the viewpoint of effect, effect is positive and cause is negative; but they are one and the same, just as the right side and the left side of one are the same reality. Kant wrote a bulky book, The Critique of Pure Reason, to solve the problem, how synthetic judgments *a priori* are possible. He was troubled by this problem, because he regarded cause and effect two distinct realities or processes. But now we see that Kant misunderstood the whole problem, and that his whole Critique was an unnecessary work. We shall see later that there are no synthetic judgments *a priori*—all *a priori* judgments are analytic. The mind does not have to go outside of the concept cause to think of effect; the mind cannot think of cause without thinking of effect, the concept effect is already involved in the concept cause, because cause and effect are one and the same. Thus we see that philosophers started out with a false idea of cause and effect. One false idea begets other false ideas. Having started out with a false idea of cause and effect, the philosophers conceived cause and effect under other false ideas. This we shall presently see.

CAUSE AND EFFECT ARE SIMULTANEOUS AND INTERDEPENDENT

15. Cause appears to be prior to and independent of effect, while effect appears to be posterior to and dependent upon cause. The problem was: how could cause be followed by an

effect? We shall presently see that, because cause and effect are one and the same, they are simultaneous and interdependent. Cause depends upon effect, as effect depends upon cause; without a cause there can be no effect, and without an effect there can be no cause; they are simultaneous as they are interdependent. An illustration will make it clear.

I take a piece of wax and expose it to the rays of the sun. In time the rays of the sun will melt the wax, the wax will become a fluid mass. The rays of the sun produced this effect on the wax, the rays of the sun were the cause of the melting of the wax. Thus the rays of the sun, as the cause, were prior to and independent of the effect, while the melting of the wax was posterior to and dependent upon the rays of the sun. This is what it appears, and this is what philosophers regard to be the case. We shall presently see that this is an illusion. It is true that the rays of the sun existed before they melted the wax, and they were independent of the wax, but until the rays of the sun came into contact with the wax they were not yet a cause; the rays of the sun became a cause only when they came into contact with the wax. What took place when the rays of the sun came into contact with the wax? All realities in existence consists of numerous particles of matter that perpetually move about one another with certain velocities. The wax consists of numerous particles of matter that move about one another with a certain velocity—a velocity much smaller than the velocity of the rays of the sun. The rays of the sun move with a velocity of 186000 miles per second. When the rays of the sun came into contact with the particles of the wax, the rays of the sun imparted part of their greater velocity to the particles of the wax, and the particles of the wax then began to move with a greater velocity than before. This greater velocity manifested itself in the melting of the wax. Thus the rays of the sun were the cause of the melting of the wax. But what happened to the rays of the sun? Before the rays of the sun came into contact with the particles of the wax they moved with a velocity of 186000 miles per second; but after they came into contact with the particles of the wax their velocity was greatly diminished; and now the rays of the sun and the particles of the wax move with the same velocity. And so, while the rays of the sun caused the particles of the wax to move with greater velocity, the particles of the wax caused the rays of the sun to move with a lesser velocity. Thus we see that each was the cause of the other, and each was the effect of the other. Which, then, was cause, and which was effect? Next notice this: the cause and the effect arose simultaneously. The rays of the sun became the cause of the melting of the wax only when the wax began to melt; before that the rays of the sun were not yet a cause. And the rays of the sun did not become a cause until they also became an effect, the slowing down of their velocity. Thus we see that a cause cannot produce an effect without itself becoming an effect, and an effect cannot be produced by a cause without itself becoming a cause; and all this takes place simultaneously. Thus we see that cause and effect are not only one and the same, but they are also simultaneous and inter-dependent.

THERE ARE NO PROXIMATE CAUSES

16. Philosophers speak of proximate causes as distinguished from ultimate causes. Even Spinoza, who started out with the Cause of Itself, and who all along proved that God is the only direct, immediate and immanent cause of all effects, even he speaks of proximate causes as distinguished from the remote or ultimate cause. We shall presently see that there are no proximate causes, and that even Spinoza had no adequate idea of cause.

A stone fell to the ground. The stone could not fall to the ground unless some cause determined it to fall to the ground. What was the cause? The answer is: the attraction of the earth. Inherent in matter is a force by virtue of which every particle of matter attracts all other particles of matter in the universe. The earth consists of infinite particles of matter, and the stone consists of numerous particles of matter. Between them there is an attraction. As the number of particles of matter composing the earth is infinitely greater than the number of particles of matter composing the stone, the greater prevailed over the lesser, and the stone was attracted by the earth, and the stone fell to the ground. Several questions present themselves. First, how can the particles of matter attract one another at a distance without any intermediary? Second, how did matter come to possess this infinite and universal power of attraction? One particle of matter attracts all infinite particles of matter in the universe? Third, how did this power of attraction come into existence, did it create itself, is it the cause of itself? Finally, what is matter? To understand why the stone fell to the ground, it is necessary to know the answers to these questions. Thus far, neither science nor philosophy answered these questions. This means that neither science nor philosophy could explain this simple phenomenon, the fall of the stone to the ground. Since science and philosophy could not explain so simple a phenomenon, they could not explain any phenomenon, and this means that the phenomena are still a mystery. And now let go a step further.

A perfectly elastic ball has the property by virtue of which it can impart its motion to another elastic ball, and itself to remain at rest. From the ceiling I suspend ten elastic balls at such distance from one another in a straight line that, when I set in motion the first ball in the direction of the other balls, it will strike the second ball, the second ball will strike the third ball, and so with the rest, until the tenth ball is struck. With my hand I strike the first ball in the direction of the other balls, imparting to the first ball a motion. The first ball will strike the second ball, imparting its own motion to the second ball, and itself remaining at rest. The second ball then strikes the third ball, imparting to it its own motion, and itself remaining at rest. This is repeated until the tenth ball is struck and set into motion. I now ask the tenth ball, what caused it to move? Its answer will be: the ninth ball caused it to move. I then ask the ninth ball, what caused it to move? Its answer will be: the eighth ball caused it to move. And so with the other balls, until I come to the first ball. I ask the first ball, what caused it to move? Its answer will be, my hand caused it to move. Here, then, we have ten separate causes that produced ten separate effects. Yet, when the matter is examined more closely, it will be seen that there was only one cause that produced these ten separate effects, and that one cause was my hand. The other causes which may be called proximate causes were no causes at all, they were only the means through which my hand imparted its own motion to the ten balls.

And now the question is: was my hand the cause that set the ten balls into motion? This would be so, if my hand created itself and endowed itself with the power to set the ten balls into motion. But my hand did not create itself, it did not endow itself with the power to set the balls into motion, and it did not determine the nature of the elastic ten balls. My hand is only a part of my body. Now, my body did not create itself, it did not endow itself with energy, and it did not determine the nature of the ten elastic balls. What cause created my body, and what cause endowed my body with energy to set the balls into motion? My body received its energy, directly and indirectly, from the sun. Hence it was the sun that, through my body, set the balls into motion. But was the sun the cause of the motion of the balls? This would be so, if the sun had created itself and had endowed itself with energy. But the sun did not create itself and it did not endow itself with energy. What cause created the sun and endowed it with energy? Consider the infinite energy of the sun. The sun radiates 360 million tons of mass-energy every day. For countless millions of years the sun radiated every day 360 million tons of mass-energy. Where did the sun get this infinite energy? Some scientists claim that the sun gets its infinite energy directly from existence; other scientists claim that the sun gets its infinite energy from itself, from the disintegration of its elements. The first position at once solves the problem, for it tells us that the energy which I imparted to the ten balls came directly from existence. But let us consider the second position. The sun gets its energy from itself, from the disintegration of its elements. Did the sun create itself, did it create its elements, did it endow its elements with energy? The sun was created by some cause, and that cause endowed its elements with infinite energy. Hence, whether the sun gets its infinite energy directly from existence or from the integration of its elements, it is clear that the sun was not the cause that set the ten balls into motion. Hence existence itself was the cause that set the ten balls into motion, and it was existence itself that determined that the stone should fall to the ground, and it was also existence that caused my hand to set the ten balls into motion.

But it will be argued: granted that all energy in existence originates in existence itself, but was there not an independent cause that determined my hand to set the ten balls into motion, and was not that cause my will? Assuming that the infinite energy of the first cause was the condition, without which I could not move the ten balls, was not my will the cause that gave to that infinite energy a definite direction? Now, it is clear that without the infinite energy emanating from the first cause I could not set the balls into motion; but what is my will? My will is nothing else than a part of the infinite energy of the first cause. I did not create myself, I did not endow myself with a will, and I did not determine its nature. My will was given to me just as the energy was given to the sun and as the nature of the elastic balls was given to them by one and the same cause. That cause gave me existence, it determined my will, and determined me to set the ten balls into motion. Have I not a free will that is independent of the first cause? My answer is: I have neither a free will nor a will that is independent of the first cause. I have no more freedom of will than I have freedom of existence; all is determined by the first cause. The first cause is the direct, immediate and immanent cause of all infinite effects in existence. There are no proximate causes; there is only one cause of all effects, and the idea of proximate causes is an illusion and false. What appear to be proximate causes are only effects. Thus we learned the following. Cause and effect are one and the same; cause and effect are simultaneous and inter-dependent; finally, the first cause is the only cause in existence—all else are effects. In other words, the first cause manifests itself in infinite effects.

The First Cause is the Cause and Effect of Itself

17. Spinoza tells us that the first cause is the cause of itself. To be the cause of itself means to be the effect of itself. Hence the first cause is the only cause in existence, and is itself the only effect in existence. This is clear. Since cause and effect are one and the same, it follows that the first cause is also the first effect of itself. Spinoza tells us that the first cause, the cause of itself, involves existence. The term involve must be understood in the mathematical sense, and in mathematics the term involution means the multiplication of a number by itself. Thus the number 5, by involution, becomes 25, 125, 625, and so on to infinity. And here we come to consider another postu-late of the monistic philosophy, namely: What is one, infinite, eternal and absolute is one, infinite, eternal and absolute in every part thereof; for the one, infinite, eternal and absolute cannot be composed of the many, finite, temporary and relative parts, nor can it resolve itself into many finite, temporary and relative parts; but infinitely and eternally is and remains one, infinite, eternal and absolute in every part thereof. Let us consider a few cases.

Number begins with one. One is unity which becomes an infinite number of ones; the one becomes in succession two, three, four, five, and so on ad infinitum. Let us consider the successive numbers. Two consists of two ones, three consists of three ones, four consists of four ones, five consists of five ones, and so on ad infinitum. In all these infinite numbers, the nature and unity of the first one did not change, but in all cases remained absolutely one—each one of the infinite numbers is absolutely the same as the first one. Now, the first one is infinite, for it becomes infinite ones; implicit in the first one are infinite ones. And the same is true of every one of the infinite numbers. Any one of the infinite numbers is infinite, it can become infinite numbers, and implicit in it are infinite ones. The first one is also eternal, it never ceases to exist, and continues to exist in all infinite ones that come out of the first one. And this is true of every one of the infinite ones. Every one of the infinite ones is infinite and eternal. Finally, the first one is absolute, it exists in itself and by itself and independently of everything else in existence. And the same is true of every one of the infinite ones that come out of the first one. Thus we see that that which is one, absolute, infinite and eternal is and remains one, infinite, eternal and absolute in every part thereof.

Consider a more concrete case. I take an acorn and put it into the ground. In due time, the acorn becomes an oak tree, reproducing thousands of acorns. These thousands of acorns are exactly like the first acorn. I put the thousands of acorns into the ground. In due time, they becomes thousands of oak trees, reproducing millions of acorns. I can continue this process, and in infinite time there will be infinite oak trees, reproducing infinite acorns. All these oak trees and acorns came out of the first acorn, and all have the same nature, they are absolutely the same. Here, again, we find the same situation. The first acorn, which seemed to be a finite and perishable thing, turned out to be an infinite and eternal thing. Likewise, every one of the infinite acorns, which came out from the first acorn, is infinite and eternal: each one can become infinite oak trees, reproducing infinite acorns. Finally, the acorn is absolute; it is in itself and by itself independently of all else in existence. If all else in existence be annihilated, and only the one first acorn remained, the first acorn, as part of absolute, infinite and eternal substance, would fill the universe with infinite oak trees and acorns. And this is true of every one of the infinite acorns that came out of the first acorn. The same is true of all realities in existence.

And now consider another case. I conceive an idea. This

idea, like a seed, will germinate and become a system of ideas; each idea of the system of ideas can become a system of ideas, and so out of one idea an infinite number of ideas can arise. Each idea is absolute, infinite and eternal. Consider the idea of the first wheel conceived by some primitive savage. It was a crude idea, as the wheel he created. Yet, follow up the evolution of this crude idea of the wheel, and you will find that it gave rise to infinite ideas of infinite wheels, and all the wonderful machines which mankind already brought out and all wonderful machines which mankind will bring out in all future time—all came out of the first idea. These illustrations give us an idea of the first cause. The first cause is absolutely one, infinite, eternal and absolute. Implicit in the first cause are all infinite realities and processes, and in infinite time and space they manifest themselves. Each reality, is, like the first cause, absolute, infinite and eternal, because each reality involves the first cause. The first cause is the cause of itself; that is, it is the effect of itself. Just as besides the first cause there is no other cause, so besides the first cause there is no effect.

The Progressive Multiplication of Effects

18. Philosophers wrote much about the multiplication of the effects of a given cause. One cause produces many effects, the effects of a cause are followed by other effects, and so, once a cause produced an effect, the effects continue to multiply one after another. Suppose a bomb was dropped from an aeroplane, destroying several houses and killing hundreds of persons. The explosion, not only destroyed these houses and killed these hundreds of persons, but it also affected the neighboring houses and also affected the relatives, neighbors of the hundreds of persons killed. And, if we follow up the progressive multiplication of the effects upon the children, grandchildren, and so on, we shall find that the one explosion produced numerous effects. Here we see again the case of one acorn becoming many oak trees and numerous acorns. Now, philosophers tell us that each

effect becomes, in turn, a cause of the subsequent effects; but
this is an illusion. The explosion of the bomb is the direct, immediate and immanent cause of each and every subsequent
effect. I say, the explosion of the bomb is the cause, but this
is only to show that between the explosion of the bombs and
each of the subsequent effects there is a direct and immediate
relation; but the explosion of the bomb itself is but an effect of
some cause; and, as we saw before, the cause of the explosion
is the first cause itself.

THE REGRESSIVE MULTIPLICATION OF CAUSES

19. John Brown had a father and a mother. His parents had four
parents; his grandparents had eight parents; and so, if we trace
back the ancestral tree of John Brown, we shall find that he had
an infinite number of parents. An infinite number of men and
women had to unite to bring John Brown into existence. A
union of a man and a woman is in itself an effect of numerous
concurring causes. Hence John Brown is the effect of infinite
causes. But is it true that John Brown had infinite ancestors?
As we trace back the ancestral tree of John Brown, we find
the number of men and women becomes ever smaller, until we
reach one man and one woman, say, Adam and Eve. In turn,
John Brown may become the ancestor of infinite descendants.
And so, John Brown is a point between a progressive multiplication of effects and a regressive multiplication of causes. And yet
in all these cases there was but one cause and one effect, or a
cause which was also an effect. Let us see. Were the infinite
ancestors of John Brown the cause of of the existence of John
Brown? Not in an eternity could they create John Brown; the
infinite ancestors were only the means through whom the first
cause created John Brown. Again, John Brown will never be
the cause of his children and grandchildren. Not in an eternity
will John Brown be able to create a human being. Again, consider the explosion of the bomb. That a bomb might be dropped
from an aeroplane, destroying several houses and killing hun-

dreds of persons, there had to be a world war involving hundreds of millions of human beings. That a world war should take place, an infinite number of antecedent causes and events had to take place. Next, that a bomb might be dropped from an aeroplane, the whole human race had to work and struggle for thousands of years to bring out the sciences, the arts and the industries to create an aeroplane and a bomb. And so, when we trace the explosion back to its antecedent causes and events, we find that an infinite number of causes and events had to concur to produce the explosion. But did an infinite number of causes and events concur to produce the explosion? Did men create themselves, did they endow themselves with knowledge and understanding, did they plan their evolution and history, and did they determine to have a world war? All this was determined by the first cause. Thus we see that the first cause is, not only the only cause in existence, but also that it is the only effect in existence. An effect can be separated from the cause only when the cause produces an effect on something else, upon something which is not the cause. But, besides the first cause, there is absolutely nothing else in existence. The first cause is the substance of all realities and processes in existence; the first cause is all the realities and processes in existence. Only now we understand the cause of itself. The first cause is the cause of itself, because it is the effect of itself. There is no other cause, and there is no other effect.

THE FIRST CAUSE IMPLIES THE ABSOLUTE

20. The first cause is cause and effect. Cause and effect are correlatives, they imply each other, neither can exist without the other. Correlatives imply a third reality of which they are correlatives. The first cause is both cause and effect of itself. What is the third reality which is implied in the first cause? The third reality is the Absolute. What is the Absolute? The Absolute is substance. The term substance means to stand under. Substance is that which underlines all realities and processes in existence;

all realities and processes in existence are carved out of one absolute, infinite and eternal substance. But what is that substance? Suppose we examine a table. The table appears to be made out of wood. The wood appears to be a solid body of matter, and is nothing else than wood. Yet, when we examine the wood more closely, we find that it is neither solid nor wood. The wood is nothing else than a mass of carbon, oxygen, nitrogen, and other chemical elements, which are relatively to their size as far apart from one another as the earth is from the sun, and these elements are perpetually moving about one another. Thus the table is neither wood nor a solid body. And what about those chemical elements? These chemical elements themselves consist of protons and electrons. Thus the wood and the chemical elements disappear. And what about the protons and the electrons? They are nothing else than forms of energy. Thus all matter disappears. And what about the energy? This is the problem. Before we take up this problem, we must notice the following. All realities in existence, like the table, are nothing else than forms of energy. All realities and processes are carved out of one infinite and eternal energy. This infinite and eternal energy is substance.

What, then, is substance? Spinoza defines substance as that which is in itself and is conceived through itself. What, then, is it which is in itself and which is conceived through itself? All realities and processes in existence exist in substance and are conceived through substance; but substance is in itself, because there is nothing else besides substance; and is conceived through itself, because there is nothing else through which it can be conceived. What, then, is this substance? The answer is: substance is absolute thought—thought without form. All realities and processes are in something else, but thought is in itself. Again, all realities and processes are conceived by thought, but thought can be conceived only by itself. Thought comprehends time, space, matter, motion, force, and so on indefinitely; but thought itself is neither in time, nor in space, nor in matter, nor in anything else, it is in itself. Absolute thought—thought without form—is the substance of all realities and processes in existence. This substance is the Absolute. The Absolute is absolute thought without form. Of the absolute thought we have a direct and intimate consciousness; we are conscious of the thought in us, we think by thought and we live by thought. From the infinite and eternal absolute thought flows through us a stream of absolute thought. If this stream of absolute thought should cease to flow through us, we will cease to exist. The absolute thought is our substance, it is our life, it is our consciousness; so long as this absolute thought flows through us, we live, we are conscious, we think and we act. We become conscious of the absolute thought when it assumes a form, when it assumes the form of a perception, a concept, an idea, a feeling or a state of our body and mind. Absolute thought is in itself, it is implicit in itself. As such it is neither cause nor effect. The Absolute becomes both cause and effect when it becomes explicit, when it comes out from its implicitness and manifests itself explicitly. This explicit manifestation of the Absolute is the first cause and the first effect. Thus we have a trinity: The Absolute, the First Cause and the First Effect. This trinity runs through all infinite and eternal existence. Each and every reality in existence is a manifestation of this trinity. To know and understand any reality or process, we must perceive in it this primordial trinity. I defined knowledge as the comprehension of cause and effect. Now we can make the definition more explicit. Knowledge is the comprehension of the Absolute, the First Cause and the First Effect. Our next step is to consider the Absolute more closely.

CHAPTER III

The Absolute Is Knowable

21. The Absolute is substance, and substance is absolute thought —thought without form. The Absolute, then, is absolute thought without form. Spinoza tells us that substance by its nature is prior to its affections, or modifications. What is the affection or modification of substance? Since substance is absolute thought without form, the primordial affection or modification of substance is the assumption of form. This means that absolute thought assumes a form. When absolute thought assumes a form, then it becomes an idea. An idea, then, is the form of thought. It may be said that the definition of the Absolute as absolute thought without form is a contradiction in terms, for a definition already implies form. This is true: the Absolute implies form. Notice this. Spinoza tells us that substance by its nature is prior to its affections or modifications (which are forms); but Spinoza does not say that substance is prior to its affections or modification. The Absolute, as absolute thought, never was without form; but by its nature it was prior to its forms. Form already presupposes substance, for only substance can assume a form. We can conceive substance without form, although this will be a vague and abstract conception; but without substance form cannot be conceived. Hence we start out with the idea that the Absolute started out as absolute thought without form. How did the Absolute assume form? Thought by its nature thinks, and thinking requires an object of thought. The Absolute by its nature thinks, and the Absolute required an object for its thought. Since, however, besides the Absolute there is nothing else in existence, the Absolute thinks of itself, it comprehends itself in its own thought. This self-reflexion of

the Absolute gave the Absolute an idea of itself, and an idea is a form of thought. Thus the Absolute, by acquiring of an idea of itself, comprehended itself in a form. This primordial idea, which comprehended the Absolute in a primordial form, Spinoza calls the Infinite Intellect, and the Kabbalah call the Kether, the Crown. Just as the crown comprehends the head, so the Kether comprehends the Absolute, or as the Kabbalah calls it, the Ain-Sof—the Absolute, Infinite and Eternal. Thus the Absolute clothed itself in form; substance assumed a form.

We saw that what is absolute, infinite and eternal is absolute, infinite and eternal in every part thereof; for the absolute, infinite and eternal cannot be composed of relative, finite and temporary parts, nor can it resolve itself into relative, finite and temporary parts; but is and remains absolute, infinite and eternal in every part thereof and in every form of manifestation. The Infinite Intellect, therefore, is also absolute, infinite and eternal. We saw that one becomes an infinite number of ones, and each one of the infinite ones is itself also infinite. The Infinite Intellect is an absolute, infinite and eternal idea of the Absolute, that is, it is an absolute, infinite and eternal form of the Absolute. The Infinite Intellect becomes infinite ideas, which are forms of substance. A form of substance is a reality. Thus all infinite realities in existence came into existence. We saw that thought can be conceived only by thought. Likewise, an idea can be conceived only by an idea. By means of ideas we can comprehend the realities of existence, and by means of ideas we can comprehend absolute thought. To comprehend the Absolute is nothing else than to comprehend the absolute thought in us. And we already saw that we are conscious of the absolute thought in us. Thus the Absolute is knowable. Since the Absolute is knowable, then all manifestations of the Absolute are knowable. At the outset, I stated that the ultimate problem which presents itself to the human mind is: what is cause itself. Now we know what the ultimate cause is, and therefore what cause is. The Absolute assuming the form of the Infinite Intellect, this is the ultimate cause, it is the first cause. Thus the ultimate problem is solved. Once the ultimate problem is solved, then all proximate problems can be solved. Now we comprehend both cause and effect. Since, however, philosophers convinced themselves that the Absolute, the First Cause, is un-knowable, we must go a step further to justify our conclusion.

22. We saw that the knowledge and understanding of an effect depend upon and involve the knowledge and understanding of the cause; for, if we do not know and understand the cause of an effect, we cannot know and understand the effect itself. All realities and processes in existence are only effects of the first cause. To know and understand any reality or process in exist-ence, we must know and understand the first cause. The first cause implies the Absolute. This means that to know and under-stand any reality or processes, we must know and understand the Absolute, substance. Since, however, the philosophers tell us that the first cause, the Absolute, substance, is and forever will remain to the human mind unknowable, it follows that we cannot know and understand any reality or process in existence. Why, then, did the philosophers write many bulky books to show what they knew and understood about the realities and the processes of existence? The truth is this: men are wiser in their conduct than they are in their philosophy; for, while through their conduct life itself speaks, through their philosophy speaks their immature mind. It is clear that there must be a fundamental fallacy in the reasoning of the philosophers. It is therefore necessary to expose this fallacy. For this purpose I will consider the argument of Spencer.

Spencer starts out with the Unknowable. He starts out by showing that all human knowledge is and necessarily must be relative. We can know one fact only with relation to another fact, we can understand one truth only with relation to another truth: but we cannot know a fact by itself, and we cannot understand a truth by itself. Assuming that we begin to inter-pret the realities of existence in terms of matter, and then we reinterpret matter in terms of motion, and then we interpret motion in terms of force; when we then try to interpret force itself, we fail, because there is no longer any other reality in terms of which we can interpret force itself. Hence force itself must remain unknowable. Spencer then tells us the following: "If, to use an algebraic illustration, we represent matter, motion and force by the symbols X, Y, and Z, then we may ascertain the value of X and the value of Y in terms of Z, but the value of Z can never be found: Z is the unknown quantity which must forever remain unknown, for the reason that there is nothing in which its value can be expressed." Applying this illustration to the problem before us, Spencer argued that, since all human knowledge is and forever will remain relative, we can know the realities of existence only with relation to the ultimate reality, but the ultimate reality must forever remain to the human mind unknowable. Let us examine the argument.

23. The problem resolves itself into an equation. Take the following equation: X equals Y. X is a symbol of quantity, but is not quantity itself; X does not tell us what quantity it represents. But we are not concerned about X, we are concerned about the quantity that it symbolizes. How can we find out the quantity which X symbolizes? This we can find out by bringing X into a quantitative relation to Y. When we bring X into a quantitative relation to Y, we discover that X equals Y. In this equation, X stands in the relative aspect, because it reveals its value with relation to Y; but Y stands in the equivalent aspect, because Y, as it stands by itself, is a definite quantity; and X, by telling us that it is equal to Y, tells us that the quantity which is hidden behind its symbolic garment, is equal to Y just as Y is. And, while the quantity which X symbolizes is thus revealed, the quantity for which Y stands is not revealed; for, if we take away X and ask, what is the quantitative value of Y, we cannot tell. This is what the nature of an equation seems to be, and upon this Spencer based his argument that the ultimate reality is and forever will remain unknowable. We shall presently see that this argument is involved in an inadequate

idea of the nature of an equation. Let us again consider the equation: X equals Y. We found that the quantitative value which X symbolizes is revealed to be equal to Y, but this equation does not tell us what is the quantitative value of Y, and we do not know what is its value. And yet, notwithstanding this, we immediately proceed to use Y instead of X, or we use them interchangeably. If, indeed, we do not know what the value of Y is, how can we use it interchangeably with X? The answer is this: the equation, X equals Y, tells us, not only that X equals Y, but it also tells us that Y equals X. This arises from the fact that an equation is of a double nature: direct and indirect. In the nature of things this must be so, for action and reaction are equal and opposite in direction. Thus far we considered the direct aspect of the equation. Let us now consider the indirect aspect of the equation.

X is only a symbol of quantity, the quantity is hidden behind its symbolic garment. To reveal the quantity which is hidden behind the symbolic garment of X, we place X into a quantitative relation to Y. Now Y stands in front of X like a mirror, and X sees itself reflected in Y, and finds that the quantity hidden behind its symbolic garment is equal to Y just as it appears. But, while X was making this direct equation, Y also made an indirect equation; it equated itself, not to X, but to the quantity symbolized by X; and Y found that it, just as it appears, is equal to the quantity which is symbolized by X. Y says: I, just as I am and appear, am equal to the quantity which is hidden behind the symbolic garment of X. In this manner both X and Y reveal that they are equal to each other. Hence now we can substitute Y for X, and we can use them interchangeably. Let us now apply this analysis to the case before us.

Philosophers perceived that the knowledge and understanding of an effect depend upon and involve the knowledge and understanding of the cause; but they did not perceive the converse of this proposition, namely: the knowledge and understanding of a cause depend upon and involve the knowledge and understanding of the effect; for, if the effect is not known and understood, the cause cannot be known and understood. This must be so, since cause and effect are correlatives, neither of which can exist without the other. From this follows that the knowledge and the understanding of the one is possible only with the knowledge and understanding of the other. Take away cause, and there will be no effect; take away effect, and there will be no cause. Take away the knowledge and understanding of the one, and the knowledge and understanding of the other will be impossible. Now, the first cause is the cause of all effects, and we are one of the effects. But cause and effect are one. This means that the first cause and we are one. Just as we cannot be without the first cause, so without us the first cause cannot be. Let all effects cease to be, and the first cause will cease to be. The Absolute is an absolute only with relation to the relative, just as the relative is a relative only with relation to the Absolute. Without the Absolute there would be no relative, but without the relative there would be no Absolute. It is true that we can know ourselves only with relation to the first cause, the Absolute, substance; but for this very reason we can know the first cause, the Absolute, substance, with relation to ourselves.

We are the X, and the Absolute is the Y. Standing in front of the Absolute, we perceive that the essence which we symbolize, and which is hidden behind our symbolic garment, is equal to the Absolute—absolute thought without form. Absolute thought is our substance, our life and our consciousness. Thus we perceive that the absolute thought which is our essence and which is hidden behind our symbolic garment is the same as the absolute thought of the Absolute. And, while we make this direct equation, the Absolute also makes an indirect equation. The Absolute says: I, just as I am, am absolute thought, and that I am the same as the absolute thought which is hidden behind our symbolic garment. Thus the truth is revealed that the Absolute and the absolute thought which we symbolize are one and the same. To know and understand ourselves, we must know and understand the Absolute; and to know and under-stand the Absolute, we must know and understand ourselves.

The Absolute is absolute only with relation to us, and we are relative only with relation to the Absolute. As stated before, the Absolute did not exist for an instant without manifesting itself in form; substance did not exist for an instant without form. The Absolute is absolute, infinite and eternal, and therefore manifests itself in absolute, infinite and eternal forms, and these forms are the realities and processes of existence. The more of the forms of absolute thought we know and understand, the more we know and understand the Absolute. In turn, the more we know and understand the Absolute, the more we know and understand the realities and the processes of existence. Hence Spinoza tells us: The more we understand individual things, the more we understand God. Thus all knowledge and understanding mean self-knowledge and self-understanding. Know thyself —this is the beginning and end of all knowledge and understanding. The Absolute is knowable, and for this reason the relative is knowable. Knowledge, which implies understanding, comprehends the Absolute and the relative, cause and effect, substance and form, absolute thought and idea. A true monistic philosophy begins with the Absolute and ends with the Absolute. And now let us briefly sum up what we have learned thus far.

Man was created last. When man came into existence, the world had already been created. At first, man began to acquaint himself with the things around him. Gradually he began to investigate the nature, origin and cause of things. Men discovered the causes of things; but, upon examination, the causes revealed themselves to be but effects of some hidden causes. Men searched further and deeper to find true causes. At last they reached the first cause. Men then reflected on the first cause and reached the conclusion that the first cause is and forever will remain to the human mind unknowable. But we went further. We found that the first cause is the cause of itself and the effect of itself; cause and effect are correlatives, they imply each other, neither can exist without the other; they are only two aspects of one and the same reality or process. Cause and Effect, being correlatives, imply a third reality of which they are correlatives. The third reality is the Absolute. The Absolute is absolute thought without form, it is the substance of all realities and processes in existence. Absolute thought is in us, it is our substance, our life and our consciousness. Thought thinks, and thinking requires an object of thought. Absolute thought thinks and requires an object of thought. As besides the Absolute there is nothing else, the Absolute thinks of itself. This self-reflexion gives rise to an idea of the Absolute. The Absolute forms an idea of itself. This idea comprehends the Absolute, and thus the Absolute becomes clothed in a form. An idea is nothing else than a form of absolute thought. Thus substance acquired a form. This primordial idea and form is the Infinite Intellect. The Infinite Intellect, being an absolute, infinite and eternal idea manifests itself in infinite ideas, each of which is absolute, infinite and eternal. These ideas and their forms are the realities and processes of existence. Thought is in itself and is conceived through itself. Thought comprehends time, space, matter, motion, reality and process, but thought is not comprehended by time, space, matter, motion, reality and process. An idea comprehends thought and itself. By a knowledge and understanding of ourselves we attain to a knowledge and understanding of the Absolute and the realities and processes of existence. The Absolute is knowable, and so are all effects of the Absolute knowable. Thus we acquired an adequate idea of knowledge, which implies understanding. Men began with a surface and inadequate knowledge of things, but gradually they penetrated deeper into the nature, origin and causes of things. The destiny of mankind is to attain to an adequate knowledge and understanding of the Absolute, God, Existence, Man, Society and History. The monistic philosophy here presented is a heuristic propaedeutic to such adequate knowledge and understanding.

CHAPTER IV

The Genesis of the Absolute

24. Inherent in the human mind is the postulate: Something cannot arise out of nothing, and something cannot disappear into nothing. The Absolute is the substance and form of all realities and processes in existence, it is the beginning and end of existence. How did the Absolute come into existence? It is said that the absolute is eternal and infinite, and eternity and infinitude have neither beginning nor end. But this does not answer the question. No matter how often we may repeat to ourselves that the Absolute has no beginning and no end, the question persists: how and when did the Absolute come into existence? This question arises not only in the mind of thinkers, it arises also in the mind of ordinary men, even in the mind of children. Whether the question is: how and when God came into existence, or how and when the first cause came into existence, or how and when substance came into existence, it is ultimately the question, how and when did the Absolute come into existence? This question cannot be suppressed, it inevitably arises in the human mind when it reflects on the nature and origin of things. Religious thinkers commanded men not to inquire after the origin and nature of God, but accept on faith that God exists, that he created the world, and that he concerns himself about men. On the other hand, philosophy tried to prove that the ultimate reality is and forever will remain to the human mind unknowable, and therefore it is in vain for men to try to find out how and when the Absolute came into existence. Notwithstanding all this, the human mind refuses to acquiesce in ignorance. A true monistic philosophy cannot evade this problem.

How did the Absolute come into existence, did it arise out of an absolute vacuum, out of absolute nothing? And how and by what necessity did the Absolute come into existence? But what is an absolute vacuum? Can we conceive of an absolute vacuum, can we conceive the absolute absence of space? But what is space itself, how did it originate? Space is usually conceived to be the absence of material objects, but space is not merely the absence of material objects, space itself is a reality, and we cannot conceive the absence of space. What, then, is space? To explain gravitation, light and other phenomena, science at one time postulated the existence of an ether. Science assumed that the ether fills infinite space. But what is the ether? Science tried hard to find out what the ether is, and failed. In despair, science abandoned the assumption that there exists an ether. And since there is no ether, gravitation, light and other phenomena remain a mystery as they were before. What, then, is space? Space is absolute thought—thought without form. Space is substance, it is the Absolute. The Absolute is the eternal and infinite space in which all realities and processes live, move and have their being. And here I call attention to a very remarkable fact. The ancient Jewish thinkers referred to God as Space. "Blessed is Space; Blessed is Space who gave us the Torah." By Space they meant God. This is worthy of notice, because it shows that the ancient Jewish thinkers had a deep insight into the nature of existence. Space is the Absolute, it is absolute thought. When considering Spinoza's definition of substance, we saw that substance is absolute thought; it is in itself and is conceived through itself. All realities and processes of existence exist in space, but space exists in itself; all realities and processes can be conceived by thought in space, without space we cannot conceive any reality or process; but space is conceived by thought without anything else. A vacuum, then, is nothing else than space without realities or processes, but it does not mean the absence of space. We cannot banish from thought space, because thought itself is space, and thought cannot banish itself. While all realities in existence have forms, space itself has

no form. It has no form, because it is absolute thought. Thus
we see that we live, move and have our being in the Absolute.
The Absolute is the infinite and eternal space in which all infinite and eternal realities and processes exist, move and have their
being. This gives us a more definite idea of the Absolute. The
moment we become aware of space, we become aware of the
Absolute. We do not look for the Absolute somewhere outside
of space, the Absolute is the space of which we are always
aware.

This brings us to the original question: how and when did
the Absolute come into existence: or, how and when did space
come into existence? This question the human mind cannot
answer, for the following reason. The human mind is a form
of absolute thought: it originates in absolute thought, it functions within absolute thought and by means of absolute thought.
The human mind cannot transcend absolute thought, it cannot
go outside of the Absolute, outside of space, outside of substance, to perceive what was before the Absolute. Therefore
the human mind cannot solve this problem. But this raises
another question: Why does the problem of the genesis of the
Absolute persist in the human mind? The answer is: the human
mind is concerned about its own origin, how did it come into
existence? In endeavoring to find out its own origin, it endeavors
to find out the origin of things, the origin of the first cause and
the origin of the Absolute. When the human mind reaches the
Absolute and perceives that it is only a form of absolute
thought, that as absolute thought it is the same as the Absolute,
then it knows and understands itself and the Absolute. But
beyond this the human mind cannot go: it cannot transcend
its own form and become absolute thought without form, for
then it will cease to be a human mind, it will become substance,
absolute thought, the Absolute. The problem as to the origin
of the Absolute is nothing else than the problem of the origin
of the human mind itself. This is the reason why it persists in
the human mind of ordinary men as well as in the mind of
thinkers.

WHAT IS REALITY?

25. Reality is form, for form determines the nature and function of a thing. Let us consider a few illustrations. Out of a mass of iron I make a hammer, a saw, a drill, and many other kinds of instruments. They are all made of iron, yet they differ from one another in their functions; the hammer cannot perform the function of the saw, the saw cannot perform the function of the hammer, and so on with all instruments. What determines the function of a tool? It is its form. I can make a hammer of wood, of stone, of iron, of copper, of gold, and so on; but no matter what be the material out of which I make the hammer, so long as it has the form of a hammer, it performs the function of a hammer, and is a hammer. On the other hand, if I destroy the form of the hammer, by this I destroy the hammer, although this does not affect the substance out of which the hammer was made. Now, iron, wood, copper, silver, gold, and all other material substances are themselves only forms of substance. Suppose we destroy the iron, the wood, the silver, the gold, and so on, by this we destroy the forms of substance, but substance itself is not in the least affected by this: substance itself cannot be destroyed, it is absolute thought, it is the Absolute, and the Absolute cannot be destroyed, and it cannot be affected by the destruction of the forms of absolute thought. Thus we see that reality is nothing else than the form of absolute thought. When absolute thought assumes a form, it becomes a reality. But what is form itself? Form is nothing else than an idea, an idea is a form of absolute thought. Before I can make a hammer, I must first conceive an idea of a hammer, and then I realize this idea by giving to substance a form corresponding to the idea in my mind. And even after I have made the hammer, I must continue to have the idea in my mind to use the hammer as a hammer. If the hammer should fall into the hands of primitive men, who had no idea of a hammer, the hammer in their hands will not be a hammer, and it will not perform the function of a hammer. And this is true of all realities in exist-

ence. To use any reality in existence we must first have an idea of its nature and form, for form determines function, and this constitutes the nature of a thing.

Form determines the function of a thing, and this is its nature. Form itself is an idea—a form of absolute thought. An idea, then, is the essence of reality, and the destiny of an idea is to realize itself in material form. Matter is nothing else than the manifested form of absolute thought. An idea is the essence of reality. What is essence? Essence is that without which a reality cannot exist. When the essence is given, the reality will exist; when the essence is taken away, the reality ceases to exist. Let us consider the electric lamp. It consists of a material body and electricity. The material body and the electricity must cooperate in a definite way that they may constitute an electric lamp. The material body alone or the electricity alone could not be an electric lamp. It would therefore seem that the material body and the electricity are both the essence of the electric lamp. Yet we shall presently see that they are not the essence of the electric lamp. The material body is part of the eternal and infinite matter in the universe; likewise, the electricity is part of the eternal and infinite energy in the universe. The matter and the electricity existed eternally and infinitely, and yet there was no electric lamp. Why? Because the essence of the electric lamp was not in existence. What, then, is the essence of the electric lamp? It is an idea. This idea was crystallized by Edison. Once Edison crystallized the idea of the electric lamp, an infinite number of electric lamps came into existence. So long as this idea will live in the mind of men, so long there will be infinite electric lamps. When this idea will cease to live in the mind of men, then there will no longer be electric lamps. Thus we see that the essence of the electric lamp is neither the material body nor the electricity, but it is the idea.

And now the question arises: Did Edison create the idea of the electric lamp? This seems to be so, and this is what is universally believed; but we shall presently see that Edison did not and could not create the idea. The idea of the electric lamp involves the nature of matter and the nature of electricity, and their natures are involved in the nature of substance, in the nature of absolute thought. For Edison to have created the idea of the electric lamp, he would have to create absolute thought and determine its eternal and infinite nature. Could Edison achieve this in an eternity? Hence, all that Edison accomplished was only this: he discovered the idea which was already inherent in absolute thought from eternity. And even this discovery was not made by Edison; he could not discover this idea in an eternity. This idea was revealed to him by the Absolute. Thus we see that the essence of the electric lamp is an idea.

26. And now let us consider another case. An acorn is a small and perishable thing. I put the acorn into the ground. In time it becomes an oak tree, reproducing thousands of acorns. The thousands of acorns are exactly like the first acorn. I put the thousands of acorns into the ground, and in due time they become thousands of oak trees reproducing millions of acorns. I can continue the process indefinitely, and thus the original acorn will become numberless oak trees reproducing numberless acorns. And now the question is: what was there in the original acorn which in time became numberless oak trees and numberless acorns? Let us examine the first acorn. It consists of a material body and life. It is clear that the material body alone or the life alone could not become an oak tree and reproduce acorns. The material body and the life in it had to cooperate that they might become an oak tree reproducing acorns. It would therefore seem that the material body and the life in it were the essence of the acorn. Yet we shall presently see that they were not the essence of the acorn. The material body of the acorn is part of the eternal and infinite matter in the universe, and the life in the acorn is part of the eternal and infinite life in the universe. Matter and life existed eternally and infinitely, and yet there was no acorn. Why? Because the essence of the acorn did not exist. What is the essence of the acorn? It is an idea. When the idea of the acorn was created, then an

infinite number of acorns and oak trees came into existence. So long as this idea will live, so long there will be infinite oak trees and acorns. When this idea will cease to live, then there will no longer be acorns and oak trees. By whom was this idea created? It was created by the first cause. The idea was inherent in the Absolute from eternity, and the first cause brought it into explicitness. Thus, again, we see that an idea is the essence of reality, whether the reality be a material object or a living being.

An idea is a living, conscious and thinking form of absolute thought. Let us consider the following case. After years of study and reflexion, I crystallized an idea. I wish to communicate this idea to others. I take paper, pen and ink and write a book, presenting my idea in all its fulness. I give the mansucript to the printer, and he prints ten thousand copies. I then distribute the ten thousand books. Ten thousand persons receive this book. Each one receives a different copy, a different material embodiment of my idea, but all copies contain one and the same idea. It is now clear that the essence of the book is the idea, for without the idea there would be no book. Assume that the idea is of a revolutionary nature; it will revolutionize the thoughts, beliefs and ideas of ten thousand persons. The idea will determine them to become active and to spread my idea. They will then reprint the books into hundreds of thousands of copies, they will translate it into many languages, and in time hundreds of millions of human beings will become revolutionized in their thoughts, beliefs, ideas, and they will organize themselves to effect a revolutionary transformation in society. Now, universal experience shows that this is not an uncommon case. Consider the Bible, Marx' Capital, Hitler's Mein Kampf, and so on, to see that this is not unusual. This was the history of Judaism, of Christianity, of Marxism, of Nazism, and so on. These ideas revolutionized the beliefs, thoughts, ideas, actions and attitudes of countless millions of human beings and revolutionized society. Assume, then, that the idea which I embodied in my book is of the same nature. The question is: What was there in my idea which affected mankind so fundamentally?

There was in my idea life, consciousness and thought; my idea was a form of life, consciousness and thought. An idea is a living, conscious and thinking soul. A soul is nothing else than an idea. By reading my book, the readers embraced the soul which I embodied in the book, and that soul revolutionized them. An idea, is a living, conscious and thinking soul; and, because of this, it is the most powerful in existence. Consider what Judaism, Christianity, Mohammedanism, Marxism, and even Hitlerism, accomplished against infinite opposition and obstacles. Armies, navies and forts are as nothing against ideas. The messengers of ideas might have been poisoned, stoned, crucified and destroyed, but their ideas conquered the world. An idea is so powerful, just because it is a living, conscious and thinking soul. When an idea embodies itself in matter, it becomes a living being. When the idea leaves the body, the body ceases to exist. Thus we see that an idea is the essence of reality, it is the essence of all realities in existence, it is the essence of existence itself. The idea which is the essence of eternal and infinite existence is the Infinite Intellect—the absolute, infinite and eternal idea of the Absolute.

27. And now let us consider another case. I take you to the Garden of Eden and show you Adam and Eve, just as they came out of the hands of God, perfect and beautiful. Adam and Eve had children, their children had children; and so, in the course of time, an infinite number of human beings descended from Adam and Eve. I bring them all back to life, I separate the males from the females, I place the males behind Adam, one after the other, an infinite line; and I place the females one after the other behind Eve, an infinite line. And now look at them. All males are in form like Adam, and all females are in form like Eve. And now let us consider them more closely. All were conceived in the same manner, all were born in the same manner, all grew and developed in the same manner, all had the same human nature, the same desires, the same passions, the same emotions, the same aims and purposes, they all had the

same experiences, they all suffered pain, they all enjoyed pleasure, and in the end they all died. The question now is: what determined them all to be alike? The answer is: an idea of the Infinite Intellect. This idea had two aspects: a masculine and a feminine aspect. This idea, like a seal, was stamped by the Infinite Intellect upon matter and life, and thus determined the forms, the natures and the destinies of the males and the females. All infinite human beings were only the impressions of one and the same idea of the Infinite Intellect, and for this reason they were all alike. So long as this idea of the Infinite Intellect lives, so long there will be infinite human beings; when this idea will cease to live, then there will no longer be human beings. Thus we see that, whether it is an electric lamp, or an acorn, a tool, or a human being, or any and all realities in existence, the essence of reality is an idea, which is a living, conscious and thinking soul. It is a living, conscious and thinking soul, because it is an idea of the Infinite Intellect, and the Infinite Intellect is a living, conscious and thinking idea of the Absolute.

The Infinite Intellect is God

28. The Infinite Intellect is the first cause and the first effect. The reader probably had no difficulty to follow the argument thus far. The reason is this. When we speak of the Absolute, substance, the Infinite Intellect, and the first cause, we speak of what, at first, seem to be abstractions, and no great objections can be raised against abstractions. One may accept them or reject them. But, when we come to speak of God, we are confronted with a definite Being. God implies a being that is conscious and rational. Since God is the cause of all effects, all effects ought to manifest consciousness and rationality, and this seems is not the case. Driven by the laws of thought and the nature of the human mind to postulate some ultimate reality as the cause and substance of all realities and processes in existence, we take refuge in abstractions. We call the ultimate reality the first cause, the cause of itself, substance, and the like—

they are all Unknowables. But God is not an Unknowable, an unknowable cannot be our God. Since most thinkers reached the conclusion that the ultimate reality is Unknowable, they could not speak of God, and some of them denied the existence of God. On the other hand, religion demanded that men believe in God; but thus far religion did not prove that God exists, and that he concerns himself about men. And thus it came to pass that, while mankind professed to believe in God or in many gods, no one was convinced that God exists. Let us consider the matter more closely.

Inherent in the human mind is the postulate: ex nihilo nihil—something cannot arise out of nothing. If something exists, it must have arisen out of something else; some cause determined its existence. Now, we exist. This means that some cause determined that we should exist. But we not only exist, we are also conscious, we think and we reason. We no more determined that we should be conscious, to think and to reason than we determined that we should exist; the cause that gave us existence also gave us consciousness and the powers to think and to reason. Now, a cause must be commensurate with its effect, the cause cannot be less than the effect; for, if the cause is less than the effect, part of the effect will be without cause, and this is impossible. Hence the cause that gave us existence, consciousness and the powers to think and to reason must itself exist and possess consciousness, and the powers to think and to reason. The cause that gave us existence, consciousness and the powers to think and to reason also gave existence to all infinite realities and processes in existence. That cause is absolute, infinite and eternal. And we already saw that that which is absolute, infinite and eternal is absolute, infinite and eternal in every part thereof. Now, a being that eternally exists, and is eternally and infinitely conscious, thinking and reasoning—this is God. Spinoza tells us that from the necessity of the divine nature infinite numbers of things in infinite ways, that is to say, all things which can be conceived by the Infinite Intellect, must necessarily follow. The Infinite Intellect is God. God is an infinite intellect, who conceives infinite things and processes in infinite ways, and all these constitute existence.

Hegel tells us that to him who looks upon the world rationally, the world presents itself as a rational process. Whatever the human mind contemplates, be it space, time, matter, motion, force, life, thought, and so on, it perceives that thought and reason pervade the whole of existence; that all realities and processes in existence live, move and have their being in thought and reason. Thought and reason are the substance and essence of existence; and this is so, because God, who manifests himself as existence, is a conscious, thinking and rational being. That most men do not perceive the rationality of existence, this is not surprising. Everything is measured by itself: length is measured by length, weight is measured by weight, color is measured by color, and reason is measured by reason. Most men have not yet attained to reason. That they seem to be rational, this is due to the fact that men that had attained to reason created a wonderful world, and in this world even men who had not yet attained to reason can live more or less rationally; and thus appear more or less rational. But, in fact, they are not rational. This painfully manifests itself when they have to decide on any course of conduct. So long as they follow the methods already crystallized by rational persons, so long even the ordinary men appear to be rational. But, when they have to decide upon a course of conduct that was not already determined for them by science, religion and philosophy, they invariably act irrationally. Is it any wonder that they cannot perceive thought and reason in existence? And even scientists are limited in their perception of the rationality of existence, just because science itself is limited. It requires the height and universality of philosophy to perceive that all existence lives, moves and has its being in thought and in reason. Every one according to the degree that he attained to reason, to that extent does he perceive the rationality of existence. Existence is rational. But existence is the manifestation of God. God manifests himself as existence, God is existence, God is everything in existence, and

God everywhere. Not only all realities and processes in existence live, move and have their being in God, but also God
lives, moves and has his being in all realities and processes in
existence. Just as the whole sun reflects itself in a drop of water,
so God reflects himself in every reality, be it infinitely great
or infinitesimally small. Once and for all, we must emancipate
ourselves from the superstition that God is separate and above
from the world; we must discard the notion that God created
the world, then retired into his holy abode, and left the world
to take care of itself. God did not create the world, God is the
world, and God is eternally and infinitely in the world. If God
should for an instant separate himself from the world, the world
would at once cease to exist. God not only became the world,
but God eternally and infinitely continues to be the world. We
do not have to fly on the wings of thought to find God, just
as we do not have to fly on the wings of thought to find space.
God is everywhere and is everything.

> There is no great and no small
> To the soul that maketh all;
> And where it cometh, all things are,
> And it cometh every where.—*Emerson.*

CHAPTER V

The Purpose of Creation

29. The ancient Jewish thinkers believed that God created the world to manifest himself, so that he should be recognized, honored and loved. God created man in the essence and form of God. Since man is the highest being created by God, and God endowed him with reason, it is the duty of man to recognize God, to honor and to love him. Hence the commandment: Thou shalt know Jehovah thy God, and thou shalt love him with all thy heart, thy mind and thy soul. But this belief is rejected by philosophers. I will not stop to consider those philosophers who, like Schopenhauer, postulate an unconscious cause of existence, and who therefore deny any purpose in existence. These thinkers did not realize that they involved themselves in an inherent contradiction. An unconscious cause cannot bring out conscious and thinking beings, and cannot bring out a rational world. Now, these thinkers were conscious, they were thinking and they believed themselves to be most rational. This was why they wrote big books, to manifest themselves, to be honored and to be loved. How could an unconscious cause bring out such mighty thinkers? I leave it to these philosophers to answer this question. I am concerned here about such philosophers, as Spinoza. Spinoza, in his Ethics, tried hard to prove that God exists, that he is the direct, immanent and eternal and infinite cause of all realities and processes in existence. And yet, Spinoza denied any purpose in existence, he denied that God created the world to realize any purpose. According to Spinoza, God is absolutely and supremely perfect and self-sufficing; he lacks nothing and desires nothing, and therefore he has no purpose to realize. The world came into existence, because

from the necessity of the nature of God infinite things followed in infinite ways. Hence, the question before us is this: Did God create the world, or became the world, to realize some purpose; and, if so, what was that purpose?

30. At the outset, we must be clear about purpose itself. Purpose is defined as an idea or ideal kept in the mind as an end of an effort or action; it is a plan, design or aim. It is clear that only a conscious and thinking being can have a purpose. A purpose implies a desire, and desire implies something that is desired; without a desire for something there can be no purpose. Now, God is absolutely and supremely perfect and self-sufficing, he lacks nothing and he wants nothing. Is it conceivable that God should desire something; and, to satisfy this desire, he created or became the world? Hence, Spinoza maintains that there is no purpose in existence. The question—how did men come to the belief that God created the world to realize a purpose—Spinoza answers by telling us that men are so constituted that, whatever they do, they do to realize some purpose. But men are superstitious, they create a God in their own essence and form, and therefore attribute to God a human nature. Since men do everything for a purpose, they believe that God also does every thing for a purpose. Since men crave for recognition, honor and love, they believe that God also craves for recognition, honor and love. And now the question is: which is the correct view—the religious view that God created the world to realize his purpose, to be recognized, honored and loved; or the view of Spinoza is correct, that there is no purpose in existence? We shall presently see that the religious view is correct, and Spinoza's view is false. Still more, we shall see that Spinoza, unconsciously, sustained the religious view.

According to Spinoza, God is the absolute, infinite, eternal, direct and immanent cause of all realities and processes in existence. Nothing can be conceived without God. God determines the existence, the nature, the actions and the destinies of all realities and processes in existence. And the same is true of man. God determines the existence, the nature, the thoughts, the feelings and the actions of men, and he determines the consequences of their actions. Nothing can take place in existence without the determination of God, and what God determines cannot be rendered undetermined. Man must think, feel and act as God determines him to think, feel and act. God, therefore, determines men's beliefs and ideas. Even the crudest and most superstitious beliefs of men were determined by God. The light of a small candle is of the same nature as the light of the sun, although the light of the sun is infinitely greater than the light of the candle. Likewise, the thoughts and ideas of the most primitive savage were of the same nature, and were determined by God, as the thoughts of Spinoza and his ideas, although the thoughts and ideas of Spinoza were infinitely higher and more universal than those of the primitive savage. Hence it was incumbent on Spinoza to understand the crude and superstitious ideas of men, for they were determined by God. But Spinoza contemptuously rejected them, as if they were not worthy of any consideration. This was inconsistent with his own philosophy. Men believed that God created the world to manifest himself, that he should be recognized, honored and loved. Spinoza should have endeavored to understand this belief, since it was determined by God. But Spinoza did not do this, and that was inconsistent with his own philosophy.

Next, Spinoza tells us that God loves himself with infinite love? Why does God love himself with infinite love? To understand the answer, we must first understand the nature of love. According to Spinoza, love is joy accompanied with the idea of the cause of the joy. We crave for joy, and therefore we love the cause that gives us joy. What is joy? Joy is the consciousness of our passing to higher perfection. When we pass to higher perfection, we feel joy. Hence we love that which causes us to pass to higher perfection. And now let us consider God. God loves himself with infinite love. This means that God passes to infinite higher perfection. But why does God pass to infinite higher perfection and love himself? Because he is the cause of himself, because he creates and procreates the world eternally and infinitely. If God did not create and procreate the world, he would not pass to higher perfection, and he would not feel joy, and he would not love himself. Is God indifferent to his perfection, his joy and his love? God wants to pass to infinite higher perfection, he wants to enjoy supreme and eternal joy, and he wants to love himself. But God can realize all this only by creating and procreating the world, and that means by creating and procreating himself. Can we conceive a more valid purpose than this? Thus we see that God created the world to realize a purpose—to pass to higher perfection, to feel joy and to love himself.

Whatever is absolute, infinite and eternal is absolute, infinite and eternal in every part thereof. The nature of God is the nature of existence and of every reality in existence. Every being and reality in existence procreates itself to realize a purpose. Purpose was not invented by men, it was implanted in man by God. This is the reason why men cannot do a thing without a purpose. And so, in the case of other realities and beings, purpose is implicit in their existence and in their actions. The supreme aim of all human endeavors is happiness; for, as already stated, while all other states of gratification and well being are limited in scope and duration, happiness is unlimited in scope and duration. But what is happiness? Happiness is recognition, honor and love. Man is happy only then when he is recognized, honored and loved; nothing else can give him happiness. And man never strives after anything as much as he strives after recognition, honor and love, for they give him happiness. For the sake of recognition, honor and love men will work, struggle, suffer and even die. No human being ever struggled to realize any aim or purpose—whether noble or ignoble—which was not motivated by the primordial desire to be recognized, honored and loved. And what is true of men is equally true of animals, and of all realities in existence. This is the reason why every reality endeavors to clothe itself in beauty of form that it may be recognized, honored and loved. Existence in all its realities and aspects eternally and infinitely shouts: Recognize me, honor me and love me. This is so, because existence is nothing else than the manifestation of God himself. To satisfy his primordial desire, God created the world, or he manifested himself as the world, that he may be recognized, honored and loved. God loves himself with infinite love, he loves himself, and that means he loves himself in every reality and being in existence. Without existence and the realities and beings in existence, God could not love himself. God is not an automaton, unconscious of and indifferent to what flows from his eternal and infinite nature; God is eternally and infinitely conscious of what necessarily flows from his nature, and he desires what flows from his nature, and this gives him eternal and supreme happiness, and he loves himself with infinite love. Again, Spinoza should have asked the question—whence desire. Spinoza tells us that desire is the essence of man. Desire is the essence of everything in existence, and it is the essence of existence itself. But whence this eternal and infinite desire—is it not the manifestation of the eternal and infinite desire of God? If not for this desire, there would be no world. The knowledge and understanding of an effect depend upon and involve the knowledge and understanding of the cause. In turn, the knowledge and understanding of the cause depend upon and involve the knowledge and understanding of the effect. To know and understand ourselves, we must know and understand God; but, in turn, to know and understand God, we must know and understand ourselves. God created man in the essence and form of God; in turn, man creates God in the essence and form of man. Know thyself—this is the beginning and end of all knowledge and understanding. But this is anthropomorphism, and anthropomorphism is universally condemned. Therefore, before we proceed further, we must consider anthropomorphism.

ANTHROPOMORPHISM

31. Anthropomorphism ascribes to God or existence human attributes, feelings and purposes; it interprets God or existence

in terms of human nature; it identifies the nature of God or existence with the nature of man. Anthropomorphism is universally condemned by philosophers and scientists. If the philosophers and scientists had but reflected on the matter, they would have perceived that anthropomorphism is the only rational, true and possible method for knowing and understanding God and existence. We can know and understand existence only through the means of our body and our mind; we cannot cast off our body and mind and see existence as bodyless and mindless spirits. The philosphers and the scientists deceive themselves by imagining that they see existence not anthropomorphically; they always remain within their bodies and their minds, and they always see existence through their bodies and their minds; and, viewing existence through the means of the body and the mind, is anthropomorphism. If anthropomorphism is to be condemned, then all human knowledge and understanding are to be condemned; what, then, will become of philosophy and science? When the philosophers and the scientists are confronted by this question, they take refuge in the pre-Einsteinian relativity. They then tell us that human knowledge and understanding are necessarily relative, and that we cannot know existence as it is in itself. Yet this does not prevent the philosophers and the scientists from formulating theories about existence, its realities and processes. If we can never know and understand existence as it is in itself, then all the theories of the philosophers and scientists are only figments of the human mind. Are the philosophers and the scientists ready to admit this? In turn, I will ask the philosophers and the scientists this question. How do they know that all human knowledge and understanding are only relative? Since, according to their assumption, we have only relative knowledge and understanding—and this is the only kind of knowledge and understanding that we can ever have—then we should have taken this knowledge and understanding as absolute. For instance, the rustic is absolutely certain that the earth is stationary and that the sun moves about the earth; he is certain of this, because he does not know the truth. Only one who knows the truth knows that the senses are deceived by appearances. Hence, to know and understand that our knowledge and understanding of existence are relative, we must first know and understand existence as it is in itself. But, since the philosophers and the scientists tell us that we cannot know and understand existence as it is in itself, they impliedly tell us that they do not know the nature of their own knowledge and understanding of existence. What, then, is the truth about the matter?

We are not extra-mundane beings, we did not fall into the world from nowhere; we are soul of the soul, mind of the mind and body of the body of existence. We did not make ourselves, we did not determine our nature, and we did not endow ourselves with the powers to think and to reason. Just as the body manifests the physical laws of existence, so our mind manifests the mental laws of existence. Our mind no more determines its thoughts and ideas than our body determines its actions; all are determined by existence. Existence is absolutely one in essence and form of manifestation. A photon, an electron, a proton, a grain of sand or a seed is just as infinite and eternal as existence itself is; existence contains no more than what the photon, the electron, the proton, the grain of sand or the seed contains; and they do not contain less than the whole existence contains. When philosophers and scientists will adequately know and understand the photon, the electron, the proton, the grain of sand and the seed, then they will know and understand the whole of existence. And this is especially true of man, for man is the highest and most explicit manifestation of existence. To know and understand man is to know and understand infinite and eternal existence. Man is in truth the measure of all existence. In man's being, in his thoughts, feelings, actions and purposes, manifest themselves the being, the thoughts, the feelings, actions and purposes of existence itself. Man goes through an evolution, this evolution is the evolution of existence itself. Job was therefore absolutely correct when he said: Yet, through my being shall I see God. The Bible tells us that Elohim created man in the essence and form of God. Philosophers and scientists reverse this statement and tell us that men created gods in the essence and form of men. Savages created savage gods, barbarians created barbarian gods, and civilized men created civilized gods. Both statements are correct. God manifests himself in man, and man realizes himself in God. Thus we see that anthropomorphism is the only true and possible way to know and understand God and existence. And the philosophers and scientists who condemn anthropomorphism do not realize that they, too, know and understand only anthropomorphically.

32. We saw that the Absolute is absolute thought, and that absolute thought is substance. We also saw that the Absolute comprehends itself in an idea of itself, and that this idea is the Infinite Intellect, and that the Infinite Intellect is God. Again, we saw that an idea is the essence of reality, the destiny of an idea is to manifest itself in material form. God conceives infinite ideas in infinite ways, and these ideas realize themselves in the infinite realities in existence. Finally, we saw that of absolute thought we have a direct and intimate consciousness, for absolute thought is our consciousness, it is our life, and it is our thoughts. Thus by means of our consciousness we comprehend the realities of existence, existence and God and the Absolute. To confirm all this, I will quote what Eddington tells us in his work: The Nature of the Physical World. This is what he tells us:—

Take the living human brain endowed with mind and thought. Thought is one of the indispensable facts of the world. I know that I think, with a certainty which I cannot attribute to any of my physical knowledge of the world. Here then is a world fact to be investigated. The physicist brings his tools and commences systematic exploration. All that he discovers is a collection of atoms and electrons and fields of force arranged in space and time. But none of these is identical with thought. How can this collection of ordinary atoms be a thinking machine? But what knowledge have we of the nature of atoms which renders it at all incongruous that they should constitute a thinking object? Why not then attach it to thought? It seems rather silly to prefer to attach it to a so-called concrete nature inconsistent with thought, and then to wonder where the thought comes from. To put the conclusion crudely—the stuff of the world is mind-stuff. The mind-stuff is not spread in space and time. Only here and there it rises to the level of consciousness, but from such islands proceeds all knowledge. Besides the direct knowledge contained in each self-knowing unit, there is inferential knowledge. The latter includes our knowledge of the physical world. Consciousness is not sharply defined, but fades into sub-consciousness; and beyond that we must postulate something indefinite yet continuous with our mental nature. This I take to be the world-stuff. We liken it to our consciousness, our conscious feelings, now that we are convinced of the formal and symbolic character of the entities of physics, there is nothing else to liken it to. We have only one approach to a knowledge of the world, namely, through our direct knowledge of the mind. The supposed approach through the physical world leads only into the cycle of physics, where we run round and round like a kitten chasing its tail and never reach the world stuff at all. So that the crudest anthropomorphic image of a spiritual deity can scarcely be so wide of the truth as one conceives in terms of metrical equations.

The Absolute is absolute thought, existence is thought, the realities of existence are forms of thought, and we are only a form of thought. Thought can comprehend thought. When the philosophers and the scientists will realize this, they will no longer raise any objection against anthropomorphism. The truth that thought is the substance of all realities was perceived by profound thinkers long ago, but it took science a long time to perceive this truth.

CHAPTER VI

The Order of Creation

33. Modern philosophy and science tell us that the world was brought out by the process of evolution. Modern philosophy and science postulate the existence of matter in a diffused state, which in time became integrated and differentiated into stars, planets, and all other realities of existence. Modern philosophy and science do not know how matter itself came into existence, nor why it was in a diffused state. Somehow matter existed in a diffused state. Thus modern philosophy and science begin in the middle of the story. But what is evolution? Spencer tells us: Evolution is an integration of matter and concomitant dissipation of motion, during which the matter passes from a state of indefinite, incoherent homogeneity into a state of definite, coherent heterogeneity; and during which the retained motion undergoes parallel changes. This means that all realities in existence started out from a state of discrete and unorganized homogeneity and gradually integrated into states of ever higher organization and ever greater heterogeneity. We must notice this. Evolution is only a method in accordance with which realities came into existence, but evolution is not a cause. When it is said that a house was constructed in accordance with a certain plan, it is understood that, not the plan, but somebody made the plan and constructed the house. When it is said that the realities came into existence in accordance with the method of evolution, it must be understood that some cause made the plan or method of evolution, and brought out the realities in accordance with that plan or method. Evolution, then, is but an effect, and not a cause. By an effect we cannot explain the creation of the world.

However, for a time the doctrine of evolution remained un-
challenged. Then science discovered the second law of thermo-
dynamics, known as entropy. Clausins formulated the law of
entropy as follows: The entropy of the world tends towards
a maximum state; the more the universe approaches this bound-
ary state, the more do the occasions of new changes disappear;
and if this state were at last attained, no further change would
take place, and the universe would come to be in a state of per-
sistent death. According to this law, the universe started out in
a state of highest organization, and since then constantly and
inexorably ran down, degenerated and passed into states of ever
greater disorganization. This will continue until the universe
will reach the death-level of disorganization. Thus we see that,
according to the law of entropy, the genesis of the world was
by a process just the reverse of that of evolution. Eddington tells
us that, while all else in existence may be relative, the law of
entropy is absolute: all existence inevitably passes into a state
of death. Thus we have two theories of the genesis and destiny
of the world that are opposed to each other. Which of them is
the true theory? We shall presently see each theory is only half
true, each theory comprehends only one-half of the cycle of
creation. Evolution starts out with matter in a diffused state, but
evolution does not tell us how matter came into existence, and
why it was in a diffused state. On the other hand, the law of
entropy tells us that the universe is inevitably running to the
state of death. If this was so, then the universe by this time
would have been absolutely dead, for an eternity passed since
the universe came into existence. And yet we find the universe
is now just as much alive, and is just as capable of change, as
it ever was before. Again, how came the universe to be in a
state of highest organization? How came there to be a universe
altogether? Thus we see that both evolution and the law of
entropy start in the middle of the story and end in the middle
of the story. It is only by a synthesis of both theories that the
truth is revealed.

34. God started out with an infinite and eternal idea of existence. This idea was in a state of absolutely highest organization and unity, because it was one infinite and eternal idea of infinite and eternal existence. This idea then differentiated itself into infinite series of ideas, each idea of which became a separate and distinct idea, and manifested itself in a separate and distinct material form. Thus came into existence the infinite photons, electrons, protons, atoms, molecules, and groups of molecules. Matter was then in a diffused state. Thus the diffused matter came into existence as the result of the law of entropy. And now that infinite matter was in a diffused state, the process of evolution began to integrate the diffused matter, and differentiated it into the infinite realities in existence. Entropy is the downward movement from the Absolute to diffused matter, and evolution is the upward movement back to the Absolute. The universe does not tend towards absolute death, it tends back to the highest organization. When the earth was prepared for life, life appeared on the earth's surface; it started out in the form of primordial living cells, the monera; then life integrated the cells into groups of cells, and groups of groups of cells; and thus, in time, life brought out an infinite series of living beings, one higher than the other, until man was brought out. Man started as an animal, then in succession he became a savage, a barbarian, a civilized man, and he is destined to become a superman, a rational and morally autonomous person. Thus we see the eternal cycle of creation. Viewing creation in this light, we see that out of chaos and darkness emerged creation; we see the dawn of light and the appearance of life; we see the infinite forms of life following one another, rising ever higher, until man appeared. The ladder of evolution stands on the basis of diffused matter, and reaches the Absolute. Thus existence begins with the highest organization, descends to universal disorganization, and then returns back to highest organization. "And a ladder stood on the earth, the top of it reached heaven, and the angels of Elohim ascended and descended by it, and Jehovah stood above it." (Genesis: 28, 12-13.)

WHAT IS MATTER?

35. Einstein tells us: All matter in the universe is made of elementary particles of only a few kinds. It is like seeing in one town buildings of different sizes, construction and architecture, but from shack to sky-scraper only a few different kinds of bricks were used, the same in all buildings. So all known elements of our material world, from hydrogen the lightest, to uranium the heaviest, are built of the same kinds of bricks, that is, the same kinds of elementary particles. The heaviest elements, the most complicated buildings, are unstable and they disintegrate or, as we say, they are *radioactive*. Some of the bricks, that is, the elementary particles of which the radioactive atoms are constructed, are sometimes thrown out with a very great velocity, approaching that of light. Matter represents vast stores of energy, and that energy represents matter. By far the greatest part of energy is concentrated in matter; but the field surrounding the particles also represent energy, though in a comparably smaller quantity. We could therefore say: Matter is where the concentration of energy is great, field where the concentration of energy is small. The difference between matter and fields is a quantitative rather than a qualitative one. We cannot imagine a definite surface separating distinctly field and matter. Again, Eddington tells us that the atom is as porous as the solar system. If we eliminate all the unfilled space in man's body, and collect his protons and electrons into one mass, the man would be reduced to a speck just visible with a magnifying glass. All varieties of matter are ultimately composed of two elementary constituents—protons and electrons. Electrically these are the opposites of one another, the proton being a charge of a positive electricity, and the electron a charge of negative electricity. The proton has 1840 times the mass of the electron. The hydrogen is the most primitive form of matter, its atom consisting of one proton and one electron. In other atoms a number of protons and a number of electrons are cemented together to form a

nucleus; the electrons required to make up a balance are scattered like remote satellites of the nucleus, and can even escape from the atom and wander freely through the material world. The diameter of the electron is about one-fifty-thousands of the diameter of the atom. This means that the atom is fifty thousand times greater than the electron. A proton is supposed to be smaller than the atom.

Matter, then, is nothing else than concentrated energy. Energy implies motion and velocity of motion. The particles of energy which constitute the atom are perpetually in motion, and their velocities are very great. In the case of the electron, it approaches the velocity of light. As we proceed from what appears to be a solid piece of matter to the molecules, the atoms, the protons, the electrons and the photons, we pass to a form of energy that moves with ever greater velocity; the apparently solid piece of matter has the least velocity of motion. The velocity of the energy, as we proceed ever deeper into the constitution of matter, approaches the velocity of light. When the velocity of the energy reaches the velocity of light, matter disappears and becomes light; that is, the energy which until then appeared as matter, now appears as light. Einstein tells us that light is composed of energy-grains which are called photons. The photons are small portions of energy, travelling through empty space with the velocity of light. Not only matter and electric charges, but also energy of radiation has a granular structure, that is, is built up of light quanta. In addition of quanta of matter and quanta of electricity there are also quanta of energy. What Einstein tells us means this. The ultimate element or unit of matter is light. The difference between light and matter is only a difference in the velocity of motion; light travels with the greatest velocity, while matter travels with a lesser velocity. Thus we get at the secret of the nature of matter. When light lessens its velocity it becomes matter, and when matter reaches the velocity of light it becomes light. Light, then, is the ultimate element and unit of matter.

36. Now, science assumes that light travels with the greatest velocity, but this is not true. There is one reality that travels with even greater velocity, and that is thought; thought travels with infinite velocity. Of this we have a direct proof. Our thoughts can travel through infinite space and infinite time in a moment; the comprehension of infinite time and infinite space implies infinite velocity of motion. Thought has infinite velocity, because it is the Absolute. The Absolute is infinite, and therefore his thought is infinite in velocity. The substance of all realities is, as we saw, absolute thought. All forms of matter and all forms of energy are nothing else than forms of absolute thought. The differences between them are due to the differences in the velocities of their motions. The greater the velocity of motion the nearer a reality approaches absolute thought, and the smaller the velocity of its motion the nearer it approaches matter. Hence it follows that any reality can pass from one state to another state only by a change in the velocity of its motion. If matter reaches the velocity of light, it becomes light; on the other hand, when light travels with the velocity of matter, it becomes matter. Again, when light travels with infinite velocity, it becomes absolute thought. In turn, when absolute thought travels with the velocity of light, it becomes light. Thus we see how absolute thought becomes light, and light becomes matter. In turn, matter becomes light, and light becomes absolute thought. All realities travel through a four-dimensional continuum; but absolute thought transcends all realities, it is above space, time, light and matter. Therefore the velocity of motion of absolute thought is absolutely infinite. And thus we adequately realize that absolute thought is the substance of all realities and processes in existence. This prepared us to understand the physical world, which we are now to examine. In recent times, relativity revolutionized all prior knowledge and understanding of the physical world. Hence, before we take up the physical world, we must acquaint ourselves with the modern theory of relativity.

RELATIVITY

37. Relativity has revolutionized the scientific conceptions of time, space, matter, motion, force, gravitation, magnetism, electricity, heat and light. The physical world is only one of the infinite aspects of existence. Relativity does not comprehend the Absolute, Infinite and Eternal, it does not comprehend God, it does not comprehend substance and thoughts, it does not comprehend life, mind and man; it does not comprehend society and history and destiny; it does not comprehend philosophy, religion, ethics and art; and, finally, it does not know of the creation and purpose of the world, and it does not concern itself about good and evil, justice and injustice, progress and regress, and it does not comprehend the ultimate nature even of matter, motion, force, and so on. Thus we see that Relativity is limited in its scope. But, while Relativity is limited in its scope, nevertheless it involves the whole of existence in all its eternal and infinite aspects. This must be so. Existence in all its eternal and infinite extent and aspects is absolutely one and indivisible; every one of its aspects is absolutely bound up with all other aspects of existence. Hence, adequately to know and understand any one of the aspects of existence, we must know and understand all its aspects. From this follows that adequately to know and understand relativity, we must interpret it in the light of the monistic philosophy—a philosophy that comprehends all aspects of existence. Hence, the method of procedure will be the following. First, I will present the theory of Relativity as it was formulated by Einstein. Second, I will then interpret relativity in the light of the monistic philosophy.

Relativity does not concern itself about the physical world as it appears to our senses, but as it can be perceived by intuition, comprehended by reason, and interpreted mathematically. Relativity is the mathematical aspect of the physical world. For this purpose relativity brought out a mathematics of a high order. This presents to us a problem. Since relativity rests on a mathematics of a high order, and we are not mathematicians, how can we understand relativity? Indeed, there was a time, and not long ago, when it was said that only a dozen scientists understood relativity. It is true that only a dozen scientists understood relativity, but now there are thousands who understand relativity, and in due time all educated persons will understand relativity, although not all of them will be mathematicians. How will this be possible? This we shall presently see. Mathematics is absolutely essential to demonstrate a truth or a fact, but mathematics is not absolutely essential to the understanding of the truth or the fact. An illustration will make it clear. The earth rotates about its axis and revolves around the sun. The earth is about ninety-three million miles from the sun, it moves around the sun with a velocity of about nineteen miles per second, and its orbit around the sun is an elipse. These and many other facts connected with the relation of the earth to the sun and the other planets required infinite observation, thought and mathematical calculations to be demonstrated. But, once these facts were demonstrated and the scientists and astronomers convinced themselves that these facts are true, mankind could accept these facts and understand them, although they were neither mathematicians nor scientists. This is true of all sciences. With infinite observation, thought, mathematical calculations and experiments the scientists demonstrated numerous facts and truths about the realities and the processes of existences. We accept these facts and truths and we understand them, although we are not scientists. It is the same with relativity. To demonstrate the truths which relativity revealed about the physical world, it was necessary that great mathematicians and physicists should bring out a high order of mathematics and make numerous experiments. But now that the truths and facts of relativity were demonstrated and accepted by the scientists, we can accept these truths and facts and understand them. And we shall presently see that the truths and facts of relativity can readily be understood. There is another aspect of the matter which must be pointed out.

As stated before, relativity does not concern itself about

the physical world as it appears to the senses. For this reason, relativity does not affect our relations to the physical world. All that relativity accomplished was this: it revealed to us a deeper and more adequate insight into the nature of the physical world. This is true of all sciences. Let us again refer to the earth. Science demonstrated that the earth rotates about its axis and revolves about the sun. We know that this is true. Notwithstanding this, to our senses the earth still appears to be at rest and the sun moves around the earth. Again, we know that the sun is a thousand times the size of the earth and is ninety-three million miles from the earth. Yet the sun appears to us small and near. It is so with relativity. Relativity revealed to us a deeper and more adequate idea of the physical world, yet the physical world remains to us just as it was before. The reason is this. The physical world as it appears to our senses is not an illusion, as some thinkers believed. On the contrary, the physical world as it appears to us is to us even more real than the physical world which relativity reveals. Things in existence may not be what they appear to us to be, but what they appear to us to be are the real world to us, and we are most vitally concerned about the things as they appear. Things in themselves are neither good nor evil. For instance, sugar in itself is not sweet, and poison in itself is not dangerous; but sugar to us is sweet, and poison to us is dangerous. Hence, while we may be able to make a better use of things the more adequately we understand them, yet the things concern us only as they appear to us. Relativity will help us much to understand the physical world more adequately, and to that extent we shall be able to make a better use of things; but the physical world that will always concern us will be the physical world as it appears to our senses and comprehended by our understanding.

CHAPTER VII

The Special and the General Theory of Relativity

38. The following is a brief outline of Relativity based on Einstein's book: The Special and the General Theory of Relativity, published in 1920, by Henry Holt and Company, New York.

Einstein tells us: "A most fundamental problem, for thousands of years wholly obscured by its implications, is that of motion." Indeed, the problem of motion is the most fundamental problem that confronted the human mind. All realities in existence—the largest as well as the smallest—are perpetually in a state of motion. Without this perpetual motion, the realities could not exist. Assuming that the realities could exist in a state of absolute rest, they would not affect us, and we would not be aware of their existence. Again, if we were in a state of absolute rest, we could not exist, and we could not be conscious of anything. Thus we see that the problem of motion is the most fundamental problem of existence. Next, Einstein tells us: "It was at all times clear that, from the point of view of the idea it conveys to us, motion must only be considered as relative motion." What we must notice is the following. Einstein does not tell us that motion itself is relative. Science does not know whether motion in itself is relative or absolute. It is only from the point of view of the idea it conveys to us, motion must only be considered as relative motion; for we can perceive something moving only with relation to something else as a body of reference. For instance, a train is travelling with uniform motion in a straight line. If we stand on the embankment, we shall see the train in motion; but, if we sit in the train, we shall see the embankment in motion. The embankment will appear to us to be in motion even when we are fully aware that we and the train are in motion. This is so in all cases.

And now consider the following case. While we sit in the train that is travelling with uniform motion in a straight line, we drop from the window a stone without throwing it. We look out from the window and see that the stone falls to the ground in a straight line. But a man standing on the embankment will see the stone fall to the ground in a curved line. Consider another case. The first law of motion, as formulated by Newton, is known as the law of inertia. According to this law, a body persists in the state in which it is. If it is at rest, the body will persist to remain at rest; if it is in motion, it will persist to move with uniform motion in a straight line. This means that a body resists any change in its state or direction and velocity of its motion. Now, a body far removed from other bodies, so that no other bodies or forces can affect it, will remain at rest if it is at rest, or it will move with uniform motion in a straight line if it is in motion. The stars are very far from one another, and they are not affected by one another. According to the law of inertia, the stars should move in uniform motion in straight lines. Yet to us they appear to move in circular orbits. We see the sun rise in the morning at the horizon, then rises to the zenith in the sky, and towards evening it comes down again. And the same is true of the stars. They appear to be moving in circular orbits. But we know that they do not move in circular orbits around the earth. But because we stand on the earth, which is our body of reference from which we view the motions of the sun and the stars, they appear to us to be moving around the earth. Thus we see that motion appears to us to be relative to the body of reference from which we view the motion. This was known all the time; it was not discovered by relativity, and is not the starting point of relativity.

39. And now consider the following case. We sit in the train that is moving with uniform motion in a straight line. A raven is flying in the air with uniform motion in a straight line. We

look out from the window and see the raven flying with uniform motion in a straight line. A man standing on the embankment also sees the raven flying in the air with uniform motion in a straight line. Notice the difference between this case and the case of the stone falling to the ground considered before. To us sitting in the train moving with uniform motion in a straight line, the stone will appear to be falling to the ground in a straight line; but to one standing on the embankment, the stone will appear to be falling to the ground in a curved line. But in the case of the raven moving with uniform motion in a straight line, it will appear to be moving with uniform motion in a straight line both to us who are sitting in the train that is moving with uniform motion in a straight line and also to the man standing on the embankment. But notice the conditions. First, the raven itself must be flying in the air with uniform motion in a straight line. Second, the train itself must be moving with uniform motion in a straight line. Only in this case will the flying of the raven appear to be with uniform motion in a straight line both to us who are sitting in the moving train and to him who is standing on the embankment. But, if the raven is not flying in the air with uniform motion in a straight line, or if the train is not moving with uniform motion in a straight line, the raven will not appear to be moving with uniform motion in a straight line both to us sitting in the train and to him that is standing on the embankment. This is called the principle of *restricted* relativity, because it is restricted to motions that are uniform and in a straight line. But what about the stone falling to the ground which we considered before? The stone was not falling to the ground in a straight line. While in our hands, the stone was moving together with us and the train in a uniform motion in a straight line; that is, the train was carrying us and the stone in a uniform motion in a straight line. The stone embodied a momentum which carried it forward. When we dropped the stone from the window, its momentum carried it forward, at the same time the gravitation of the earth pulled it downward. The result was that the stone fell to the ground in a curved line. We sitting in the moving train also moved together with the train forward; that is, we moved forward with the same velocity as the stone was moving forward. Therefore the stone appeared to us to be falling to the ground in a straight line. For this reason the principle of restricted relativity does not apply to the case of the stone. But bear this in mind. The principle of restricted relativity was not a discovery of relativity, nor is it its starting point. This principle was known even before the theory of relativity was brought to the fore. Thus we learned about the relativity of motion in general, and we also learned about the principle of restricted relativity. And now let us go a step further.

40. A train is moving with uniform motion in a straight line. A man in the train is moving or walking in the direction of the motion of the train. Let us say that the train is moving with a velocity of sixty miles an hour, and the man is walking with a velocity of three miles an hour. A man standing on the embankment will see that the man is walking with a velocity greater than that of the train. The reason is this. The train is moving with a velocity of sixty miles an hour. The man is walking in the direction of the motion of the train with a velocity of three miles an hour. But, while he is walking with a velocity of three miles an hour, the train carries him with a velocity of sixty miles an hour. Thus the man is moving with a greater velocity than the train is moving. Hence with relation to the embankment the man will traverse a greater distance than the train will traverse in a given time. And now let us consider another case. Light travels with a uniform motion in a straight line with a constant velocity of 186,000 miles a second. The velocity of light neither increases nor diminishes: it is constant. And now let us suppose that a ray of light travels along the train that is moving with a velocity of sixty miles an hour in a straight line. According to the previous case, the ray of light should travel with a greater velocity than 186,000 miles a second. Yet, it is shown mathematically that in this case the ray of light will travel with a velocity

less than 186,000 miles a second. The physicists were thus confronted with a problem. They were confronted with this alternative: either to abandon the principle of restricted relativity, or to assume that light does not travel with the constant velocity of 186,000 miles a second. But the physicists could not do either, because the principle of restricted relativity and the constancy of the velocity of light were demonstrated beyond any doubt. At this juncture relativity entered the arena. The endeavor to reconcile the constancy of the velocity of light with the principle of restricted relativity gave birth to the theory of relativity. As we shall presently see, the theory of relativity reconciled the constancy of the velocity of light with the principle of restricted relativity. To understand how relativity achieved this, we must first consider the relativity of space and time.

41. Time is measured by clocks, and space is measured by measuring-rods. Prior to relativity, time and space were assumed to be absolute; but relativity showed that time and space, like motion, are relative to the body of reference from which they are viewed. Consider the following case. A lightning struck the embankment at two points far apart from each other. Suppose that by clocks and mirrors we convince ourselves that the lightning struck the embankment at the two points simultaneously. And now let us assume that, while the lightning struck the embankment at the two points, a long train was travelling along the embankment so that the lightning struck also the train at two points opposite the two points on the embankment. The question is: will the men sitting in the train also convince themselves that the lightning struck at the two points in the train simultaneously? We shall presently see that to them the lightning strokes at the two points in the train will not appear to have been simultaneous. That the men sitting in the train should see the two strokes of the lightning, the light from the two points must travel to their eyes, and only when the light reaches their eyes do they see the strokes of the lightning. Now, the train is moving away from the point in the rear and is moving towards the point in

the front. The light from the point in the front will have to travel a shorter distance than the light from the rear will have to travel; therefore the passengers will see the point in the front sooner than they will see the point in the rear. Thus to the passengers it will appear that the lightning did not strike both points simultaneously. Thus we see that, while from the embankment the lightning will appear to have struck both points simultaneously, to the passengers in the train it will appear that the lightning did not strike both points simultaneously.

Again, suppose we want to measure the distance between these two points on the embankment and on the train. With the measuring-rod we measure the distance on the embankment, and we find that the distance is five-hundred feet. And now we measure the distance between the two points on the moving train. Will we also find the distance on the moving train to be five-hundred feet? The answer is, no, and the reason is this. Matter in motion contracts. The measuring-rod in the moving train will also be in motion, and therefore will contract. Therefore on the moving train the distance will appear to be more than five-hundred feet long. Again, suppose we want to measure the time it took the train to pass from one point to the other point. Let us assume that, when measured by the clock on the embankment, it will show that it took thirty seconds. And now let us measure with the same clock the time on the moving train. Will the clock show the same time on the moving train? The answer is, no, and the reason is this. Clocks in motion slow down. Matter in motion contracts, and clocks in motion slow down. By our senses we cannot detect this, but this is demonstrated by mathematics. Referring again to the case of the ray of light travelling along the moving train, we saw that the ray of light with relation to the moving train will move with a lesser velocity than its constant velocity of 186,000 miles a second. Can this be detected by the senses? The answer is, no; this is demonstrated by mathematics. As this is universally accepted by the scientists, we also accept these facts as demonstrated. We must bear this in mind. The whole theory of relativity rests on mathematics,

and cannot be demonstrated to the senses. It is our task to understand it.

42. The theory of relativity grew out of the endeavor to reconcile the principle of restricted relativity with the constant velocity of light. The reconciliation was achieved through the discovery that matter in motion contracts and clocks in motion
slow down. Before the advent of relativity physics postulated
the following assumptions:—

(1) The time interval between two events is independent of
the condition of the body of reference, whether it is at rest or
in motion;

(2) The distance between two points on a rigid body is
independent of the condition of the body of reference, whether
it is at rest or is in motion.

But relativity demonstrated that both assumptions are false.
Matter in motion contracts, and clocks in motion slow down.
The measuring-rod in the moving train will become shorter, and
the clock in the moving train will slow down. They thus compensate each other. Hence, in fact, the distance traversed by the
train as measured in the train will appear to be the same as measured on the embankment, and both distances will be traversed
in the same time as measured by the clock on the moving train
and on the embankment. And thus there is no longer any contradiction between the principle of restricted relativity and the
constant velocity of light. This reconciliation between the principle of restricted relativity and the constant velocity of light
is called the principle of *Special Relativity*. The principle of
special relativity declares: Every general law of nature is so constituted that it is transformed into a law of the same form with
reference to a body of reference that is at rest as with reference
to a body of reference that is in uniform motion in a straight
line. We must, however, carefully notice this. The principle of
special relativity, like the principle of restricted relativity, applies only to motion that is uniform and in a straight line; it does
not apply to other forms of motion. But in existence there are

all kinds of motion, such as accelerated motion, curvilinear motion, and so on. To these different kinds of motion the principle of special relativity does not apply.

43. Before we proceed to consider motions that are neither uniform nor in a straight line, we must pause to consider the question: why does matter contract when in motion, and why do clocks slow down when in motion? We saw that the atom is as porous as the solar system is. All matter consists of electrons and protons; the protons are positive electric charges, and the electrons are negative electric charges. The measuring-rod is nothing else than a swarm of electrical particles rushing about and widely separated from one another. The particles keep a certain average distance from one another, so that the whole volume remains relatively steady. When the rod is set into motion, these electrical forces change. Electricity in motion constitutes an electric current, and the electric current gives rise to magnetic forces. The electrical particles will come closer together, and thus the rod contracts. The contraction increases as the velocity of the motion increases. When the velocity of the motion reaches that of light, the matter contracts to zero, and the matter disappears. Why do clocks slow down when in motion? A material body consists of numerous particles of matter, of electrons and protons. The greater the velocity of motion of a body the slower becomes the movement of its component parts. And so it is with the clock. The clock is a material body consisting of numerous particles of matter and of parts of the clock. When the clock as a whole is set into motion, its component parts slow down their motions. When the velocity of the motion of the clock should reach that of light, the clock will stop altogether. The deeper reason for this is the following. We saw that, by virtue of inertia inherent in matter, a body persists to remain in the state in which it is; it resists any change either in its state of rest or in its state of motion, or a change in the direction and the velocity of the motion. The greater the velocity of the motion the greater is the inertia, that is, the greater will be the re-

sistance. When the velocity of motion reaches that of light, the resisting inertia becomes infinite, so that no force in existence can overcome the inertia. Hence the parts of the body come to a standstill, and the body itself disappears. The resisting inertia causes the particles of matter to come ever nearer and closer to one another. Since the particles of matter are only electrical charges, the particles fuse together and become light. Matter occupies space; but when matter reaches the velocity of light it no longer occupies space.

When a body is at rest, its parts freely move about one another within certain distances from one another; but, when the body is set in motion, their individual motions are transmitted and transformed into a motion of the whole body; and so what the body as a whole gains in motion its individual parts lose in motion. Hence the greater the velocity of motion of the clock the slower will be the motion of its individual parts. And, when the velocity reaches that of light, all parts of the clock come to a standstill, and the clock itself disappears. Spencer already perceived the transformation of the motions of the individual parts into the motion of the whole body. Spencer tells us: "If concrete matter arises by the aggregation of diffused matter, then concrete motion arises by the aggregation of diffused motion. That which comes into existence as the movement of masses implies a cessation of an equivalent molecular motion. The advance is from the motion of simple molecules to the motion of compound molecules, from molecular motions to the motions of masses, and from the motions of smaller masses to the motions of larger masses." What Spencer means is this. When a body is at rest, its particles move freely about one another and have a wide range of motion, and then they are far apart from one another. But, when the body is set into motion, the motions of the individual parts are transformed into motion of the whole body; the particles come closer to one another, the range of their motions becomes ever more limited, they become integrated, and their individual motions slow down. Thus, when the velocity of motion of the whole body reaches that of light, the individual parts become integrated into what is no longer matter, and all motion stops. It is so with a body of men. In a state of peace, the individuals move freely about one another and each one has a wide range of motion; but, when an emergency arises which requires cooperation or struggle, then the motions of the individuals become integrated into a motion of the whole aggregate of individuals; and so what the whole body of men gains in motion the individuals lose in motion.

44. Before the advent of relativity science knew of two laws of conservation: the conservation of matter and the conservation of energy. Matter was regarded as distinct from energy; matter was regarded as being passive, while energy was regarded as active. But relativity demonstrated that matter and energy are one and the same. In the sense in which previously matter was regarded it does not exist, Matter is nothing else than a form of energy. Since matter is energy it follows that there is only one law of conservation, namely, the conservation of energy. Relativity, therefore, no longer speaks of matter and energy, it speaks of mass, by which it means matter and energy. We saw that the principle of special relativity, as well as the principle of restricted relativity, pertains to uniform motion in a straight line. But in existence there are all kinds of motion; some are uniform, some are accelerated motions; some are in a straight line, and some are curvilinear. What about these different kinds of motion? This problem was solved by Einstein, and his solution constitutes the General Theory of Relativity. Our next step is to consider the general theory of relativity.

The General Theory of Relativity

45. Suppose two bodies are acted upon by the same force, and suppose that one body is three times as massive as the other body is. Since the same force acts upon both bodies, the smaller body will move faster than the larger body. This is clear. But this is not the case of gravitation. Gravitation affects all bodies with

the same accelerated velocity, no matter how the bodies may differ from one another in size, shape and mass. If from a high tower and through a vacuum several bodies of different sizes, shapes and masses were dropped, they will all come down to the earth with the same accelerated velocity at the same time. This shows that gravitation is proportional to the mass of the body. The reason is this. Gravitation acts, not on the mass of a body as a whole, but on each particle of matter. Therefore, whether the body consists of few particles of matter or of many particles of matter, gravitation will pull down all particles of matter with the same accelerated velocity and at the same time. For this reason all bodies, no matter how they may differ in size, shape and mass, will through a vacuum come down to the earth in the same time. Now, Newton postulated that gravitation acts at a distance simultaneously. Every particle of matter attracts every other particle of matter in the universe, no matter how far apart they may be from one another, and no matter how devoid the intervening space may be of all matter. But how do the particles of matter attract one another at infinite distances through empty space? Modern physicists convinced themselves that this is impossible. Hence they were compelled to assume that the infinite space in the universe is filled with a substance, called ether, and that by means of this ether the particles of matter attract one another. But investigation showed that there is no such substance as ether in the infinite space of the universe. Thus the original question presented itself: how is gravitation possible? The answer which general relativity gave is this. Gravitation is like magnetism. How does a magnet attract a piece of iron? The magnet radiates a magnetic field. When a piece of iron comes into the range of the magnetic field, the magnet attracts the iron. It is the same with gravitation. Every body radiates a gravitational field. The earth radiates a gravitational field. When a body comes within the range of the gravitational field of the earth, the earth by means of its gravitational field attracts the body. Thus gravitation does not act through empty space, it acts through a gravitational field. Thus the sun and the planets attract one another by means of their gravitational fields. And so all the infinite bodies in the universe attract one another by means of their gravitational fields. And thus the general theory of relativity revolutionized our idea of gravitation.

Next, the general theory of relativity revolutionized our ideas of space and time. Prior to the advent of this theory, space and time were regarded as two separate and distinct entities or, according to Kant, intuitive perceptions. For instance, geometry comprehends space, but it does not comprehend time. But the general theory of relativity showed that space and time constitute one continuum. Whatever exists or takes place, exists or takes place in both space and time. Matter was defined as that which occupies space, but now we see that matter occupies both space and time. Matter is perpetually in a state of motion. Matter is extended, which means that it occupies space. Do away with extension, and matter is no longer in existence. Again, matter is perpetually in a state of motion. Motion is possible only in space and time. Matter cannot move without moving from one point in space to another point in space; and matter cannot move from one point in space to another point in space without moving also from one moment to another moment of time. Hence, motion not in time is just as inconceivable as motion not in space. All realities and processes in existence live, move and have their being in a space-time continuum. All natural bodies in existence are spherical in form. This is true of stars, planets, electrons, protons, grains of sand, seeds and living cells. A spherical body radiates a spherical field of gravitation, and motion in a spherical gravitational field is necessarily curvilinear. Hence all motions in existence are curvilinear. What appears to be motion in a straight line is due to the fact that we see only a small segment of the line in motion. If we cut up a curved line into small segments, the segments will appear to be straight lines. Thus the general theory of relativity shows us the following. First, it shows that motion in existence is neither uniform nor in a straight line. Second, the gravitational force is equal to the inertia of the bodies, for it acts on all bodies with the same accelerated velocity of motion. Third, it shows that all motions are in a space-time continuum. Since the general theory of relativity does away with uniform motions in a straight line, the problem presents itself: How can the non-uniform motions and which are not in a straight line be comprehended under a general law of nature? We started out with the fact that all motion is relative, depending upon the body of reference from which the motion is viewed. If we stand on the embankment, we see the train in motion; and, if we sit in the train, we see the embankment in motion. But what is the truth? Science could not answer this question. The general theory of relativity answered this question. How did it answer this question? By doing away with all bodies of reference; it revealed the laws of nature independently of the bodies of references from which they are viewed. This was the achievement of Einstein. How did he achieve this? This we shall presently see.

46. As stated before, relativity rests on a mathematics of a high order. Mathematics of a high order works with imaginary quantities upon the basis of imaginary assumptions. Now, imagine a large portion of empty space, and so far removed from the stars and other material bodies that in this space there is no gravitational field. According to the law formulated by Newton, in this space the law of inertia is absolute. If a body is at rest, it will remain at rest; if a body is in motion, it will continue to move with uniform motion in a straight line. And now imagine a spacious chest resembling a room with an observer inside who is equipped with apparatus and other things. Gravitation does not exist for this observer. The chest and the observer are in this vast empty space. To the middle of the chest externally a hook with a chain are attached. Some power pulls the chest upward by the chain with an accelerated velocity. The chest and the observer inside are pulled upwards with an accelerated velocity. In time the velocity will reach immense speed. How does the man in the chest regard this process? The accelerated motion of the chest is trans-

mitted to him by the reaction of the floor of the chest on which
he stands. He takes up the pressure of the floor by his legs. He
is then standing on the floor of the chest in the same way as we
stand on the floor of a room on the earth. And now notice the
following. The man and the chest are in empty space wherein
there is no gravitation. Together with the chest he is being
pulled upward with an accelerated velocity. Yet he will not feel
or perceive that he is being pulled upward. He will regard himself and the chest at rest, just as we feel when we stand on the
earth and regard the earth as at rest. The pressure of the floor
of the chest he will feel, but he will regard it as the pressure of
his body on the floor, just as we feel that by the pressure of our
body's weight we press against the earth. And so, though the
man in the chest is not in a gravitational field, yet he will feel
that his body is pulled downward by gravitation. And now he
takes out from his pocket an apple and lets it go. So long as the
apple was in his pocket it was pulled upward together with the
pocket. But now that the apple was taken out of the pocket and
let go, the apple will remain hanging in the place in which it was
left, because there is no gravitational field in the empty space.
But the chest is being pulled upwards, the floor of the chest will
rise towards the apple, and therefore to the man in the chest it
will appear that the apple fell to the floor, that it was pulled down
by gravitation, just as an apple falls from the tree to the ground.
Again, suppose that the man in the chest fixes a rope to the inner
side of the lid, and that he attaches a body to the free end of the
rope. The result will be that the rope will be stretched, so that
it will hang vertically downward. But notice this. The rope will
be stretched because it is pulled upward by the top of the chest;
and, since the body is attached to the free end of the rope, the
body will be pulled upward by the rope, and the result will be
that the rope will be stretched. But how will it appear to the
man in the chest? To him it will appear, just as it would appear
to us on the earth, that the body was being pulled down by
gravitation, and thus stretched the rope. Notice this. The man
and the chest are in empty space where there is no gravitational

field, yet to him it will appear that he is in a gravitational field. If he looks out from the chest, he will see the stars in motion about the chest just as we see the stars in motion about the earth; and, though he is being pulled upward together with the chest with an accelerated velocity, yet he will regard himself and the chest as at rest.

47. From this imaginary case we learn the following. The laws of nature behave in their own way, and they are independent of the bodies of reference from which we see the motions of bodies. Thus an old problem was solved. Motion always appears to be relative, relative to a body of reference from which the motion is viewed. This is inevitable: we cannot see motion otherwise. But the human mind refuses to accept this; the human mind demands to know what is the truth about motion? Which moves, the train or the embankment? Does the stone fall to the ground in a straight line or in a curved line? The senses cannot reveal to the human mind the truth. For thousands of years the human mind struggled to find out the truth about motion and other phenomena. At last, relativity solved the problem. The solution is this: the laws of nature act according to their own nature, independently of bodies of reference from which they are viewed. Whether the bodies of reference be in motion or at rest, and whether they move with uniform motion in a straight line or with an accelerated motion in a curved line, the laws of nature will appear from all bodies of reference just the same. We already saw that the shortening of the measuring-rod in motion and the slowing down of the clock in motion compensate each other, so that whether we measure the distance between two points on the embankment or on the train, the time and the distance will in both cases be the same. This truth was perceived by profound thinkers long ago, and Spinoza revealed the reason for this truth. Spinoza tells us that the order and connexion of ideas is the same as the order and connexion of things. Whether we contemplate existence and its laws from the viewpoint of ideas or from the viewpoint of material realities, we shall see the

same order and connexion. All aspects of existence are the manifestations of the attributes of God, and all attributes agree among themselves. What Spinoza demonstrated philosophically, Einstein demonstrated scientifically. Relativity emancipated us from the material bodies of reference. This is the great achievement of relativity. And now let us consider the final aspect of relativity.

48. Space is three-dimensional, time is one-dimensional; together they constitute a four-dimensional continuum. Until the advent of relativity matter was regarded as distinct from space and time; space was regarded as the relations of coexistence of material realities, and time was regarded as the succession of events. Since space and time are only relations among realities, it follows that space and time are organically bound up with the material realities. Hence, not only space and time constitute a continuum, but also space, time and matter constitute a continuum. Now, all natural realities are spherical in form. Since space is organically bound up with the material realities, it follows that space, like material realities, must be spherical in form. But until the advent of relativity space was regarded as infinitely extended in all direction. But infinitely extended space is inconsistent with spherical matter. Hence Einstein was bold enough to postulate that space is spherical. Since space, time and matter constitute one continuum, it follows that the universe is a sphere. Now, a sphere may be infinite, yet it is finite, because it has a spherical form, and form is finite. In a sphere there is neither beginning nor end, and in a sphere there are no boundaries. Hence Einstein reached the conclusion that the universe is finite but unbounded. By this Einstein solved several other problems. First. Light travels with great velocity. If space were infinitely extended, then by this time all light radiated by the stars would have disappeared in infinite space. Second. Matter is energy, and energy radiates just as light radiates in all directions. If space were infinite, by this time all energy would have passed into infinite space. And, since matter is energy, this means that all matter would have radiated into infinite space, and there would be left in the uni-

verse neither matter, nor energy nor light. But because the universe is spherical, light, energy and matter have been preserved. Beyond the periphery of the universe, light, energy and matter cannot go; eternally and infinitely they remain within the universe. Third. According to Newton, the universe must have a center in which the density of matter is a maximum, and as we proceed outward from the center the density of matter diminishes, until it is succeeded by an infinite region of emptiness. The stellar universe ought therefore to be an island in an infinite ocean of empty space. But the fact is that there are stars everywhere, so that the density of matter, although very variable, is nevertheless on the average everywhere the same. However far we may travel through space, we will find everywhere an attenuated swarm of fixed stars approximately of the same kind of density. All this shows that the universe is a sphere. In a universe that is spherical, motion cannot be in a straight line. Hence all motion in the universe is curvilinear, circular, cyclic. Light travels with very great velocity. No matter where it originates, and no matter how far it may travel through unlimited time, it comes back to the starting point, or it remains within the universe. The universe eternally and infinitely conserves itself. The foregoing is a brief outline of relativity. As we proceed with the consideration of the physical world in the light of the monistic philosophy, we will have occasions to refer to relativity again and again. Relativity revolutionized our ideas of the physical world. Since the physical world is but one of the infinite aspects of existence, and all aspects of existence are but aspects of an existence that is absolutely one and indivisible, it follows that, on the one hand, relativity also revolutionized our ideas of other aspects of existence; on the other hand, that relativity itself must be reinterpreted in the light of the monistic philosophy. This is our next step.

CHAPTER VIII

The Philosophical Interpretation of Relativity

49. Science was born of the perception that things in the phenomenal world are only appearances of realities. The function and aim of science were to discover the realities behind the appearances of things. For this purpose, science broke up things into their minutest parts and analyzed the parts. In the course of time, science discovered that all things consists of molecules, the molecules consist of atoms, the atoms consist of electrons and protons, the electrons and protons are only electric charges, and the electric charges are only forms of energy. Thus all material things are only forms of energy. And what about this universal energy? Here science stopped. Did science discover the realities behind the appearance of things? By no means. Let us consider a few cases.

A rose is beautiful and radiates a sweet aroma. According to science, the rose is only the appearance of a reality. To find out the reality which appears as a rose, science broke up the rose into its minutest parts, and found that it consists of molecules, atoms, electrons, protons, electric charges, which are only forms of energy. What, then, is the reality of the rose? Is it energy? Ultimately, all realities are forms of energy. What, then, distinguishes the rose from all other realities? Why is the rose different from all other realities? Consider another case. Here is an animal; it lives, it feels, it thinks and acts to preserve itself. According to science, the animal is only an appearance of reality. What, then, is the reality of the animals? To find out the reality of the animal, science dissected the animals into the minutest parts, analyzed them, and found again that it consists of molecules, atoms, electrons, protons, electrical charges, which are only forms of energy. Here, again, is energy an animal? What distinguishes the animal from the rose and from other realities? Again, consider the human mind. Science tells us that the human mind is only a function of the brains. The brains are composed of molecules, atoms, electrons, protons, electrical charges, which are only forms of energy. Is the human mind only a form of energy? What distinguishes the human mind from the animal or from the rose?

Things in the world are classified into orders, genera and species. Science tells us that the orders, genera and species are not realities, they are only mental concepts; they are aggregates of individuals. The individuals themselves are only forms of energy. What, then, distinguishes one order from another order, one genus from another genus, or one species from another species? And it is so in all cases. Science reduces all things to forms of energy. If we reduce all things to one universal energy, then we thereby destroy the world of realities. And so, instead of creating a world of realities, science destroyed the world of realities. For a long time science was not aware of this, but since the advent of relativity, this became ever more manifest. To confirm this, I quote from Eddington's book: The Nature of the Physical World. He tells us the following:—

"Let us then examine the kind of knowledge which is handled by exact science. If we search the examination papers in physics and natural philosophy for the more intelligible questions, we may come across one beginning something like this. An elephant slides down a grassy hill. The experienced candidate knows that he need not pay attention to this: it is only put up to give an impression of realism. He reads on. The mass of the elephant is two tons. Now we are getting down to business; the elephant fades out of the problem, and a mass of two tons takes its place. What exactly is this two tons, the real subject matter of the problem? It refers to some property or condition which we vaguely describe as ponderosity occurring in a particular region of the external world. The two tons is the pointer when the elephant was placed on a weighing-machine.

Let us pass on. The slope of the hill is 60 degrees. Now the hill-side fades out of the problem, and the angle of 60 degrees takes its place. What is 60 degrees? 60 degrees is the reading of a plumb-line against the division of a protractor. The softly yielding turf on which the elephant slid is replaced by a coefficient of friction. And so we see that the poetry fades out of the problem, and we are left only with pointer readings. If, then, pointer readings or their equivalents are put into the machine of scientific calculation, how can we grind out anything but pointer readings? But that is just what we do grind out. The whole subject-matter of exact science consists of pointer readings and similar indications. Although we seem to have very definite conceptions of objects in the external world, those conceptions do not enter into exact science, and are not in any way confirmed by it. From the point of view of exact science, the thing that did really descend the hill can only be described as a bundle of pointer readings. I should like to make it clear that the limitation of the scope of physics to pointer readings and the like is not a philosophical craze of my own, but is essentially the current scientific doctrine. It is the outcome of a tendency discernible far back in the last century, but only formulated comprehensively with the advent of the relativity theory.

50. Eddington makes the case even stronger than I stated. I stated that science reduces everything to energy, but Eddington shows that science reduces everything to pointer readings. For the purpose of science, the elephant, the hill, the grass and all else are of no concern; of concern to science are the pointer readings. What is true in this case is true in all cases. Science is concerned only about pointer readings, figures and statistics. And what about the scientist himself? Let us again hear what Eddington tells us about the scientist.

I am standing on the threshold about to enter a room. It is a complicated business. In the first place, I must shove against an atmosphere pressing with a force of fourteen pounds on every square inch of my body. I must make sure of landing

on a plank travelling at twenty miles a second round the sun—
a fraction of a second too early or too late, the plank would
be miles away. I must do this whilst hanging from a round
planet head outwards into space, and with a wind of ether blow-
ing at no one knows how many miles a second through every
interstice of my body. The plank has no solidity of substance.
To step on it is like stepping on a swarm of flies. Shall I not
slip through? No, if I make the venture, one of the flies hits
me and gives a boost up again; I fall again and am knocked
upwards by another fly, and so on. I may hope that the net
result will be that I remain about steady; but, if unfortunately
I should slip through the floor or be boosted too violently up
to the ceiling, the occurrence would be, not a violation of the
laws of Nature, but a rare coincidence. These are some of the
minor difficulties. I ought really to look at the problem four-
dimensionally as concerning the intersection of my world-line
with that of the plank. Then again it is necessary to determine
in which direction the entropy of the world is increasing in
order to make sure that my passage over the threshold is an
entrance, not an exit. Verily, it is easier for a camel to pass
through the eye of a needle than for a scientist to pass through
the door. And whether the door be barn door or church door,
it might be wiser that he should consent to be an ordinary man
and walk in rather than wait till all the difficulties involved in a
really scientific ingress are resolved.

51. Eddington endeavored to show that science is not concerned
about realities, and yet the supreme function and aim of science
were just this, to discover the realities behind the appearance of
things. We saw that the essence of a thing is an idea; the destiny
of an idea is to realize itself in material form. Since the destiny
of an idea is to realize itself in a material form, it follows that the
material form of a thing is a reality, whose essence is an idea.
We saw that substance is absolute thought without form. That
which has no form is not a reality, it is not a thing. Out of one
absolute, infinite and eternal substance all infinite realities were

carved out. Substance becomes a reality when it is comprehended by a form, and an idea is the form of absolute thought. But a thing is not merely substance and a form; a thing may imply numerous intervening forms. The electron is a form of substance, so is a proton, an atom, a molecule, a group of molecules, a mass, a group of masses, and so on indefinitely. And so forms are superimposed upon forms, until we get the final form of a thing. But each form is a reality. The rose is just as much a reality as the molecules, the atoms, the protons, the electrons and the energy of which the rose is composed. The rose is to be found in the rose itself, just as it appears in its beauty, color and form and its aroma. We need not go deeper to find out what the rose is; deeper than the rose as it appears there is no longer a rose. Deeper we shall find molecules, atoms, protons, electrons and energy, but we shall not find a rose. This is true of all realities and of all living beings. By breaking up the rose into its constituent parts, we destroy the rose, and there is no longer a rose. Hence when science assumed that, by breaking up the rose they will discover the reality of the rose, science acted just as a child acts when it breaks up a watch into minute parts to find the watch. The watch is not to be found in its minute parts; the watch is what it appears. And so it came to pass that, starting to find out the realities behind the appearances of things, science destroyed all things. No wonder that science discovered a world consisting only of abstract pointer readings. What happened to science generally also happened to relativity.

Relativity started out with the assumption that the nature of an event depends upon the material frame of reference from which the event is viewed. When we stand on the embankment, we shall see the train move; but, when we sit in the train, we shall see the embankment move. The frame of reference is something outside of us. Now, since the nature of an event depends upon the frame of reference from which it is viewed, we cannot know the true nature of an event. And the same is true of things. If the nature of things depends upon the frame of reference from which they are viewed, we cannot know the true nature of things. And therefore we cannot know the true nature of the laws of existence. Hence relativity proceeded to find out a material frame of reference from which the laws and processes of existence would reveal themselves in their true nature. At last relativity did find this material frame of reference; but what was it? It was an iron chest hanging in an infinite vacuum. And relativity believed that from this frame of reference the laws and processes of existence could be seen in their true nature. But this is an illusion? Is there an infinite vacuum in existence? Can we conceive of an infinite vacuum? Can anything exist or take place in an infinite vacuum? Assuming that we and an iron chest could be hanging in an infinite vacuum, do we know how things would appear to us? And the whole general theory of relativity rests on this infinite vacuum! Yet, the general theory of relativity served a very good purpose, namely, it destroyed the basic assumption that things and events depend upon the material frame of reference from which they are viewed. The general theory of relativity destroyed the whole theory of relativity. Einstein and the relativists are not aware of this, hence they are still groping in the dark. The trouble with the scientists is this: they do not realize that science by its very nature must start in the middle of the story and end in the middle of the story. To know and understand the realities of existence, we must start with the beginning and end with the beginning. Hence science will never understand the realities of existence or the events that take place in existence. Let us, then, examine the theory of relativity in the light of the monistic philosophy.

52. Eddington tells us: The quest of the absolute is the best way to understand the relative appearances. The relativity of the current scheme of physics invites us to search deeper and find the absolute underlying it, so that we may see the world in a truer perspective. It is a mistake to suppose that Einstein's theory of relativity asserts that everything is relative. Actually it says: there are absolute things in the world, but you must look deeply for them. Einstein and Eddington realized that the physical

world is only a manifestation of the real world, yet they did not comprehend the real world. They studied the relative aspect of the phenomenal world, without at the same time correlating the relative aspect of the phenomenal world to the real aspect of the transcendental world; they studied the effects, without knowing and understanding the cause of the effects. They did not realize that the absolute and the relative are correlatives, they imply each other; neither can exist without the other, and the knowledge and understanding of either imply the knowledge and understanding of the other. Hence the assurance that Einstein and Eddington believed that there is an absolute means nothing. Since the relativists did not know and understand the absolute, they did not know and understand the relative.

Relativity starts out with the premise: reality and truth are what they appear with relation to a frame of reference. The frame of reference is outside us, it is a material frame of reference. An event is taking place, something is moving. If we stand on the embankment, the train will appear to be moving; on the other hand, if we sit in the train, the embankment will appear to be moving. If we ask, what in fact is moving? The answer is: this is a meaningless question. We cannot ask, what is moving? All that we can ask is this: with relation to given frame of reference, what is moving? Eddington tells us: Frames of space are relative; distance, lengths, volumes—all quantities of space-reckoning which belong to frames—are likewise relative. A distance is reckoned by an observer on one star is as good as a distance reckoned by an observer on another star. We must not expect them to agree; the one is a distance relative to one frame, the other is a distance relative to another frame. Absolute distance, not relative to some special frame, is meaningless. All other quantities of physics go along with the frame of space, so that they are also relative. Consider an electrically charged body at rest on the earth. Since it is at rest, it gives an electric field, but no magnetic field. But for the physicist on some distant nebula (which moves with a velocity of 1000 miles a second) it is a charged body moving at 1000 miles a second. (To the nebular physicist the earth will appear to be moving with a velocity of 1000 miles a second, and so will also the electrically charged body on the earth.) A moving charge constitutes an electric current which gives rise to a magnetic field. How can the same body give and not give a magnetic field? The answer is: magnetic fields are relative. There is no magnetic field relative to the terrestrial frame of space; there is a magnetic field relative to the nebular frame of space. The nebular physicist will duly detect the magnetic field with his instruments, although our instruments show no magnetic field. Is there really a magnetic field or not? There is one specification of the field relative to one planet, another relative to another. There is no absolute specification. Thus we see that, according to relativity, everything depends upon the frame of reference from which we view it. Let us, then, consider the frame of reference more closely.

53. Eddington tells us that the nebular physicist will detect a magnetic field, while the physicist on the earth will not detect the magnetic field. This is only an assumption based on speculation of mathematical physics. Eddington does not know what the nebular physicist would actually perceive. Let us, however, confine ourselves to our earth. A frame of reference is some material object outside us. The question is: what has the material frame of reference to do with our views of what exists or of what takes place? We must bear this in mind. Our views of things are not only perceptions, they are also judgments. When I stand on the embankment, I not only perceive the train moving, but I also judge that the train is moving. On the other hand, when I sit in the train, I not only perceive the embankment moving, but I also judge that the embankment is moving. How does the material frame of reference determine my perception and judgment? Relativity postulated this, without even attempting to explain the reason why. We shall presently see that the material frame of reference has nothing to do with our perceptions and judgments. It is true that our perceptions and

judgments are determined by a frame of reference, but that is a frame of reference of which the relativists were completely ignorant. What is that frame of reference with relation to which we perceive and judge things and events? That frame of reference is our own mind; our mind perceives and judges according to its own ideas. Our mind is ego-centric; it regards itself as at rest and in the centre of the world. It therefore makes no difference whether we stand still or move, our mind regards itself as at rest. When I stand on the embankment, I do not think of the embankment at all, I think of myself; my mind feels that it is at rest. But something outside me is moving; that something is the train. On the other hand, when I sit in the train, I do not think of the train, I think of myself; my mind feels that it is at rest. But something outside me is moving; that something is the embankment. Hence the frame of reference with relation to which the mind perceives and judges is the mind itself. Now, this is not very manifest in the cases of the embankment and the train. Hence we must go deeper into the matter.

Relativity revolutionized our conception of the physical world. One who studied and understood relativity sees a physical world which differs fundamentally from the physical world which others see and which all saw before the advent of relativity. Now, Einstein and Eddington were not born with the theory of relativity. Until they crystallized the theory of relativity the physical world appeared to them as it appeared to all other human beings. But, when they crystallized the theory of relativity, the physical world appeared to them in an entirely different aspect. The question is: what determined Einstein and Eddington to see the world in a different aspect? Was the frame of reference from which they see now the world changed? They still stand on the earth as before. And yet, since they crystallized the theory of relativity the whole world assumed to them a different aspect. What, then, determined the change in their views of the physical world? It was nothing else than this very theory of relativity. Before they crystallized the theory of relativity, their minds had different ideas about the physical world; and now they have ideas of the physical world which are different from the previous ideas. Hence, the frame of reference in this case was, not the material earth or some other material frame of reference, it was the theory of relativity—a system of ideas in their minds. A change in ideas changes our view of the world. This is a universal experience.

Consider the following. The primitive savage, the barbarians and the present civilized men—all lived and live on the same earth, and all see the world, as far as their senses are concerned, in the same aspect. The earth appears to be stationary, the sun and the stars appear to be moving around the earth, and so on. Yet, to the barbarians the world appeared different than it appeared to the savages, and to the civilized men the world appears to be different than it appeared to the barbarians and the savages. And, when we consider the Einsteins, the Spinozas, the Platos, the Jesuses and the Moseses, we see that to them the world appeared entirely different from what it appears even to the civilized men. And yet all of them lived and live in the same world, and all of them stand on the same material frame of reference. Consider another case. In an apartment house in the City of New York there live Catholics, Protestants, Jews, Buddhists, Mohammedans, communists, capitalists, democrats, and workers. In many respects they live and think more or less alike. But let the question be religion, economics, politics, and the like, and behold, they violently disagree with one another. What one regards as right, another regards as wrong; what one regards as good, another regards as evil; and so on indefinitely. On these questions their differences are so fundamental that they are ready to fight, to kill and even to die for their beliefs and ideas. On these questions, the world appears to each of them different from what it appears to the rest. Why do they differ from one another, when these questions arise? Because with relation to these questions, they have different ideas; they perceive and judge the world with relation to their ideas; their ideas are the frame of reference with relation to which they perceive and judge the world and everything that exists and takes place. Thus we see that the frame of reference with relation to which we perceive and judge is not a material frame outside us, but is our own mind. Since, however, relativity starts out with the assumption that the frame of reference is a material object outside us, relativity started out with a false assumption. Upon the basis of a false assumption, a true theory cannot be built. Now, relativity served a useful purpose; it revealed deep truths concerning the realities of existence. But this is not surprising. Many false assumptions or hypotheses served useful purposes. A hypothesis need not necessarily be true, provided we know that it is only a hypothesis; but when we take the hypothesis as a truth, then the consequences will be illusion. We shall presently see the useful purpose which relativity served.

54. Relativity started out with material frames of reference; but by the law of dialectics it reached just the opposite: the negation of all material frames of reference, and it remained hanging in an infinite vacuum. Men are like the monads of Leibnitz. Each man lives in a world of his own; it is a closed world, without doors and without windows; one man cannot see what is in the world of other men. Each man in his own closed world meets realities and witnesses events. He endeavors to understand them, and thus acquires a knowledge of his own world. What he knows about his own world he regards as good and true. But as the world of one man differs from the world of another man, so also differ the views of one man from the views of another man, so also differ the views of one man from the views of another man about the realities and processes in existence. Each one judges according to the ideas which he has in his own mind, which is his frame of reference. But men must enter into relations with one another. When they meet, they discover that they differ from one another in their judgment of the world, reality and truth, what one believes to be true and good, another believes to be false and evil. Thus arises among them misunderstanding, which gives rise to struggles, wars and revo-

lutions, and which bring upon mankind suffering and destruction. All this was known all the time. Philosophers and thinkers tried hard to overcome this misunderstanding and its consequences, but in vain. And now came relativity and showed that men differ on their views of the world, because they view the world from different frames of reference. Are they all deceiving themselves? Do they all have false views of the world? Relativity showed that all views are true with relation to the different frames of reference from which they are viewed. But this did not solve the problem. Granting that each view is true with relation to a particular frame of reference, since there can be infinite different frames of reference, there will be infinite different views of the world. Each view will be true, and yet the views will be different from one another. Thus the ancient misunderstanding will remain, and so also will its consequences continue. What has relativity accomplished? The human mind is not content to know that its own views, with relation to a particular frame of reference, are true; the human mind demands to know what is the truth in itself, independently of frames of reference. To see the world as it is, we must view the world from an absolute frame of reference; then all men will see one and the same world, they will all have the same views, and they will all agree with one another. But what is the absolute frame of reference?

Relativity shows that, though different external frames of reference will reveal things and events in different aspects, yet all views will be true. But true in what sense? Eddington asks the question: Is it really true that a moving rod becomes shortened in the direction of its motion? We often draw a distinction between what is *true* and what is *really true*. A statement which does not profess to deal with anything except appearances may be true; but a statement which is not only true but deals with realities beneath the appearances is *really true*. It is not a statement about reality (the absolute), but it is a true statement about appearances in a frame of reference. Thus, according to Eddington, relativity and science deal only with appearances, and not realities. Now relativity may repeat an infinite number of times that everything is relative to a particular frame of reference, and that it is meaningless to ask for the reality and truth of anything independently of a frame of reference, but the human mind will never accept this; the human mind demands to know what is the reality and the truth. All things in existence perpetually move about one another. The embankment and the train move together with the earth, the sun and the stars, but this is not what concerns the human mind. The human mind demands to know this: with relation to each other, which is moving, the train or the embankment? I have to go to a certain city. I come to the railroad station to take the train to that city. I stand on the platform to wait for the train. According to relativity, it should make no difference to me whether I remain standing on the platform or enter the train, for either is moving with relation to the other. Suppose that my mind worked in this manner, where would I land? Can this principle of relativity be accepted by the human mind? Can we exist in the world with relativity? The assurance that every view with relation to a particular frame of reference is true is of no significance; the mind demands to know the truth itself, independently of all frames of reference. Now, relativity, unconsciously, was trying hard to find the absolute frame of reference, but it failed. All that it accomplished was to abolish all frames of reference; it remained hanging in an infinite vacuum. Thus science started out to find the realities behind the appearance of things, and ended by negating all reality. It thus ended in an absolute negation.

55. A negation implies an affirmation; they are correlatives, neither can be conceived without the other, and neither can exist without the other. Spinoza tells us: Determinatio est negatio—an affirmation is a negation. Hegel added: Negatio est determinatio—a negation is an affirmation. Since relativity abolished all frames of reference and science generally negated all reality, by this they impliedly affirmed all reality and pointed to the

absolute frame of reference. What is the absolute frame of reference? It is the Absolute, it is God. Once we take God as the absolute frame of reference from which to view existence, then we see the world in its true nature, and then we shall all agree. God is the only direct, immediate and immanent cause of all effects and the substance of all realities. God determines our existence, our nature, our thoughts, feelings and actions, and determines our destiny. All human evolution was in the direction of this absolute frame of reference. All sciences tended to become one science, all religions tended to become one religion, all philosophies tended to become one philosophy, all economic systems tended to become one economic system, and the whole human race tended to become one human society. This will continue until mankind will attain to the absolute frame of reference. The absolute frame of reference will not be something external to us, it will be the human mind itself. When mankind will attain to this absolute frame of reference, then they will see the truth, the truth will make them free, and they will realize their destiny. By negating all reality and abolishing all material frames of reference, science and relativity prepared the ground for the absolute frame of reference. We saw that, while science deals with time, space, matter, force, light, electricity, and so on, science does not comprehend them, and this for the reason that science begins in the middle of the story and ends in the middle of the story. It is therefore the task of the monistic philosophy —which starts with the absolute beginning and ends with the absolute beginning—to reveal the true nature of these ultimate realities. At the outset, we must be clear about the two worlds: the transcendental world and the phenomenal world.

The Transcendental and the Phenomenal World

56. The transcendental world transcends the phenomenal world. And, first, what is the phenomenal world? As the term implies, a phenomenon is that which shines, which manifests itself. The phenomenal world is a world of realities which manifest them-

selves, they are realities that manifest themselves in material forms. On the other hand, the transcendental world is the world of ideas. An idea, as an idea, does not manifest itself. An idea is the essence of reality, and manifests itself in material form. This is the destiny of an idea. An idea transcends its material form; first, because the essence transcends the material form through which it manifests itself; second, because an idea transcends the senses, the senses cannot perceive an idea. Thus the transcendental world and the phenomenal world are only two aspects of one and the same world. The transcendental world is the world of thought, and the phenomenal world is the world of extension. Neither thought alone nor extension alone is reality. Thought and extension are correlatives, they imply each other; neither can exist without the other. The transcendental world does not exist somewhere far and high in existence; the transcendental world is right here together with the phenomenal world. In ourselves we have both the transcendental world and the phenomenal world. In so far as we have ideas in our mind, in so far we have in our mind the transcendental world. And in so far as we realize our ideas in material forms, we have the phenomenal world. It is with the transcendental world as it is with God. Just as we did away with the superstition that God resides somewhere in infinite space, far from this world; so we must do away with the superstition that the transcendental world is somewhere far in infinite space. The monistic philosophy rejects both superstitions. Existence in all its infinite aspects is absolutely one and indivisible.

What is the dividing line between these two worlds? It is the velocity of light. The transcendental world begins with the Infinite Intellect, God, and ends where the ideas of God become light. The phenomenal world begins where the ideas become light and ends with matter. This profound truth was revealed in the Bible. The Bible tells us that Elohim began creation with light. Elohim said: Let there be light, and there was light. Once Elohim brought out light, then all material realities were created. Light is the ultimate unit of matter. This profound truth is now confirmed by relativity. Relativity shows that all material realities are nothing else than energy, that this energy radiates; and when this energy attains the velocity of light it disappears as matter and becomes light. On the other hand, light becomes matter when its velocity is reduced. Consider this. Since creation the stars radiated infinite light. What became of the light? The answer is: the infinite light became matter. And so the eternal process goes on: light becomes matter, and matter becomes light. Light, then, is the dividing line between the transcendental world and the phenomenal world, between the world of ideas and the world of material forms of the ideas. And now we proceed to consider light itself and its correlative darkness.

CHAPTER IX

Light and Darkness

57. What is light? Two theories about light came down to us: the corpuscular theory of Newton, and the undulatory theory of Huygens. According to Newton, luminous bodies emit, in all directions, an imponderable substance, which consists of molecules of an extreme degree of tenuity; these are propagated in straight lines with an almost infinite velocity. Penetrating into the eye, they act on the retina, and determine the sensation which constitutes vision. According to Huygens, all bodies are filled by an extremely elastic and subtle medium, which is called the luminiferous medium or ether. The luminosity of a body is due to an infinitely rapid vibration of its molecules, which, when communicated to the ether, is propagated in all directions in the form of spherical waves, and this vibratory motion, being thus transmitted to the retina, calls forth the sensation of vision. The vibrations of the ether take place, not in the direction of the line in which the wave is travelling, but in a plane at right angles to it. An idea of this may be formed by attaching one end of a rope to something, and by taking hold of the free end of the rope and shaking it. The vibrations, or to and from movements of the particles of the rope are at right angles to the length of the rope, but the onward motion of wave's form is in the direction of the length. According to Newton, the propagation of the light is effected by a motion of translation of particles of light thrown out from the luminous body, as a bullet is discharged from a gun. According to Huygen's theory, there is no propagation of the particles themselves, but only of the state of the disturbance which was communicated by the luminous body, and this is transmitted by the vibratory motion of the

particles of the luminous body. Now, the optic nerve is insensible to a large number of wave-lengths. It can apprehend only those waves that form the visible spectrum. If the rate of undulation is slower than the red or faster than the violet, though intense motion may pass through the humours of the eye and fall upon the retina, yet we shall be utterly unconscious of the fact, for the optic nerve cannot take up and respond to the vibrations which exist beyond the visible spectrum in both directions. Hence these are termed invisible or obscure rays. It is the same with sound. The vibrations of the air below or above certain rates do not affect the auditory nerve; it can only take up and transmit to the brain vibrations lying in a certain range of frequency.

58. For a time the scientists accepted the undulatory theory of Huygens, because it explained the phenomena of light better than the corpuscular theory of Newton. But relativity showed that both theories are true. According to relativity, light is both a corpuscle and a wave. Light consists of a unit, called photon, which acts as a particle and also as a wave. Einstein tells us: there are phenomena which can be explained by the quantum theory, but not by the wave theory. Photo-effect furnishes an example, though other phenomena of this kind are known. There are phenomena which can be explained by the wave theory, but not by the quantum theory. The bending of light around an obstacle is a typical example. Finally, there are phenomena, such as the rectilinear propagation of light which can be equally explained by the quantum and the wave theory of light. Eddington tells us the following. Consider the light-waves which are the result of a single emission by an atom on the star Sirius. These bear away a certain amount of energy with a certain period. The period is carried by the waves without change, but the energy spreads out in an ever-widening circle. Eight years and nine months after the emission, the wave-front is due to reach the earth. The light-waves reach the eye of a man; their energy would seem to be dissipated beyond recovery

over a sphere of fifty trillion miles' radius, and yet it enters the retina as a single quantum, and the man is able to see the star Sirius. How is this managed?

How is this managed, asks Eddington. Indeed, suppose we know that light is a photon, a particle and a wave, do we know what light is? Science has revealed numerous wonderful facts about light, but thus far has failed to reveal what light itself is. What is light itself, how does light originate, and what becomes of light? Science does not know. As in all cases, so in this case science begins in the middle of the story and ends in the middle of the story. Let us approach the problem from the opposite side, namely, from the side of matter. Matter resolves itself into electric charges—forms of energy; matter is concentrated energy, and light is also a form of energy. Matter, electric charges, energy, radiation and light—all have a granular structure, they are corpuscles of a definite quantum, and at the same time they are also waves. The atom emits light continuously in a discontinuous manner. It sends out a long train of waves and then stops. It has to be restored by some kind of stimulation before it emits again. This applies to light absorbed by an atom as well as to light emitted, the absorption being also discontinuous. Light is both a corpuscle and a wave; likewise the electron is both a corpuscle and a wave. Einstein tells us that, viewed as an elementary quantum of matter, it is an electron; but, viewed as a quantum of energy, it is photon. We thus see that matter and light are only different forms of energy. Now, matter in motion contracts; and, when the motion reaches the velocity of light, the matter disappears. What becomes of the matter? Something cannot disappear into nothing as something cannot arise out of nothing. Relativity does not tell what becomes of the matter when its velocity reaches that of light. But the answer is perfectly clear. When the motion of matter reaches the velocity of light, it becomes light. In the words of Einstein, viewed as an elementary quantum of energy, it is a photon; and, when viewed as an elementary quantum of matter, it is an electron. Again, relativity shows that the velocity of light is not constant, as was assumed by pre-relativity physics; light slows down. What becomes of light when it slows down? The answer is now clear: light becomes matter. Again, relativity shows that light does not travel with the greatest velocity in existence. Since light slows down, this means that light also originates in something that has even a greater velocity than light. What is that in which light originates, and which has a greater velocity than light? The answer is: it is absolute thought. Absolute thought has an infinite velocity. When absolute thought slows down, it becomes light; and, when light slows down, it becomes matter. Thus we see that light is only an intermediary state between absolute thought and matter. What, then, is light?

Eddington asks: Matter disintegrates and its energy is set free in radiation. Is there no counter-process by which radiation collects in space, evolves into electrons and protons, and begins star-building over again? Eddington does not give a positive answer. But from all that we learn from relativity it is clear that light and matter are only different degrees of velocity of absolute thought. Consider this. Since the beginning of creation infinite light was radiated by the material bodies in existence. Light is a corpuscle and a wave, just as matter is a corpuscle and a wave. What became of the infinite light that was radiated by the material world, did it disappear? The answer is: the infinite light slowed down and became matter. Light is the ultimate unit of matter, with light begins the material world. I already referred to the significant statement in the Bible. Elohim said: Let there be light, and there was light. Once light was created, then out of light the whole material world was created. Absolute thought becomes light, and light becomes matter. In turn, matter becomes light, and light becomes absolute thought. This is the eternal cycle of creation, it is the cycle of entropy and evolution. But this does not yet reveal to us the true nature of light. What is light itself? Before this question can be answered, we must first consider its correlative, darkness.

WHAT IS DARKNESS?

59. Science and philosophy bestowed infinite thought on light, but they completely ignored darkness; they assumed that darkness is only the absence of light. But this is a false assumption. Darkness is the correlative of light, they imply each other, neither can exist without the other, and neither can be conceived without the other. Now, correlatives are realities, there can be no correlation between a reality and the absence of reality. Since light and darkness are correlatives, darkness is just as much a reality as light is. Next, science and philosophy naively assumed that in existence there is really an absence of light, but this is a false assumption. What we call darkness is only invisible light—the light which the human eye cannot perceive. But we know that the human eye can perceive only those rays of light that are within the spectrum; but there are infinite rays, above and below the spectrum, which the human eye cannot perceive. Next, the human eye is not the only eye in existence; there are eyes that can see in what to the human eye appears to be darkness. Animals can see in the darkness far more distinctly than men can see. Insects see in complete darkness just as we do in day light. Most insects live under ground, in plants and in trees; and yet they build for themselves homes, form societies, distribute food, eliminate dead and waste matter, defend themselves against enemies, and procreate themselves—all just as if they lived on the surface of the earth. Again, consider the human body. It consists of infinite living and conscious cells. They constitute a vast society, they have a division of labor, a regulating, controlling and governing system; they take in food and drink, distribute them and assimilate them; they reproduce themselves, they maintain fighting armies to fight against enemies, and maintain the human body in health; they eliminate dead and waste matter, and thus preserve the life of the human body. All this takes place in what to us would be complete darkness; yet these living cells are not in darkness. Again, by means of ingenius photographic instruments we detect light beyond, above and

below the spectrum, just as by the radio we detect sounds beyond the capacity of the ears. Since matter absorbs light and emits light, since there is going on a transformation of light into matter and matter into light, it is clear that in the universe there is no darkness. What, then, is darkness? Darkness is nothing else than the light which transcends the human eyes. The spectrum reveals to the human eye only an infinitesimal part of the infinite light that fills the universe. Darkness is what the Kabbalah calls the dark light; the light is so intense that the human eye cannot perceive it, and therefore it appears as darkness. And now let us consider light and darkness more closely.

60. Absolute thought is infinite light; hence existence is filled with infinite light. Since light is absolute thought reduced in velocity to the velocity of light, it follows that in our own thought we must be conscious of light and darkness. Hence, to understand the true nature of light and darkness, we must consider our own thought. We shall presently see that light is reason, and darkness is intuition. Reason is visible light, intuition is invisible light. What, then, are reason and intuition? When I shall come to speak of man, I will consider reason and intuition fundamentally; but for the present purpose I will state the following. Intuition perceives individual realities, but not the relations among them. On the other hand, reason perceives the relations among the realities, but it does not perceive the individual realities themselves. Intuition must first perceive the individual realities that reason may afterwards perceive the relations among them. Intuition supplies the substance of knowledge, and reason supplies the form of knowledge. When intuition and reason cooperate, only then is knowledge born. The intuitive perception of the realities is invisible light, it is darkness; the perception by reason of the relations among the realities is visible light, it is light. This was the reason why mankind always spoke of the light of reason, but of the intuitive perceptions they spoke as of mysteries. A mystery is darkness. Reason, like light, makes itself manifest; but intuition, like darkness,

does not make itself manifest. It is only when reason sheds its light upon a mystery of intuition, that it ceases to be a mystery and becomes knowledge. To understand the relation of reason to intuition, let us consider a case.

Columbus intuitively perceived that, by sailing westward, he could reach land. This was only an intuitive perception, because he had nothing to show him that this was the case. A problem then presented itself to him. A problem involves many elements. Columbus needed the necessary means and help to discover the new continent. Intuition perceived the several elements, but it did not perceive the relations among them; how to bring the several elements together so that they should realize the desired purpose. At that time, the mind of Columbus was in darkness, it was puzzled and oppressed. Now, if intuition had not revealed to Columbus the possibility of discovering a new continent, there would be no problem in his mind. But intuition did reveal to him this possibility, but not how this possibility could be realized. This gave rise to the problem. Intuition alone could not solve the problem. Then reason came to the fore and showed the relations among the elements involved in the problem. Once these relations were perceived by the mind of Columbus, the problem was solved. What before was darkness now turned into light. This was and is the case of all problems that confronted the human mind. A problem arises when intuition perceives something, and the problem is solved when reason shows how the problem can be solved. Hence in proportion as men attain to reason, in that proportion they perceive the light that pervades the universe, and in that proportion can they solve the problems that present themselves to them. On the other hand, in proportion as men attain to intuition, in that proportion is their mind confronted with problems, and in that proportion it is in darkness. If intuition did not perceive realities, the human mind would be neither in darkness nor in light.

Consider the following. Religion is a product of intuition, philosophy is a product of reason. Religion perceives transcendental realities and truths, but not the relations among them.

Hence religion deals with mysteries, and it brings darkness to the human mind. Religion lives in a closed world—a world without windows. One religion does not know what is in another religion. For this reason, religion is intolerant; one religion cannot tolerate another religion. But it is just the reverse with philosophy. Philosophy is the perception by reason of the relations among realities and truths. Philosophy dwells in light, it is in open relation with the world, it is inherently tolerant, and loves the light. That which in religion is a mystery, becomes in philosophy knowledge. Thus we see that intuition is darkness, reason is light.

61. We saw in a previous chapter that, by the process of entropy, absolute thought became matter. Matter then was in a diffused state. The electrons and protons were separate from one another, and there was chaos and darkness. This was the work of intuition. Then reason came to the fore. Creation and evolution began with the appearance of reason. Reason integrated the diffused matter, and brought out the material world. Reason integrated the diffused matter because reason comprehends the relations among realities. This is what the Bible tells us. In the beginning there was chaos and darkness. Matter in a diffused state is chaos and darkness. Then Elohim said: Let there be light, and there was light. Elohim—this is Reason, the mother of all creation. Intuition is entropy, Reason is evolution. This agrees with what St. John tells us. In the beginning was the word, and the word was with God, and the word was God. All things were made by him; and without him was not anything made that was made. The word—this is reason. The word is the product of reason. Language is not merely individual sounds; language is a relation among sounds. Hence, while intuition brought out the infinite matter in a diffused state, reason created out of the diffused matter the material world. Intuition is entropy, reason is evolution. As we proceed, I shall have occasions to elaborate this more adequately.

Light and darkness are correlatives, and correlatives imply

a third reality of which they are correlatives. What is the third reality of which light and darkness are correlatives? We saw in a previous chapter that the primordial trinity is: the Infinite Intellect, that is, God; thought and extension. The Absolute is absolute thought. The Absolute reflects on itself and forms of itself an idea. This is the Infinite Intellect, God. The Infinite Intellect reflects on the absolute, and perceives the Absolute in the attributes of thought and extension. Thus the Absolute becomes the primordial trinity. This primordial trinity manifests itself in all infinite realities and processes in existence. The Infinite Intellect, God, conceives the attribute thought in infinite ideas, and it conceives the attribute extension in infinite forms. The infinite ideas constitute the transcendental world, and the infinite forms constitute the phenomenal world. The infinite ideas in the transcendental world are infinite light, the material forms in the phenomenal world are finite light. Our senses cannot perceive the infinite light, but they can perceive the finite light. We saw that the velocity of light divides the transcendental world from the phenomenal world. Above the velocity of light is the transcendental world of ideas and infinite light; below that velocity is the phenomenal world of material forms and finite light. The infinite light in the transcendental world is intuition, the finite light in the phenomenal world is reason. Thus light and darkness are correlatives inherent in the Infinite Intellect, in God. God is light, and God is darkness.

CHAPTER X

Space and Time

62. What are space and time? Are they entities which are independent of the realities of existence, and which existed and would exist even if no realities had existed; or, are they relations of coexistence and succession among the realities of existence, and therefore without the realities of existence there would be neither space nor time; or, finally, are they only forms of perception of the human mind, so that outside of the human mind there is neither space nor time? All philosophers agreed that space and time are not entities independent of the realities of existence, but the philosophers differed on the following. Kant and others maintained that space and time are only forms of perception of the human mind. The human mind is so constituted that it perceives the realities of existence in relations of coexistence and succession; the perceptions of the relations of coexistence are space; and the perceptions of the relations of succession are time. Hence outside of the human mind there is neither space nor time. On the other hand, Spencer and others maintained that the relations of coexistence and succession exist among the realities themselves, and the human mind perceives these relations as space and time. Hence the relations among the realities of existence exist independently of the human mind, and would exist even if there was no human mind to perceive them. These philosophers did not tell us what is eternity. Spinoza did tell us what eternity is. At the outset, we must consider what these philosophers told us about space, time and eternity.

63. According to Kant, space and time are only forms of perception of the human mind. In this view is involved the whole

philosophy of Kant. According to Kant, there are no realities in existence; in existence there is only an unknowable Thing in Itself. What the Thing in Itself is, the human mind will never know. The human mind carves out of the Thing in Itself certain forms, and these forms appear to the human mind as the realities of existence. The human mind creates the realities, and exist only in the human mind; outside of the human mind there are no realities. Likewise, outside of the human mind there are no relations among the realities. The human mind creates the realities, and it perceives these realities in relations of co-existence and succession, and these perceptions are space and time. If there was no human mind, there would be neither realities nor relations among the realities, and therefor there would be neither space and time. At this occasion it is not necessary to examine Kant's philosophy critically. For the present purpose it is enough to state that Kant's philosophy rests on an illusion. The realities of existence were not created by the human mind, as the human mind did not create itself; the realities of existence existed before there was a human mind, and will exist even after there will no longer be a human mind. Likewise, the relations among the realities existed and will exist independently of the human mind; the human mind only perceives these relations. Hence, Kant did not understand space and time.

According to Spencer, the realities of existence and the relations of coexistence and succession among them exist independently of the human mind; they existed and will exist even if there was no human mind to perceive them. The human mind perceives the realities and the relations among them. The relations of coexistence among the realities is space, and the relations of succession among the realities is time. Hence space and time would exist even if there was no human mind to perceive the relations among the realities of existence. Thus far, Spencer was right; but he was wrong in the following. According to Spencer, the human mind derived the perceptions of space and time from the experiences with the realities of existence. Now, a perception derived from experience must necessarily be limited

as the experience is. If the human mind derived the perceptions
of space and time from experience with the realities of existence, then the perceptions of space and time would be limited.
But this is not so: space and time present themselves to the
human mind as unlimited, infinite. How did the human mind
come to possess perceptions of what are infinite? Next, Spencer
maintained that the perceptions of space and time were derived
by the human mind from the experiences with the realities of
existence, but this is not the case; the perceptions are the absolute conditions to experience. If the human mind did not possess
these perception *a priori*, it could not even begin to have experience; for all experience with the realities already presupposes
space and time. It is therefore clear that the human mind did
not acquire the perceptions of space any time from experience,
as Spencer maintained; but they were *a priori* perceptions, as
Kant maintained. Thus we see that Spencer did not understand
space and time.

64. And now let us consider what relativity tells us about space
and time. The world in which we live is four-dimensional. Space
is three-dimensional, time is one-dimensional; together they constitute a four-dimensional continuum. What is a continuum?
Matter consists of ultimate units. Before the advent of relativity, the atom was regarded as the ultimate unit of matter; but
relativity showed that the atom itself is composed of electrons
and protons. Again, before relativity matter and energy were
regarded as distinct from each other; but relativity showed that
matter is energy, and energy is matter. What appears as matter
is called the electron, and what appears as energy is called the
photon. Thus energy, light and matter consist of ultimate units.
The ultimate unit is called quantum. Hence the ultimate units
are quanta. The quanta are both corpuscles and waves. For this
reason Eddington calls the quanta wavicles. Now, the quanta
coexist with relation to one another. Every quantum has many
other quanta in its neighborhood among which there is a correlation of coexistence. The electrons and protons constitute the

atom; many atoms constitute the molecule; many molecules constitute a material body; and so on infinitely. The units of matter
are separated from one another. Relative to their sizes, they are
as far apart from one another as the planets are from one another. But, while the units are separated from one another by
great distances, they are held together, just as the planets are
held together in the solar system. This holding together constitutes their coexistence, and this coexistence is space. Space does
not exist apart from and independently of the units; space is
only a general term for the distances between the units of
matter. Take away the units of matter, and there will be no
space. To use an expression of Spencer, space is the abstract of
coexistence.

The units of matter are perpetually in motion about one another, and at great distances from one another. Now, motion
is in succession, and is discontinuous. There is no continuous
motion in existence. All motion in existence is pulsation, vibratory, rhythmic, consisting of motions and pauses or intervals.
The motion of a unit is called an event. Hence between the
motions of events there are pauses or intervals. Motion is wave-
like. A wave's motion is discontinuous; there are intervals between the crests and the troughs of a wave. The events follow
one another in succession. Each event has many events in the
neighborhood, some events preceding it and other events following it. Thus the events are separated from one another by intervals, yet at the same time they are connected by the intervals
in succession. The intervals which separate and connect the
events is time. Thus time does not exist separate from and independently of the events; that is, time does not exist separate
from and independently of the motions of the units of matter.
If the units did not exist or they would not be in motion, there
would be no succession of events, and therefore there would
not be time. To use an expression of Spencer, time is the abstract
of succession. The distances between the units of matter coexisting together is space, and the intervals between events is time.
The units coexist in three-dimensional space, and their motions

succeed one another in a one-dimensional time. Thus all matter exists and moves in a four-dimensional continuum. What is true of the ultimate units of matter is true of all material realities in existence; they all exist and move in a four-dimensional continuum. What we must carefully notice is this. According to relativity, space is not an infinite volume of extension in which things exist and move; space is only the distances between the units of matter or material bodies. Likewise, time is not an infinite duration in which events succeed one another; time is only the intervals between the events which succeed one another. Take away the distances between the units of matter and there will be no space; take away the intervals between the events and there will be no time. This is what relativity tells us about space and time.

65. And now a problem presents itself. All units of matter and all material bodies in existence are separated from one another by great distances relative to their sizes, and yet they are held together in definite relations. What holds them together? According to Newton, they are held together by gravitation. Gravitation is a universal force by which every unit of matter attracts all other units of matter in the universe. It makes no difference how great the intervening distance is, or whether the intervening distance is filled with matter or is an absolute vacuum. The physicists were compelled to assume that infinite space is filled with an ether by virtue of which units of matter attract one another. But investigation showed that there is no ether. Then the original question arises: how can the units of matter attract one another, or how can they be held together in definite relations? We saw before how relativity answered this question. Relativity showed that every material body radiates a gravitational field, and by virtue of the gravitational field do the material realities attract one another and hold together in definite relations. Now, the gravitational field, like the magnet field, is a form of energy, and matter itself is only a form of energy. Einstein tells us: From the relativity theory we know

that matter represents vast stores of energy, and the energy represents matter. We cannot, in this way, distinguish qualitatively between matter and field, since the distinction between mass and energy is not a qualitative one. By far the greater part of energy is concentrated in matter; but the field surrounding the particles also represents energy, though in an incomparably smaller quantity. We could therefore say: matter is where the concentration of energy is great, field is where the concentration of energy is small. The difference between matter and field is a quantitative rather than a qualitative one. We cannot imagine a definite surface which separates field from matter. Now, what Einstein tells us about field and matter comes into conflict with the quantum theory. The quantum theory postulates ultimate units of matter, but now we see that there are no ultimate units of matter. A unit of matter is continuous with its gravitational, magnetic or any other field. Then there are no longer quanta. This was known to the ancients long ago, and Spinoza already demonstrated that there are no units of substance; but substance is one continuous, indivisible and infinite. Some of the relativists already began to perceive that there are no quanta in existence. Schroedinger tells us (as quoted by Eddington in his book: The Nature of the Physical World):—

Imagine a sub-ether whose surface is covered with ripples. The oscillations of the ripples are a million times faster than those of visible light—too fast to come within the scope of gross experience. Individual ripples are beyond our ken; what we can appreciate is a combined effect—when the convergence and coalescence of the waves conspire to create a disturbed area large enough compared with the individual ripples, but small from our point of view. Such a disturbed area is recognized as a material particle; in particular it can be an electron. Accordingly, the electron is only a disturbed surface of the sub-ether. This means that the electron is not an infinitely small individual unit of matter, it is only a disturbed area of the sub-ether. Now, a ripple on the surface from the water is not separate and distinct from the water; it is only a state of the water itself. Thus all material realities are only ripples on the surface of the infinite energy which fills the universe. Hence the continuum is not the distances between the units of matter and the intervals between their motions; the continuum is the infinite energy itself; it is infinite in extension and in duration. There is no vacuum between the units of matter, and there is no hiatus between the events. There is but one absolute, infinite and eternal substance. What, then, are space and time?

66. According to the theories which we have considered, space and time are not entities separate and distinct from the material realities, in existence; space is only an abstract of coexistence, time is only an abstract of succession. All these theories rest on the assumption that between the units of matter there is a vacuum, and between the motions of the material realities there is a hiatus. But now we see that there are no individual units of matter, separate and apart from one another. This means that there are no quanta in existence. There is only one substance which is eternal and infinite. The perception of the infinite extension of substance is space, and the perception of the eternal duration of substance is time. The infinite extension and the eternal duration of substance is the four-dimensional continuum; the infinite extension is coexistence, and the eternal duration is succession. Now, coexistence and succession are correlatives, they imply each other; neither can exist without the other. Let us consider, by way of illustration, number. We begin with one. The one becomes two, three, four, five, and so on to infinity. Here we see succession, but this succession implies coexistence. Take the number five. The number five is the result of a succession: one became five. The number five consists of five ones that are coexisting together. And so we see that, as the one becomes an infinite succession of numbers, each of these numbers is also a coexistence of many ones. Five is a coexistence of five ones, ten is a coexistence of ten ones, and so on to infinity. Thus we see that coexistence and succession are correlatives. This means that space and time are correlatives, they

imply each other; neither can exist without the other, and neither can be conceived without the other. Hence relativity is correct when it tells us that we live in a four-dimensional continuum; but relativity does not understand that continuum. The continuum is not the distances between the units of matter and the realities of existence and the intervals between motions or events; the continuum is substance itself. Substance is coexistence and succession; the human mind perceives this coexistence and succession of substance itself, and this constitutes the perception of space and time. We must consider this more closely.

Succession implies change, and change implies permanence; only that which is permanent can change; that which is not permanent does not change: it comes and goes, but it does not change. The realities themselves are not permanent; only substance is permanent. Substance, in succession assumes infinite forms, and these forms are the realities of existence. The human mind perceives this succession in substance, and this perception constitutes time. Thus time is a perception of succession in substance, and therefore time does not pertain to the realities of existence. The same is true of coexistence. There is no coexistence among the realities in existence. All realities perpetually move about one another and perpetually change their relative positions. Hence there is no coexistence among the realities. The coexistence is in substance itself. Space is the perception by the human mind of the eternal coexistence of substance itself. Hence Kant was right when he maintained that time and space do not pertain to the realities of existence, but he was wrong in assuming that they are merely perceptions of the human mind. Indeed, they are perceptions of the human mind, but they are perceptions of the succession and coexistence of substance itself, or, as he called it, The Thing in Itself. Space and time are correlatives, and correlatives imply a third reality of which they are correlatives. What is the third reality of which space and time are correlatives? The third reality is eternity. Our next step is to consider eternity.

67. What is eternity? Spinoza tells us that eternity is existence itself, so far as it is conceived to follow from the definition of an eternal thing. Eternity cannot be explained by duration of time, even if the duration be conceived without beginning and end. We must notice the following. Eternity is existence itself; existence is eternal, and that which is eternal is neither created nor destroyed. Second, eternity is fundamentally different from time. Time itself may be eternal, yet it is not eternity. Time is succession, and succession is change; but eternity does not change. Spinoza uses the triangle as a symbol of eternity. The triangle stands before as an eternal reality. We cannot conceive a time or space when and where there was no triangle, or when and where there will be no triangle. The triangle stands before us as: I Am; from eternity unto eternity the triangle is, was and will remain absolutely the same, it never changes. But existence is not merely I Am; existence is also I Am Becoming. That which in existence is permanent, which never changes, which is not created and which is not destroyed—this is eternity. This means that the Absolute, God, the infinite attributes of substance—all these are eternal, for they do not change; but all their manifestations perpetually change. Therefore, in their esssence they are eternal, eternity; but in forms of manifestation they are temporary, time. Eternity is the third reality of which time and space are correlatives. We considered space and time with relation to each other. Now, we must consider space and time with relation to eternity. And, first, the relation of time to eternity.

Substance is, form is becoming; substance is eternity, form is time. Substance has no past, and it has no future; substance is eternally in the present. Substance does not carry within itself the past, because it never existed in the past; and substance has no future, because it does not change. Eternity, then, is the present. But men are in the habit of speaking of the past, the present and the future. This, of course, relates to time. Let us, then, consider time. Time has no present, and we cannot grasp the present. That we may become aware of what takes place in existence, time must pass. In whatever way we are affected by external things, whether by light or sound or in any other way, it takes time before our mind becomes aware of the effection. Hence we cannot become aware of what actually takes place in the present; we can become aware only of what took place in the past. And even of our own states of mind we can become aware only when they are no longer in the present. This is so, because we can become aware of a state of consciousness only with a subsequent state of consciousness. Again, we cannot grasp the past. We can grasp the past only in the present. Suppose we reflect on our own experiences in the past. That we may think of our past experiences, we must think of them as they appear to us in the present. Suppose we think of the time when we went to school. We recall the school, the teachers, the school-mates, and the subjects we studied. While thinking of them, we bring them back to the present and we see them right now before us; we cannot see the past as in the past. Likewise, when we read history. Suppose we read in the Bible how Moses was leading the flocks of Jethro—his father-in-law—to Mount Horeb; how he saw the thorn-bush in flames, and yet was not consumed by the fire. We read that Moses said to himself. I will turn to see this marvel, why is not the thorn-bush consumed by the fire. As we read all this, Moses, the flocks, Mount Horeb and the burning thorn-bush—all appear before us in the present, we see them right now before us; otherwise, we cannot understand what we are reading. And what about the future? The future is again the eternal present becoming the present. We always existed in the present, and always exist in the present, and always will exist in the present. What, then, are the past and the future? The past is the recollection of the forms as they were in the past present, and the future is the anticipation of the forms as they will be in the future present.

And now let us consider eternity and space. We saw that there is no succession among the realities, and there is no coexistence among the realities. Space is the perception of the infinite extension of eternal substance. Space symbolizes eternity; space is absolute, without form. In a previous chapter I referred to the fact that the ancient Jewish thinkers referred to God as Space. We can now see the reason for this. Space is absolute thought—thought without form; and space is conceived as eternal present. We saw that absolute thought, when it assumes a form becomes a reality. This is true of space. When space assumes a form, it becomes a reality. One form excludes another form. This is the reason why the realities of existence exclude one another, and they appear to be distinct from one another. Eternity pertains to the transcendental world, space and time pertain to the phenomenal world. The velocity of light is the dividing line between them. The transcendental world is the world of ideas, and the phenomenal world is the world of material forms in which the ideas realize themselves. Now, eternity is infinite; are time and space also infinite? We shall presently see that time and space are both finite and infinite, relative and absolute.

68. Imagine a disk having a diameter like that of the earth, resting on a pivot in the center. The disk can be made to rotate with such speed that at the circumference of the disk the velocity will be like that of light. Let us place two young men, each twenty years old, one at the centre of the disk, and the other at the circumference. Let us provide them food, drink and other necessaries of life to last them for fifty years. And now, by means of machinery, let us cause the disk to rotate about its pivot with such velocity that at the circumference it will reach the velocity of light, and let the disk rotate for fifty years, and then let us stop the rotation of the disk. We now go up to the young man at the centre of the disk, what will we find? We will find an old man of seventy, gray and bent, and all the food and drink that he had were consumed by him. And now let us go to the young man at the circumference of the disk, what will we find? We will find the young man just as he was fifty years ago; he has not grown older by one day, and he has not

touched the food and drink which we had provided for him. What is the reason for this difference? This we already learned from relativity. A clock in motion slows down; and, when the velocity of the motion reaches that of light, the clock stops altogether. What is true of the clock is true of all processes in existence. All motions and all processes in existence, when they reach the velocity of light, stop completely. The young man at the circumference of the disk was moving with a velocity of light; therefore all life-processes in him completely stopped. During the fifty years he was in a state of eternity. On the other hand, the young man at the centre of the disk moved with a slow velocity, therefore he grew older by fifty years. Time and change exist only up to the velocity of light; beyond that velocity there is no longer time and change—it is eternity.

And now notice this. When the disk was rotating, at the circumference its velocity was that of light, but at the centre its velocity was small. Between the velocity at the centre and the velocity at the circumference there were infinite different velocities; it was least at the centre and greatest at the circumference. These different velocities manifested themselves in different times and different changes; the further from the centre the slower was the time, and also the slower was the change. Thus we see two things. First, time is relative to the velocity of motion. Second, while time is relative to the velocity of motion, motion itself is absolute. This we shall see in the next chapter. For instance, the motion of the electron is absolute. This means that time is both relative and absolute. And now the question is this: Is time finite or infinite? The answer is, time is both absolute and infinite. We already saw that the absolute and the relative are correlatives, and the same is true of the infinite and the finite, they are correlatives, they imply each other; neither can exist without the other. First, time is finite and relative. Time is only up to the velocity of light; above the velocity of light there is no longer time. But below the velocity of light time is infinite, because the phenomenal world existed infinitely and eternally. There never was a time when there was no phenomenal world and there will never be a time when there will not be a phenomenal world. Substance eternally and infinitely manifests itself in material forms. Thus time, like eternity, is infinite and eternal. The difference between them is this: eternity is the transcendental aspect of substance, time is the phenomenal aspect of substance. The ideas in the transcendental world are eternal, they do not change; but the material forms which the ideas assume in the phenomenal world perpetually change. Consider the triangle, the circle, the square, the sphere. As ideas in the transcendental world they are eternally the same; but as material forms in the phenomenal world they perpetually change. And now let us consider space.

69. What is true of time is true of space. Space is both finite and infinite, absolute and relative. Let us again use the disk for an illustration. We take two blocks of iron, each weighing a ton. We place one block of iron at the centre, and the other block of iron at the circumference. We cause the disk to rotate as before, so that at the circumference its velocity will be like that of light. What will become of the blocks of iron? The block at the centre will remain intact as before, but the block at the circumference will disappear. This is so because, as we saw before, matter when it reaches the velocity of light shortens to absolute zero, it disappears. Matter occupies space. When matter contracts to zero, the space which it occupied also contracts to zero. Hence with the disappearance of the block of iron also the space which it occupied will disappear. Between the centre of the disk and its circumference, as we saw before, there will be infinite different velocities. This means that, if we placed many blocks of iron between the centre of the disk and the circumference, the different blocks of iron would contract in different degrees. This means that the spaces occupied by the different blocks of iron would contract in different degrees. Thus we see that space, like time, is relative to the velocity of motion. But motion itself is absolute, and extension of substance is absolute and infinite. Thus we see that space is both relative

and absolute; it is relative in the phenomenal world, it is absolute in the transcendental world. Again, with the contraction of matter to zero, space in the phenomenal world disappears. Space exists in the phenomenal world, but not in the transcendental world. Thus space is finite. But the phenomenal world is infinite; therefore space is infinite. In other words, with relation to the transcendental world, time and space are relative and finite, because they do not exist in the transcendental world; but in the phenomenal world time and space are infinite and absolute.

Finally, time is thought, space is extension. Of time we have an inner consciousness, of space we have an outer consciousness. We have a consciousness of the flow and succession of thought in us, and we have a consciousness of the external realities coexisting outside of us. We now see the primordial trinity in another aspect. The Infinite Intellect Thought and Extension now reveal themselves as eternity, time and space. In a previous chapter I quoted the statement of Einstein: A most fundamental problem, for thousands of years wholly obscured by its implications, is that of motion. Much has been said and written about motion, but thus far the true nature of motion has not yet been revealed. Hence our next subject of inquiry must be: what is motion?

CHAPTER XI

Motion and Rest

70. Motion implies a force, and means that something is impelled by a force to move. Motion involves space and time. First, motion means that something moves from one point in space to another point in space. Second, it means that something moves from one moment of time to another moment of time. Hence all motion takes place in a space-time continuum. Motion is usually conceived with relation to material things, but motion pertains to all infinite aspects of existence, it pertains to thought, and it pertains to existence itself. All motion, as said, implies a force. The force which causes all motion is the Absolute itself. The Absolute is eternally and infinitely in a state of motion. There are two kinds of motion: dynamic and static. Dynamic motion is a motion of translation, that is, it is from one point of space to another point of space, and from one moment of time to another moment of time. Static motion is called space-occupying motion. A material body consists of numerous particles: molecules, atoms, protons and electrons; they are held together by a force; otherwise, the particles of matter would fly asunder from one another. But just as motion implies a force, so a force implies a motion; a force that is not in motion is not a force. The particles of matter are held together by a space-occupying and time-enduring force that is in motion. Again, the infinite numbers of stars, planets, and all other bodies in the universe are held together by a space-occupying and time-enduring force that is in motion. Thus we see two things. First, motion is not limited to material things only. Second, motion is both dynamic and static.

Motion implies rest, neither can exist without the other, and neither can be conceived without the other. But is there rest in existence? All realities and processes in existence are perpetually in a state of motion. Consider a table. The table seems to be at rest, yet it is not at rest. First, the table consists of particles of matter that are in a state of motion about one another. Since the table consists of these particles of matter, and they are in motion, the table therefore is in a state of motion. The table stands on the floor of the house, but the house moves together with the earth, with the sun and with the stars. Thus we see that, while the table seems to be at rest, in fact it is in a state of motion. Again, consider the human body. The human body consists of infinite cells which are perpetually in a state of motion. Since the human body consists of these cells, the human body is also in a state of motion. Again, the human body together with the earth, the sun and the stars is perpetually in a state of motion. Consider the human mind. The human mind is never at rest, it constantly thinks; thoughts perpetually flow through the human mind, and thus the human mind is always in a state of motion. Thus we see that there is no rest in existence. But motion implies rest, they are correlatives, neither can exist without the other. Since motion is the infinite and eternal state of existence, there must be in existence infinite and eternal rest. What, then, is rest?

71. Rest is inertia. Inertia is defined as a negative property of matter, by virtue of which matter resists any change in its state of rest or motion. Newton defines inertia as follows: Every body continues in its state of rest or of uniform motion in a straight line, except as it is compelled by a force to change that state. Matter of itself cannot change its state of rest or of motion. According to this definition, inertia is a negative property of matter. Since, however, by virtue of its inertia matter resists any change in its state of rest or of uniform motion in a straight line, inertia cannot be a negative property of matter, inertia is a positive force, and a positive force is not a negative property. Relativity shows that the inertia of matter increases with the

velocity of motion; when the velocity of the motion reaches that of light, the inertia of the matter becomes infinite, so that no power in existence can overcome it. It is therefore clear that inertia is a positive force inherent in matter. Until the advent of relativity, matter was regarded as separate and distinct from energy; matter was regarded as passive, and energy was regarded as active. But relativity showed that matter is nothing else than energy, it is concentrated energy. But energy is active, it is a force, it is a positive force; energy is the force inherent in matter which resists any change in the state of the matter. This energy is inertia, and this is rest. Let us consider the matter more closely.

A material body consists of infinite particles that are held together. These particles move about one another with certain velocities and within certain range. The electrons move about the protons, the planets move about the sun, and so throughout all infinite existence. They all move with definite velocities and within definite ranges. The particles of a material body are held together by a force; and so the planets are held together by a force; and so all infinite stars and other material bodies in the universe are held together by a force. All resist any change in their velocities and range of motion. The force which holds the particles of a material body together, the force which holds the planets and the sun together, and the force which holds all infinite stars and material bodies together—this force is inertia. This inertia is rest. Rest, then, is a space-occuping and time-enduring motion. It requires force to hold the particles of matter together; it takes force to hold the planets and the sun together; and it takes infinite force to hold the whole material world together. It is this force that resists any change in the relations of the parts, their motions, the velocities of their motions and the direction of their motions. The same is true of human society. Organized society resists any change in the relations among the members of society. How great the force of that resistance is, is shown by the fact that it requires struggles, wars and revolutions to effect some change in the relations of the

members of a society. And now let us consider another aspect
of motion and rest.

72. I sit and rest. While I sit and rest, I am in fact in a state
of motion. All parts that constitute my body are in a state of
motion; the thoughts in my mind are in a state of motion; and
together with the earth, the sun and the stars I am in a state of
motion; and yet I am at rest, I feel that I am at rest. And so,
while I sit and rest, I am in fact in a state of motion. And now
I get up from my chair and begin to walk. Walking is motion.
And so, in addition to the previous motion, I now add another
motion. What is the difference between these two motions?
This is the difference. While sitting and resting, the motions of
my body and of my thoughts were not determined by me, and
I could not stop them; but the motion involved in the walking
was determined by me. The first motion is a universal and
dependent motion, the second motion is an individual and independent motion. The universal and dependent motion is rest,
the individual and independent motion is motion. There is a
correlation between these two kinds of motion, neither can
exist without the other. Every reality in existence is in a state
of double motion. On the one hand, every reality moves together with all other realities in existence; on the other hand,
every reality moves independently of the other realities. The
infinite force in existence causes all realities to move together,
and the same infinite force causes each reality to move independently of the other realities. This manifests itself in a struggle. On the one hand, each reality struggles against the universal
and dependent motion, so as to be free to move independently
of the rest of the realities. On the other hand, all realities in
existence struggle against the individual motions of each reality,
so as to keep it within the order of existence. In turn, each
motion is a condition to the other motion. If there were no
individual and independent motion, there would be no universal and dependent motion; on the other hand, if there were no
universal dependent motion, there would be no individual and

independent motion. Thus action and reaction are equal and
opposite in direction. The greater the struggle of an individual
reality for independent motion, the greater is the resistance of
all realities against the independent motion of the individual
reality; and the greater the resistance of all realities, the greater
is the struggle of each reality for independent motion. Thus
motion and rest coexist eternally and infinitely.

Correlatives imply a third reality of which they are correlatives. What is the third reality of which motion and rest are
correlatives? The third reality is force. What is force? Philosophers tell us that force is unknowable. We can interpret matter
in terms of motion, and we can interpret motion in terms of
force, but we cannot interpret force in terms of anything else,
because there is nothing else in which we can interpret force.
Therefore force is and forever will remain unknowable to the
human mind. But we did away with the unknowable, and we
shall presently see that force is knowable. I sit and rest physi-
cally and mentally. In fact, as we saw before, I do not rest; but
I rest because I am passive and move with the universal dependent motion—a motion which is not determined by me. As I
thus sit and rest, an idea comes to my mind to do something. As
soon as the idea comes to my mind I become active; my passivity
and rest turned into activity and motion. What changed me
from passivity and rest into activity and motion? It was the
idea. Now, an idea is a form of absolute thought. Before this
idea came to my mind, absolute thought was flowing through
my being; for absolute thought is my substance, my life and my
consciousness; yet this absolute thought did not stir me to action
and motion. But the moment this absolute thought assumed the
form of an idea, the idea stirred me to action and motion. Now,
absolute thought is eternally and infinitely in motion, but absolute thought becomes a force and determines action and motion
only when it assumes the form of an idea. An idea comprehends
absolute thought in a definite form, it limits absolute thought,
it causes the absolute thought to flow through a definite channel. It is this channelizing of the flow of absolute thought that

converts it into a force. Consider the ocean. If there were no winds, the earth did not rotate around its axis and it did not revolve about the sun, then the ocean would be in a state of rest. The ocean would be in a state of rest, though the particles of water would be in motion. And now, suppose that we dig a deep channel from some distance to the ocean. The moment the channel is opened, the water from the ocean would begin to flow through the channel with great force. This is the case of absolute thought. Absolute thought is an infinite and eternal ocean. Within itself it is eternally and infinitely in motion, yet it is not a force. But when the absolute thought assumes a form, when the absolute thought is channelized, then it becomes a force. Force, then, is nothing else than absolute thought flowing through an idea, which is a form of absolute thought. Thus we see that force comes into existence when absolute thought assumes the form of an idea. All forces in existence are nothing else than the idea of God—the Infinite Intellect. The Infinite Intellect is the eternal and infinite idea of the Absolute; this idea comprehends the Absolute in infinite attributes and modes, and thus the Infinite Intellect becomes the creator of the world. The realities of existence are perpetually in a state of motion just because they are the material forms of the ideas of God. In a previous chapter we saw that an idea is a living and conscious reality, and this is so because it is an idea of God. Whatever is absolute, infinite and eternal is absolute, infinite and eternal in every part thereof. An idea of God is like God; like God it lives and is conscious of itself and of its functions. And this is force.

73. We saw that the velocity of light is the dividing line between the transcendental world and the phenomenal world; the transcendental world is above the velocity of light, and the phenomenal world is below the veolcity of light. We also saw that eternity is in the transcendental world, time and space are in the phenomenal world. Again, we saw that ideas are in the transcendental world, their material manifestations are in the phenomenal world. And now we can see that force is in

the transcendental world, while motion and rest are in the phenomenal world. As we just saw, force is an idea, and an idea is in the transcendental world. Again, we saw that material bodies can move only in a space-time continuum, and matter itself exists in the phenomenal world. An idea comprehends time, space, matter, motion and rest; but an idea transcends time, space, matter, motion and rest. An idea is eternal and infinite, it does not change; only its manifestations in material forms change. Consider the triangle. There is only one idea of a triangle in eternal and infinite existence. The idea itself never changes, but this idea of the triangle assumes infinite material forms in the phenomenal world. This is true of all ideas. Take the idea of evolution. All realities in existence eternally and infinitely change in accordance with the idea of evolution, but evolution itself eternally and infinitely remains the same, it never changes. Thus we see that force is transcendental, while motion and rest are phenomenal. This was the reason why philosophers maintained that force is unknowable. Force is unknowable, so long as we do not comprehend the Absolute and we do not know the nature of an idea. But, once we comprehend the Absolute and we know the nature of an idea, then force is knowable. Now, motion and rest involve attraction and repulsion. Hence we must consider attraction and repulsion.

ATTRACTION AND REPULSION

74. In his First Principles, Spencer tells us the following. "Matter cannot be conceived except as manifesting forces of attraction and repulsion. Body is distinguished in our consciousness from space by its opposition to our muscular energies; and this opposition we feel under the two fold form of a cohesion that hinders our effort to rend, and a resistance that hinders our effort to compress. Without resistance there can be merely empty space, without cohesion there can be no resistance. We are obliged to think of all objects as made up of parts that attract and repel each other, since this is the form of our experi-

ence of all objects. By a higher abstraction results the conception of attraction and repulsion, attractive and repulsive forces pervading space. We cannot dissociate force from occupied extension, or occupied extension from force, because we have never an immediate consciousness of either in the absence of the other." Again, science tells us that universal attraction is a force in virtue of which the material particles of all bodies tend incessantly to approach each other; it is an action which all bodies, at rest or in motion, exert upon one another, no matter how great or how small the space between them may be, or whether this space be occupied or unoccupied by matter. The attraction between any two bodies is the resultant of the attractions of each molecule of the one upon every molecule of the other. This means that every particle of matter in the universe attracts all other particles of matter in the universe. Now, it is clear that, if between the particles of matter there was only attraction, then all infinite particles of matter in the universe would integrate into one infinite mass of matter, and then there would not be the infinite individual and separate realities. Since, however, matter is divided into infinite individual and separate material realities, this means that, besides attraction, there is between the particles of matter another force, namely, repulsion. Hence, as Spencer says, matter cannot be conceived except as manifesting forces of attraction and repulsion. If there was no attraction, the infinite mass of matter would forever remain in a state of diffusion. On the other hand, if there was no repulsion, there would be no realities in existence. Thus we see that in the material realities are inherent two opposite forces: attraction and repulsion. What, then, are attraction and repulsion? Since relativity showed that matter is energy, this means that attraction and repulsion are inherent in energy itself. The question, then is: with relation to energy, what are attraction and repulsion?

75. Let us begin with number. One becomes two, three, four, five, and so on to infinity. As we proceed from one to infinity,

the numbers follow one another in groups which become ever larger, until the group becomes infinitely large. One becomes two, three, four, five, and so on. Two is a group of two ones, three is a group of three ones, four is a group of four ones, five is a group of five ones, and so on to infinity. The further away a number is from one the greater is the number of ones in that number. The one is absolute, infinite and eternal. It is absolute, because in all the infinite combinations the one remains one; it is infinite, because it becomes infinite numbers; and it is eternal, because it endures forever and never changes. In all the infinite numbers, the one remains unchanged and unaffected. And now let us consider a group of ones, say, the number five. Five is a group of five ones that are organically united. Five is not merely five ones, it is five ones united in one number. Between the five ones in the number five there is the same organic relation as between the organs of a living body. If we take apart the organs of a living body, the living body is thereby destroyed. Likewise, if we take apart the five ones of the number five, the number five is thereby destroyed. We then have five ones, but not the number five. Thus we see that the one becomes, not only an infinite series of numbers, but it also becomes an infinite series of groups of ones that are organically related to one another. When we reflect on the process by which one becomes an infinite series of groups of numbers, we perceive repulsion and attraction. First, as to repulsion. To become an infinite series of numbers, the one must repel itself from itself, it moves from itself outwardly in a centrifugal motion, every new group of numbers moves away further from the one. Thus arise the infinite numbers. On the other hand, as the one becomes infinite numbers, the infinite numbers consist of groups of ones, each succeeding group consisting of ever more ones. These ones are held together in each group. This is attraction. Attraction is nothing else than the holding together of the ones in a number consisting of many ones. It is a centripetal motion. And now we will understand attraction and repulsion in their infinite and eternal aspects. The Infinite Intellect, God, extends himself out-

wardly in an infinite series of numbers; and, while he reproduces himself in infinite numbers, at the same time combines the
ones into groups of ever greater numbers of ones. This gives us
an idea of the attraction and repulsion in existence.

Between the one and the infinite series of numbers there is
also an organic continuity—it is one continuous series of numbers. But at the same time it is also an infinite series of interrup-
tions. We saw, as relativity demonstrated, that motion is discontinuous, and this is true of the motion of the one to infinity.
While the one moves outwardly to infinity, it constantly inter-
rupts itself, and thus arise separate and distinct numbers. What
is true of numbers is true of all realities in existence. One living
cell becomes an infinite number of living cells. As the one cell
moves outwardly from itself, and becomes an infinite number
of cells, it at the same time combines the cells into groups of
cells; and the groups of cells it combines into groups or groups
of cells; and so it continues to combine them into organs, and
the organs in the whole living body. It is so with ideas. An idea,
like a cell, extends outwardly in a centrifugal motion, one idea
becomes an infinite number of ideas; at the same time the ideas
are organized into groups of ideas, and so on until systems of
ideas are organized, and these systems of ideas are destined to
become organized into one monistic philosophy. The creation
of the world began with one idea—an idea of God. This idea
might have been a proton or an electron or a still more primordial form of absolute thought. This ultimate unit of reality
became an infinite number of units, which became combined
into atoms, molecules, masses of matter, and so were brought
out the infinite stars, planets, and all other material bodies.

Attraction and repulsion are the correlatives of the absolutely
one—the Absolute. We saw that between one and the infinite
numbers there is an organic continuity; just as the one, so all
the infinite numbers constitute one. It is so with the cells. Between the one cell and the whole body there is an organic continuity; just as the cell, so all the infinite cells in the living body
are one cell. And it is so with all realities in existence. Just as the

Absolute is one, so all infinite realities are one. Hence Spinoza tells us (Ethics: Part II, Lemma VII): "Thus, if we advance ad infinitum, we may easily conceive the whole of nature to be one individual, whose parts, that is to say, all bodies, differ in infinite ways without any change in the whole individual." This is now perfectly clear. Since all existence is the manifestation of God, the One Infinite Intellect of the Absolute, and is the substance of all realities, it follows that all existence, in all its infinite and eternal aspects, is absolute one and indivisible. The process of creation begins as repulsion, devolution, entropy; and then it becomes attraction, evolution and creation. Unity is in the transcendental world above the velocity of light, repulsion and attraction are in the phenomenal world below the velocity of light. In the phenomenal world, realities are divided and separated from one another. To the senses, time appears to consist of a series of intervals, space appears to be a series of distances, matter appears to be an infinite series of individual particles, and so all through. But, when we rise to the understanding, the realities appear to be integrated into groups, species, genera, orders and classes. Time and space are comprehended in vast periods and vast distances. And, finally, when we rise to reason, then all realities combine into ideas, and the ideas are infinite and eternal. There is one attribute of thought, one attribute of extension, there is but one triangle, one circle, and one sphere, and so on all through. In the one there is neither attraction nor repulsion; attraction and repulsion arise when the one differentiates itself into many ones. The Absolutely one is the Absolute. In the Absolute there is neither attraction nor repulsion. It is only when the Absolute, as God, differentiates itself into infinite ones that attraction and repulsion arise. But this takes place in the phenomenal world.

CHAPTER XII

The Infinite and the Finite

76. For thousands of years the philosophers struggled to comprehend the infinite, at the same time believing that they understood the finite. But the infinite and the finite are correlatives, they imply each other; neither can be conceived without the other. Since the philosophers did not comprehend the infinite, they could not comprehend the finite. The philosophers, therefore, deceived themselves that they understood the finite. Until Spinoza, the problem was: what is the infinite? Spinoza solved this problem. But at the same time Spinoza himself failed to understand the finite. All philosophers grant that the cause of existence is infinite. The question is: How could the infinite create the finite? In other words, how could the infinite become finite? This question Spinoza answered as follows:—

An individual thing, or a thing which is finite and which has a determinate existence, cannot exist nor be determined to action, unless it be determined to existence and action by another cause which is also finite and has a determinate existence; and, again, this cause cannot exist nor be determined to action, unless by another cause which is also finite and determined to existence and action, and so on ad infinitum.—*Ethics:* Part I, Proposition 28.

This proposition Spinoza proves as follows:
"Whatever is determined to existence and action is thus determined by God. But that which is finite and which has a determined existence could not be produced by the absolute nature or any attribute of God, for whatever follows from the absolute

nature of any attribute of God is infinite and eternal. The finite and determinate must therefore follow from God, or from some attribute of God, in so far as the latter is considered to be affected by some mode, in so far as the attribute is modified by a modification which is finite, and which has a determinate existence. Again, this cause or mode must be determined by another cause, which is also finite, and which has a determined existence; and this last cause must, in its turn, be determined by another cause, and so on continually ad infinitum."

According to Spinoza, the infinite cannot be the cause of the finite. This is clear, for the infinite cannot become the finite. How, then, did the finite things in existence come into existence? Previously, Spinoza demonstrated that God is the only direct, immediate and efficient cause of all things in existence; and without God they could not be and could not be conceived. But God is infinite. How, then, could God become the cause of the finite things? Spinoza's answer is: the infinite attributes of God must have been modified by a finite mode, and thus the finite things came into existence. What we must carefully notice is this, Spinoza does not tell us what sort of mode it was that could modify the attributes in a finite manner, so as to produce the finite things. Nor does he tell us how a finite mode could affect an infinite attribute. Spinoza merely asserts this, without any proof. It seems that Spinoza thought this was so simple that it did not require any proof. But the truth is, as we shall presently see, that Spinoza could not prove this proposition. First, I call attention to the following. In the first part of the Ethics he tells us many things about God, that he is the cause of all things, and without him nothing can exist or be conceived. In the second part of the Ethics, Spinoza at once begins to speak of the human mind. Not a word is said about the creation of the world and the creation of man. The reason is clear. Spinoza could not tell us anything about the creation of the world and of man. Hence, between the first part of the Ethics and the second part there is an infinite hiatus. The creation of the world is an infinitely more important problem than God himself is.

We may convince ourselves that God exists, and we may attain to a knowledge and understanding of God. But the problem of problems is: how did God create the world? How could God, who is absolute, infinite and eternal, create a world of relative, finite and temporary things; how could God become relative, finite and temporary things? Thus far no one demonstrated this, least of all Spinoza. Hence we must not take Spinoza's assertion seriously.

77. Spinoza was aware of the difficulty, and he met it with the following statement: "Since certain things must have been immediately produced by God, that is to say, those which necessarily follow from his absolute nature; these primary products being the mediating cause for those things which, nevertheless, without God can neither be nor can be conceived; it follows, first, that of things immediately produced by God he is the proximate cause absolutely. It follows, secondly, that God cannot be properly called the remote cause of individual things, unless for the sake of distinguishing them from things which he has immediately produced, or rather which follow from his absolute nature. For by a remote cause we understand that which is in no way joined to its effect. But all things which are, are in God, and so depend upon him that without him they can neither be nor be conceived."

Thus, according to Spinoza, God produced certain things directly and immediately. What those things are, Spinoza does not tell us. Next, the realities of existence were not produced by God directly, but through those things which he produced immediately. Spinoza speaks of proximate and remote causes. He tells us that a remote cause is in no way joined to its effect. Here Spinoza shows that he did not have an adequate idea of cause. First, we saw at the outset, that there are no remote causes; that God is the only direct, immediate and immanent cause of all things. Second, if a remote cause is not joined to the effect, then the remote cause is not the cause of the effect. Since God could not be the cause of the finite things, how did

the finite things come into existence? And yet, Spinoza con-
cludes the demonstration by telling us: But all things which are,
are in God, and so depend upon him that without him they
could neither be nor be conceived. If all things could neither
be nor be conceived without God, and that they are all in God,
is not God the direct, immediate and immanent cause of the
finite things? Hence the problem remains: How did God create
or become the finite things? We shall presently see that God
did not and could not perform such miracle: God could not
create or become the finite things. How, then, did the finite
things come into existence? This we shall presently see. Let us
consider Spinoza's proposition more closely.

78. Suppose we take any finite and determined thing. According to Spinoza, this thing was determined to existence and action
by some finite and determinate cause. In turn, this finite and
determinate cause was itself determined to existence and action
by another finite and determinate cause; and so on ad infinitum.
Now, suppose we trace the series of causes in the ascending
order until we reach the first finite and determinate cause. Let
us stop right here. We then ask the question: how did this first
finite and determinate cause come into existence? Neither God
nor the attributes of God could produce the first finite cause;
how, then, did it come into existence? A finite cause is not the
cause of itself; how could it become the cause of the finite
realities in existence? Like the philosophers generally, who hide
themselves behind an Unknowable, Spinoza hides himself behind
an ad infinitum. What, then, is the answer? The answer is this:
There are no finite things in existence. Before the problem was,
what is the infinite; and now the problem is, what is the finite.
Let us consider the matter.

The First Cause, God, is not separate and apart from the
created world; the First Cause, God is the world, he is the
realities of existence. Whatever is absolute, infinite and eternal
is absolute, infinite and eternal in every part thereof. Since the
First Cause, God, is absolute, infinite and eternal, every reality

in existence is absolute, infinite and eternal. We saw that number is absolute, infinite and eternal. One becomes infinite numbers, and every one of the numbers is infinite. Again, consider the acorn. The acorn appears to be finite and temporary; yet we saw that this acorn can in infinite time become infinite oak trees and infinite acorns, each of which is also infinite and eternal. We saw the same with ideas. Every reality is a trinity, consisting of a material form, a form of energy and an idea. The matter of a reality is part of substance, which is absolute, infinite and eternal. The form of the energy is itself absolute, infinite and eternal. The form of the acorn reproduces itself infinitely. Finally, the idea, which is the soul and essence of a reality, is absolute, infinite and eternal. Where in existence can a finite and temporary thing be found? What, then, is the difference between the infinite and the finite? The infinite is explicit in the finite, because the infinite manifests itself in infinite finite things. In turn, the finite are implicitly infinite, because every finite thing can become infinite. Again, eternity is explicit in time, because eternity realizes itself in time; and time is implicitly eternal, because it involves eternity. And the same is true of the absolute and the relative. The absolute is explicit in the relative, because the absolute realizes itself in the relative realities; and the relative is implicitly absolute, because the relative involves the absolute. The absolute and the relative, the eternal and the temporary, and the finite and the infinite—all are correlatives, they imply each other, neither can exist without the other, and neither can be conceived without the other. All realities live, move and have their being in the Absolute, Infinite and Eternal; in turn, the Absolute, Infinite and Eternal lives, moves and has its being in the realities of existence.

FREEDOM AND NECESSITY

79. The Absolute manifests itself as the Infinite Intellect, God; and God manifests himself in infinite ideas and their material forms. Is this infinite and eternal manifestation a freely deter-

mined act, or is it determined by some inherent necessity? Is the Absolute free to manifest itself, or is it determined to manifest itself by some inherent necessity? This is an old problem. For thousands of years profound thinkers struggled with this problem, but thus far the problem was not adequately solved. And, first, what is freedom, and what is necessity? Spinoza tells us: That thing is called free which exists from the necessity of its own nature alone, and is determined to action by itself alone. That thing, on the other hand, is called necessary, or rather constrained, which by another is determined to existence and action in a fixed and prescribed manner. We must at once notice this. Spinoza defines freedom in terms of necessity. This means that freedom and necessity are correlatives, they imply each other; neither can exist without the other, and neither can be conceived without the other. Without freedom there can be no necessity, and without necessity there can be no freedom. What, then, is freedom, and what is necessity? Freedom means freedom of motion, necessity means constraint of motion. That which does not move is neither free nor constrained. Since all realities in existence perpetually move, all realities are free. On the other hand, since all realities are constrained to move within certain bounds, it follows that all realities are constrained. We saw that motion has two aspects: independent motion and dependent motion. Independent motion is freedom, dependent motion is constraint. We also saw that independent motion is repulsion, and dependent motion is attraction; independent motion is centrifugal, dependent motion is centripetal. We saw that matter is inconceivable without repulsion and attraction. Consider the atom. The atom consists of electrons and protons. The electron is negative electricity, the proton is positive electricity. It is clear that neither form of electricity can exist without the other form of electricity, the positive without the negative, or the negative without the positive, is inconceivable. Hence the electrons and the protons are only two aspects of one and the same reality. Why does the energy differentiate itself into positive and negative electricity, into protons and electrons? In order to realize itself, to manifest itself, and this can be accomplished only by becoming another self. In the other self the energy realizes itself. This is the reason why the one becomes infinite ones, the cell becomes infinite cells, the acorn becomes infinite acorns, and an idea becomes infinite ideas.

Now, the energy separates itself from itself—this is repulsion. The electron acquires an independent individual motion, a centrifugal motion. But at the same time the proton holds the electron and determines it to move about the proton within a definite range. This is attraction. The repulsion is freedom, the attraction is constraint. Thus the electrons and protons are held together by constraint, yet they do not want to part from one another. It requires great force to separate the electrons from the protons. It is the same with the solar system. The solar system is nothing else than a large atom. The sun is the proton, and the planets are the electrons. By repulsion, the sun separates itself from itself, and these separated parts become the planets. The planets move with independent motion; at the same time they are constrained by the sun to move about the sun within definite ranges. But, though the planets are constrained to move about the sun, yet they resist any release from the constraint. It would require infinite power to separate the planets from the sun. Thus we see that freedom and necessity are inherent in each other, neither can exist without the other. And now let us consider another aspect of the matter.

80. Necessity implies a relation between things. For instance, between the angles and the sides of a triangle there is a necessary relation. In a triangle of equal angles the sides are necessarily equal. Nothing in creation can change this relation. Between cause and effect there is a necessary relation; a given cause must produce a corresponding effect. Nothing in creation can change this. Between conduct and consequence there is a necessary relation; between the premise and its conclusion there is a necessary relation. And this is true of all relations in existence. All organized knowledge implies the recognition of the relation of neces-

sity in things. Next, necessity is inherent in the nature of things. Everything in existence is determined to exist and act by its inherent nature. Gold is determined by its nature to exist and act as gold, iron is determined by its nature to exist and act as iron, water is determined by its nature to exist and act as water; a lion is determined by his nature to exist and act as a lion; a serpent is determined by its nature to exist and act as a serpent; a man is determined by his nature to exist and act as a man; and so it is with all infinite realities in existence. It is the same with all processes in existence. Every process in existence is determined by its nature to exist and act according to its nature. This is true of the Absolute and of God. The Absolute is absolute, infinite and eternal, and so is God. God is determined by his nature to exist and act as God. God cannot exist and act otherwise; he cannot determine himself to become relative, finite and temporary; he cannot determine himself to cease to become the world; he cannot terminate his existence. By the necessity of his absolute, infinite and eternal nature God is constrained eternally and infinitely to become the world. Thus we see that all of existence in all its infinite and eternal aspects is constrained to exist and to act by the necessity of its nature. Now, as said before, necessity implies its correlative freedom. This raises the question: In an existence that is infinitely and eternally determined by the necessity of its nature, how is freedom possible? Since, however, freedom is a correlative of necessity, and necessity exists infinitely and eternally, it follows that freedom also must exist infinitely and eternally. What, then, is freedom?

Freedom is inherent in necessity. Every reality is under the necessity to exist and act according to its nature. In this necessity is inherent its freedom. The freedom consists in this: every reality is free to exist and to act according to its nature; and nothing in creation can determine any reality to exist and to act contrary to its nature. By the necessity of its nature gold is constrained to exist and act according to its nature; and nothing in creation can determine gold to act otherwise. But this is the freedom of the gold—it is free to exist and to act according to its nature. By the necessity of his nature the lion is constrained to exist and to act as a lion; but just for this reason the lion is free to exist and to act as a lion, and nothing in creation can constrain the lion to exist and to act as a serpent or as a man. And so it is with all infinite realities in existence, and so it is with God and with the Absolute. God is constrained by his nature to exist and to act as God, but just for this reason God is free to exist and to act as God: nothing in existence can determine God to exist and act otherwise. Everything in existence endeavors to exist and to act as it is; and it does not want to be something else, exist and act as something else. An electron wants to be an electron, a grain of sand wants to be a grain of sand, a cell wants to be a cell, a lion wants to be a lion, and so on infinitely. And so it is with men. Not only does man want to be a man, but an Englishman wants to be an Englishman, a Russian wants to be a Russian, a Jew wants to be a Jew, and so it is with all races, nations and peoples of the human race. Hence, while each is constrained to exist and act according to his nature, for this very reason each one is free to exist and to act according to his nature. As the question of freedom and necessity will concern us most vitally, I shall continue the consideration of the subject when I come to speak of man. For our present purpose it is enough to know that freedom and necessity are inherent in each other, they are correlatives, neither can exist without the other. The greater the necessity the greater is the freedom, and the greater the freedom the greater is the necessity. To use an expression of Spinoza, the more reality a thing possesses the more it is constrained by its nature and the more free it is to exist and act according to its nature. A diamond is more constrained by its nature to exist and act as a diamond than a piece of coal is, and this for the reason that a diamond possesses far more reality than a piece of coal possesses. And just for this reason a diamond is far more free to exist and to act as a diamond than the piece of coal is. A great man possesses far more reality than an ordinary man possesses. For this reason, on the one hand, the great man is far more constrained by his nature to exist and to act as a great man than the ordinary man is constrained to exist and to act as an ordinary man; on the other hand, the great man has far greater freedom to exist and to act than the ordinary man has. This gives us a general idea of freedom and necessity. When we speak of the difference between realities, we impliedly refer to quantity and quality. Hence, the next subject to be considered is quantity and quality.

QUANTITY AND QUALITY

81. Things are distinguished from one another by quantity and quality. It there a causal relation between quantity and quality? Does a change in quantity give rise to a change in quality, or does a change in quality give rise to a change in quantity? According to Spencer, quality gives rise to quantity. We begin by perceiving first a difference in quality, and only then we begin to distinguish a difference in quantity. This is most strikingly shown in the difference between common sense and scientific knowledge. Common sense is primarily concerned about quality, while science is primarily concerned about quantity. Now, while it may be true as far as our perception of things goes, the question is this: How is it in existence itself, does quality give rise to quantity? On the other hand, Hegel maintained that quantity gives rise to quality. He stated this as follows: Quantitative differences beyond a certain point give rise to qualitative changes. For instance, water heated up to the boiling point becomes steam, and brought down to the freezing point becomes ice. But this, again, is to judge things as they manifest themselves to us. The question is: how is in existence itself the relation between quantity and quality, is there a causal relation between them. We shall presently see that there is no causal relation between them. Quantity and quality are correlatives, they arise simultaneously, and neither can arise without the other. There is no quantity without quality, and there is no quality without quantity. First, a reality must have some

magnitude, and magnitude is quantity. Again, a reality is not formless substance; a reality has a definite form and a definite nature. This means that a reality must have some quality. First, a reality must have a quantitative magnitude; second, it must have a qualitative magnitude. It must have a magnitude of extension and a magnitude of nature; which means a magnitude of quantity and a magnitude of quality. A reality can be distinguished from another reality both by its quantity and its quality; but the difference in quantity is itself a difference in quality, and the difference in quality is itself a difference in quantity. It is a difference in hardness, fluidity, color or taste, that quality must be of a certain degree, extent or quantity. Thus quality implies quantity, and quantity implies quality. Let us, then, consider quality and quantity.

All infinite realities are carved out of one infinite and eternal substance. Substance is absolute thought without form. Neither quantity nor quality pertain to substance. Hence, as far as the realities are substance, there is absolutely no difference between them. The realities differ from one another only in form. For instance, a triangle and a circle comprehend space, they comprehend space within boundaries. The space comprehended by the triangle and the circle is neither the triangle nor the circle; the triangle and the circle are the forms which they give to space. Now, space itself is without form, it is absolute thought. As far as space is concerned, there is no difference between the triangle and the circle. The difference is between the space comprehended by the triangle and the circle, it is a difference in the form which space is made to assume. Now, the difference between the triangle and the circle is both quantitative and qualitative. Whence the difference? The difference is inherent in their very forms. The triangle and the circle differ, not only in the quantity of space they comprehend, they also differ in their qualities, they possess different properties. And so we see that quantity and quality are correlatives, they imply each other; neither can exist without the other.

82. This brings us to the previous question: Is there a causal relation between quantity and quality? The answer is: there is no causal relation between them, as indeed there is no causal relation between correlatives, they arise simultaneously, for neither can arise without the other. Let us begin with number. One becomes two, three, four, five, and so on to infinity. When one becomes two, it changes not only quantitatively, but also qualitatively. First, it changes quantitatively; before it was one, and now it is two. Second, it changes qualitatively; two is not merely two ones, two is a unity of two ones; two is qualitatively different from one as it is quantitatively different from one. Thus we see that quantity and quality arise simultaneously, neither precedes the other, and neither determines the other. Thus the Absolute by becoming the infinite realities in existence gives rise simultaneously to both quantity and quality. But, though the Absolute manifests itself in infinite realities that differ from one another quantitatively and qualitatively, yet in all the infinite realities the Absolute remains absolute.

THE LAW OF EQUIVALENTS

83. Something cannot arise out of nothing, and something cannot disappear into nothing. Science demonstrated that the quantity of matter and energy in existence neither increases nor diminishes, but eternally and infinitely remains the same. Whatever exists arose in the Absolute and merges in the Absolute. The Absolute neither increases nor diminishes in quantity. In all the infinite forms which the Absolute assumes, and in all the transformations of the forms, the Absolute eternally and infinitely remains the same in quantity. What is true of quantity is also true of quality. The Absolute eternally and infinitely remains the same in quality; for quality, like quantity, cannot arise out of nothing and cannot disappear into nothing. The question arises: Since the Absolute eternally and infinitely remains quantitatively and qualitatively the same, how is evolution possible? The answer is: all eternal and infinite evolution was

already implicit in the Absolute from the very beginning. We saw that the Absolute, as absolute thought without form, by the process of entropy becomes matter in a diffused state. Thus far there was only entropy, a process of disorganization; and then the process of evolution reintegrated the diffused matter and brought out the material world. And we saw that what is absolute, infinite and eternal is absolute, infinite and eternal in every part thereof. One becomes an infinite number of ones, and each one of the infinite number of ones is itself, like the first one, absolute, infinite and eternal. Any one of the infinite numbers, like the first one, can become infinite numbers, and each one is absolute, infinite and eternal. The absolute, infinite and eternal nature of the Absolute is not only quantitative, it is also qualitative. The creation of the world, evolution, development and progress only bring into explicitness that which eternally and infinitely was already implicit in the Absolute. We saw that the soul, and essence of an acorn is an idea of God. This idea is absolute, infinite and eternal, and for this reason this idea can reproduce itself in infinite oak trees and infinite acorns. The infinite oak trees and the infinite acorns do not contain more than was already implicit in the first acorn. Thus the Absolute becomes the world consisting of infinite realities, and yet the Absolute eternally and infinitely remains the same in quantity and quality. We considered the process of creation. The Absolute is absolute thought—thought without form. Thought thinks, and thought requires an object of thought. As besides the Absolute there is absolutely nothing of which the Absolute can think, the Absolute thinks of itself, and forms of itself an idea. An idea is a form of absolute thought. Thus the Absolute comprehends itself in a form. This is the Infinite Intellect, God. God. being an idea of the Absolute, comprehends the Absolute in infinite attributes. God combines the infinite attributes in infinite ways, and thus gives rise to infinite ideas which realize themselves in infinite material forms. These infinite material forms are the material realities in the phenomenal world. We must now consider this transformation more closely.

AFFIRMATION AND NEGATION

84. The Absolute, as absolute thought, does not affirm itself; for, to affirm, is to define, to put within limits and boundaries, to assume a form. Without a form there can be no affirmation. The Absolute affirms itself in the Infinite Intellect, in God. God is an idea of the Absolute, and an idea is a form of absolute thought. But notice this. When the Absolute affirms itself as God, it negates itself as Absolute. Hence Spinoza tells us: Omnis determinatio est negatio—all affirmation is a negation. A few illustrations will make it clear. Consider the table. The table affirms itself as a table, yet at the same time it negates itself. It asserts: I am a table; but at the same time it negates itself, it declares: I am not a tree, I am not an animal, I am not anything else. Consider cause. How does cause affirm itself? By becoming an effect. If cause does not become an effect, it is not a cause. But, while affirming itself as cause, at the same time it negates itself as effect. It declares: I am cause, but I am not effect. But this is not all. While cause affirms itself as cause, it also negates itself as effect. Cause declares I am cause. This is my positive aspect; but I am also effect, which is my negative aspect. Without my negative aspect, effect, I could not be a cause, I would have no positive aspect. Hence, Hegel added to Spinoza's statement: Omnis negatio est determinatio—all negation is an affirmation. Consider man. For man to affirm himself as man, he must at the same time negate himself as all other things. Man declares: I am man, but at the same time man declares: I am not a thing, I am not an animal; and so on. And only because he negates himself as all other things does he affirm himself as man. It is so with the Absolute. By affirming itself as God, it negates itself as Absolute; and by negating itself as Absolute, it affirms itself as God.

What is true of the Absolute is also true of God. God affirms himself by becoming infinite ideas which realize themselves in material forms. These material forms are the material realities in the phenomenal world. But by this very negation of himself

God affirms himself as God. And thus by affirmation and negation the Absolute becomes the world of material realities. But
the process does not end there. For an idea to become a material
reality, the idea must negate itself as an idea; while the idea
affirms itself as a material reality, it negates itself as an idea.
In turn, a material reality can affirm itself only by becoming an
idea. Let us consider the process of evolution. Matter was in a
diffused state. The process of evolution integrated the diffused
matter. The electrons united with the protons and formed
atoms. What united the electrons and the protons? It was an
idea. Hence, in the atom the electrons and the protons were
negated; they ceased to be independent and separate realities.
The same was the case when the atoms united into molecules,
the molecules into masses, and the masses combined to form the
stars, the planets and all other material realities. The ultimate
units of matter are held together by ideas. If not for the ideas,
the ultimate units of matter would not be held together. And
all material realities in existence are held together by God—
the absolute, infinite and eternal idea of the Absolute. Thus we
see that the eternal and infinite process of existence is through
affirmation and negation, and in all the infinite and eternal
transformations the quantity and the quality of the Absolute
remains the same. The law of equivalents works through affirmation and negation. When I shall come to speak of man, I will
consider the law of equivalents more fully. For the present this
is enough.

CHAPTER XIII

Body, Mind and Soul

85. The Absolute, to manifest itself, differentiates itself into a trinity: The Infinite Intellect, Thought and Extension. This is the primordial trinity which inheres in every reality of existence. The Infinite Intellect perceives the Absolute in the attributes thought and extension. When the Infinite Intellect, God, comprehends thought and extension in an idea, a material reality comes into existence. A reality, then, is a trinity, consisting of an idea, thought and extension. The extension is the body, thought is the mind, and the idea is the soul of any reality. Other realities may not be conscious of this, but man is conscious of this, we saw in a previous chapter that the idea is the essence of a reality. The same is true of man. The essence of man is his soul, which is an idea of God. When God conceives the idea of man, this idea comprehends the attributes thought and extension. The extension is his body, and the thought is his mind. Up till now I spoke of the human mind, and attributed to it the powers of perception, conception and reasoning, but I did this in conformity with the universal opinion of men. But we shall presently see that this is not true. The mind neither perceives, nor conceives, nor reasons. It is the soul that perceives, conceives and reasons. The body and the mind are only the means through which the soul functions in the material world. Through the mind the soul perceives, conceives and reasons, and through the body the soul acts. The soul is a living, conscious and thinking being, because it is an idea of God.

Between the mind and the body there is a correspondence, because the soul brings them out according to its own nature.

This profound truth was perceived by Spinoza. In the Ethics, Part II, Proposition Vii, Spinoza tells us the following:

The order and connection of ideas is the same as the order and connection of things. God's power of thinking is equal to his actual power of acting; that is to say, whatever follows formally from the infinite nature of God, follows from the idea of God, in the same order and in the same connection objectively in God. We have already demonstrated that everything which can be conceived by the Infinite Intellect as constituting the essence of substance pertains entirely to the one sole substance only, and consequently substance thinking and substance extended are one and the same substance, which is now comprehended under the attribute of thought and now under the attribute of extension. Thus a mode of extension and the idea of that mode are one and the same thing expressed in two different ways. For example, the circle existing in nature and the idea that is in God of an existing circle are one and the same thing, which is manifested through different attributes; and, therefore, whether we think of nature under the attribute of extension, or under the attribute of thought, or under any other attribute whatever, we shall discover one and the same order, or one and the same connection of causes; that is to say, in every case the same sequence of things. So that, when things are considered as a mode of thought, we must explain the order of the whole of nature or the connection of causes by the attribute thought alone; and, when things are considered as modes of extension, the order of the whole of nature must be explained through the attribute of extension alone; and so with the other attributes. Therefore God is in truth the cause of things as they are in themselves in so far as he consists of infinite attributes.

The full implication involved in what Spinoza tells us here will become manifest as we proceed. What we must bear in mind is this. The soul, being an idea of God, is the essence; the mind and the body are only the means through which the soul functions in the material world. Between the ideas in the mind and the acts in the body there is a correspondence, because it is one and the same soul that thinks through the mind and acts through the body.

LIFE AND CONSCIOUSNESS

86. What is life? Spencer defines life as a continuous adjustment of inner relations to outer relations. An adjustment implies something which makes the adjustment. What is it which makes the adjustment? This Spencer does not tell. Spencer himself admits that he does not know what life itself is; but, as usual with him, he attributes it to the Unknowable. But by the Unknowable we cannot define anything; first, because the Unknowable is everything in existence; second, by an Unknowable we cannot know anything. Hence Spencer's definition of life merely tells us a function of life, but it does not tell us what life itself is. A far better definition of life was given by Spinoza. Spinoza defines life as the power by which a thing endeavors to preserve itself in its being. Everything in existence endeavors to preserve itself as it is, and this it does by the life that is in it. According to Spinoza, all things in existence possess life, all things are animate. He tells us: "For everything there necessarily exists in God an idea of which he is the cause, in the same way as the idea of the human body exists in him; and therefore everything that we have said of the idea of the human body is necessarily true of the idea of any other thing." We saw that the essence of a reality is an idea of God; the idea of God is a living, conscious and thinking being, it is a soul. This idea, which is the soul, is life itself—it is living, it is conscious, it thinks and acts, and it endeavors to preserve itself in existence. Life, then, is nothing else than the soul. When the soul comprehends thought and extension, a human being or any other being or reality comes into existence; the thought is the mind, and the extension is the body. The essence is neither the mind nor the body, the essence is the soul. We saw this in the case of the electric lamp, in the case of the acorn, and in the other cases

which I considered in a previous chapter. Since the essence of things is an idea of God, which is a living, conscious and thinking being, it follows that all existence is a living and conscious existence.

When considering light and darkness, we saw that darkness is not the absence of light, because light is infinite and eternal; darkness is a light which the human eye cannot apprehend. Hence to the human eye it appears darkness. The same is true of life and consciousness. We must not assume that, besides the life which we perceive in living beings, and besides the consciousness which we perceive in living and conscious beings, there is neither life nor consciousness. This is an illusion. Whatever the attribute of God be, it is infinite and eternal; it is infinite in extent, in degree and in nature. Hence there are forms of life and of consciousness which we cannot perceive; but this does not mean that they do not exist. Life and consciousness are eternal and infinite attributes of God. God is everything. Hence, everything is living and is conscious. God is living, conscious and thinking in and through every reality in existence, be it an electron, a star or the whole infinite and eternal material world. Consider this. Every particle of matter in existence moves in a space-time continuum in accordance with definite laws. There never was and there will never be a particle of matter that moved or will move not in accordance with these definite laws. How come the infinite particles of matter to move eternally and infinitely in accordance with definite laws, which themselves must be eternal and infinite? Who decreed these laws? Are the particles of matter conscious of these laws?

Consider the human body. The human body consists of infinite cells that are organized in a most wonderful system of cooperation. Are the cells conscious of what they do? Have the cells an idea of man? And now consider man himself. Does man know what is going on in his body? Does he know what is going on in his mind. Is man conscious of his soul? Man has gone through a wonderful evolution. From an animal he became a human being with a destiny to become a rational and morally autonomous person. Was the primitive anthropoid conscious of what he was doing and of what he was destined to become? Are even the civilized men conscious of what they are and what they are destined to become? And yet the civilized men are conscious and thinking beings. Did men create themselves, did they endow themselves with consciousness and thought? All was the work of God. God who lives, thinks and acts through men also lives, thinks and acts through all beings and realities in existence. Life and consciousness are eternal and infinite attributes of God, and therefore whatever exists is a living and conscious reality.

LIFE AND DEATH

87. Life implies death; they are correlatives, neither can exist without the other, and neither can be conceived without the other. That one being may live, other living beings must die. That man may live, he must destroy other living beings for food. Consider the human body. On the one hand, the human body is full of life. Every cell, every tissue, every organ, and the whole body—all live. On the other hand, the body is full of death. Every cell, every tissue, every organ and the whole body constantly die. Each part of the body, while it lives also dies. Life is a process of repair, death is a process of waste. Repair and waste are correlatives, neither can exist without the other. If there be no waste, there would be no repair; and, if there be no repair, there would be no waste. Let the waste in the body cease, and the repair will cease. The cessation of waste is the cessation of death; and the cessation of repair is the cessation of life. Thus life feeds on death, and death feeds on life. We saw that life is the soul, it is the power by virtue of which every reality and being endeavor to preserve themselves in existence. What, then, is death? Is death also a power, is it also a soul, is it also an idea of God? It is with death as it is with darkness. Men of thought bestowed infinite thought on light, but no thought

on darkness; they naively assumed that darkness is merely the absence of light. But we saw that this was an illusion. It is the same about death. Men of thought bestowed infinite thought on life, but no thought on death. Is death only the absence of life? We shall presently see that, just as darkness is not merely the absence of light, so death is not merely the absence of life.

A living being, so long as it lives, moves in a space-time continuum; when it dies, it ceases to move; when living, it acts; when it dies, it rests. Is life motion and death rest? We saw before, when considering motion and rest, that in existence there is no rest. We also saw that motion has two aspects: individual and independent motion, and universal and dependent motion. Now we can see that life is individual independent motion, and death is universal and dependent motion. We also saw that motion is discontinuous; motion is constantly interrupted by pauses. Motion is life, the pauses are death. But the motions and the pauses are correlatives, neither can exist without the other. If there be no motion, there will be no pauses; and, if there be no pauses, there will be no motion. Motion must pause to re-generate itself and become again motion. Hence during the pauses, motion is not absolutely at rest; it is active, but the activity is not motion, it is regeneration. Thus just as there is no absolute rest in existence, so there is no absolute death in existence. Death is only the pause during which life regenerates itself. But life is the soul. This means that the soul is eternal. An idea of God, like God, is absolute, infinite and eternal. We saw how the soul of a cell lives through infinite generations of living beings; how the soul of an acorn lives through infinite oak trees and acorns; and how an idea lives through infinite systems of ideas. Consider the idea of the wheel conceived by some primitive savage. This idea lives and will live through all the machines and inventions that mankind will create in the course of infinite time. Just as in existence there is no absolute rest, so there is no absolute death. But what about the body and the mind? When a living being dies, the body reverts back to the eternal and infinite extension, and the mind reverts back to the eternal and infinite thought; but the soul, being an idea of God, reverts back to God. What becomes of the soul after death, this we will consider when I come to speak of man. But for the present I add the following. We saw that the electric lamp consists of a material body, electricity and an idea. The lamp may function for some time, and then it is destroyed; but the idea remains in the minds of men. And so long as the idea lives in the minds of men, so long there will be infinite electric lamps. The idea which brought out the first lamp will bring out infinite other lamps. It is so with the soul. The soul is an idea of God. So long as God has this idea in his mind, so long the idea will reincarnate itself in human bodies and human minds. But an idea of God is eternal and infinite. Therefore the soul is eternal and infinite. So much for the present.

PROGRESS AND DESTINY

88. What is progress? As the term implies, progress is a movement forward. Movement implies something that moves. Progress, then, indicates that something moves forward. How can we determine whether something moves forward or backward? By the intended aim of the movement. If something moves towards the intended aim, it progresses, it moves forward; if, however, it moves away from the intended aim, it regresses, it moves backward. But even when we know the intended aim, we do not yet know whether the movement is progressive or regressive; for, though the movement may be towards the aim, yet the aim itself may be regressive. In that case, the progressive movement towards the aim is really a regressive movement. Therefore, to know whether a movement is progressive or regressive, we must first know whether the aim itself is progressive or regressive. How, then, can we determine whether the aim is progressive or regressive? This we can know by destiny. If the aim is towards the predetermined destiny, it is a progressive aim, and so also is the movement towards that aim. On the other hand, if the aim is away from the predetermined destiny, the

aim is regressive, and so also is the movement towards the aim.

But what is destiny? Existence is not merely a transformation and equivalence of matter and energy; existence has a destiny. Inherent in every reality is its destiny. For instance, inherent in the acorn is its destiny to become an oak tree and to reproduce acorns a thousandfold. Hence all transformations that take place in the acorn towards that destiny are progressive. Again, inherent in man is his destiny to become a rational and morally autonomous person. Hence all transformations that take place in man towards that destiny are progressive. On the other hand, transformations in man in a direction opposite to his destiny are regressive; man degenerates, becomes an animal and perishes. This is true of all realities and processes in existence. But what is the destiny of existence itself? The destiny of existence itself is to return to the starting point. We saw that the process of creation begins with entropy. The Absolute, by the process of entropy, disintegrates and becomes diffused matter. Then begins the process of evolution. Evolution is a process of integration. It integrates the diffused matter into atoms, molecules, masses of matter, stars, planets and the whole material world. While evolution integrates the material particles of matter, at the same time it integrates the ideas which realized themselves in the particle of matter. The result is the absolute, infinite and eternal integration of all ideas. This is God. Hence all evolution is back to God. Creation began with God, and its destiny is to come back to God. Since this is the destiny of existence, then progress—which is a movement towards destiny—is a return back to the starting point. Progress is not a movement ever further from the starting point. This is an illusion. Progress is a movement back to the starting point, back to God. As this view of progress is just the opposite to what mankind universally regarded as progress, we must consider this view fundamentally.

89. Einstein made familiar to the scientific world what the Kabbalists had perceived long ago, namely, the universe is a sphere. In a spherical universe, all natural realities must be spherical in

form, and all motions must be cyclic. A cyclic motion is a
motion towards the starting point. Suppose that from New York
I start a journey around the world. As I proceed, I move ever
further away from New York; yet, the further away I travel
from New York the nearer I approach New York. Suppose a
star emits light. The light will travel away from the star with
great speed. Suppose the light will travel for millions of years.
Since the universe is a sphere, and the light cannot travel beyond
and outside of the universe, the further away from the star the
light travels the nearer it comes back to its starting point. All
motions in the universe are cyclic, a return to the starting point.
Consider the acorn. From the moment the acorn is put into the
ground it undergoes transformations, it makes progress. But in
what direction is its progress? It is back to the starting point.
The evolution of the acorn results in the reproduction of
acorns—the starting point. This is true of all progress in life.

And now consider man. Man is destined to attain to reason.
But reason is the starting point of creation, and reason is the
starting point of man himself. Man was conceived in reason.
Reason differentiated man from the rest of created things. Man
attains to his true nature only when he attains to reason. Thus
all human progress is back to the starting point. We saw that
man begins with knowledge. All knowledge is back to the starting point. The progress of physics was towards the electron, the
photon; and they were the starting point of the physical world.
The progress of biology was towards the moneron—the primordial living cell. The progress of astronomy was towards the
Nebular Hypothesis, which starts with matter in a diffused state.
The progress of mankind generally was from a knowledge of
external things to self-knowledge, and self-knowledge is the
starting point of all knowledge. The progress of organized and
unified knowledge was towards the knowledge of God—the
starting point of all existence. And the same is true of progress
in human creation. In proportion as mankind approached the
starting point of existence, in proportion as they acquired an
ever deeper knowledge of things, in proportion as they reached

the ultimate nature of things, in that proportion they became the masters over nature and created for themselves an ever more wonderful world. In other words, in proportion as men came nearer to God, in that proportion they became like God, creators. Plato perceived a deep truth when he said that all knowledge is only reminiscence.

90. Progress and regress are correlatives, they imply each other, neither can exist without the other. Progress is a movement forward; but a forward movement implies a backward movement. We saw that motion is not continuous, motion is constantly interrupted by pauses, and a pause is a backward movement, it is a merging into a primordial state. We saw this in the case of life and death. Since all motion in existence is cyclic, there cannot be progress in a straight line onward and forward; but every step in progress is followed by a step in regress that progress may make another step forward. Consider the wheels of an automobile in motion. The upper parts of the wheels move forward, at the same time the lower parts of the wheel move backward. The wheels cannot move forward without at the same time also moving backward. The result is that the automobile moves forward. It is likewise in walking. While one leg moves forward, the other leg moves backward. It is so with all movements of man. In working, the hands must move forward and backward. Consider social progress. Mankind are destined to become one human society resting on universal communism. Now, absolute unity is the starting point of all existence. The Absolute is absolutely one. This absolute unity manifests itself in the infinite and universal communism of all realities and processes in existence; they are all conceived in communism, and they all live and move in accordance with the communist principle: from every one according to its capacity, unto every one according to its need. This gives us an idea of progress and regress. Not he is progressive who moves away from the starting point, but he who moves towards the starting point. When I

come to speak of man, society and history I will speak of progress and regress more in detail.

GOOD AND EVIL

91. According to Plato, the only realities in existence are ideas. The ideas are the prototypes of the material realities; the ideas realize themselves in the material realities. Among the material realities there is a hierarchical relation, some are of a lower nature and others are of a higher nature. Since the ideas realize themselves in the material realities, there must be among the ideas the same hierarchical relation as among the material realities; some ideas are of a lower nature and other ideas are of a higher nature. But what is the highest idea to which all other ideas are subordinated? The answer is: The highest idea is the idea of the good. The idea of the good is the ruling ideas in existence. This agrees with the Bible. The Bible tells us that whatever Elohim created he saw that it was good. He did not see that it was perfect or beautiful, but he saw that it was good. Good implies perfection and beauty; only that which is perfect and beautiful is good; and nothing can be good unless it is perfect and beautiful. Plato tells us that the idea of the good is the author of all things beautiful and right, it is the parent of light in the visible world. What Plato tells us is profound, yet it is only an abstraction. What is good, and why is the idea of the good the highest idea in existence? Plato speaks of the idea of the good, but good implies evil. Good and evil are correlatives, neither can exist without the other, and neither can be conceived without the other. If the idea of the good is the highest idea, then the idea of evil must be the lowest idea. How did these ideas come into existence, who was the author or the cause of these ideas? It is clear that both ideas were caused by the same cause that brought out existence, and that is God. God, then, is the author of both good and evil. Hence Plato was bound to account for the existence of evil as well as for the existence of good. But this he did not do.

Since the days of Plato many thinkers wrote about good and evil, yet thus far none of the thinkers adequately understood good and evil. Most thinkers, unable to account for the existence of evil, denied the existence of evil altogether. For instance, Spinoza denied any essence to evil. He regarded evil only as inadequate knowledge. Spinoza tells us: "If the human mind had none but adequate ideas, it would form no notion of evil." And Shakespeare tells us: There is nothing either good or evil, but thinking makes it so. Now, Shakespeare was not a philosopher, and we cannot argue with him. But, if thinking makes things to be either good or evil, if it depends upon thinking, why does not thinking determine that all things should be good? Many thinkers maintained that evil is only an illusion. Now, if evil is an illusion, then good is certainly an illusion, for evil asserts itself and makes itself to be felt far more than good does. Now, philosophers may persuade themselves that there is no evil in existence, but human consciousness asserts with all emphasis that evil exists and is far more real than good. Now, the verdict of human consciousness by far outweighs all logical thinking of the philosophers; and, when there is a difference of opinion, we need not hesitate to accept the verdict of our consciousness. Hence, we begin with the certainty that good and evil exist, that they are real, and that God who brought the world into existence, or rather who became the world, also created good and evil, or rather became good and evil. The Prophet Isaiah had a profounder insight into good and evil. He tells us, speaking in the name of Jehovah: I am Jehovah, and there is none else. I form the light and create darkness; I make peace, and create evil; I am Jehovah that does all these things. (Chapter 45.) And the Zohar tells us: At the time that the Holy One created the world, and revealed the deep from concealment, and light from darkness, they were contained one in the other. And so, from darkness came out light, and from concealment came out and revealed the deep, and the one came from the other. For from good came evil, from loving kindness came justice, and one is contained in the other, the good spirit and the evil spirit, the right and the left, the white and the black, and all depend upon one another. What Isaiah and the Zohar tell us is infinitely more profound and true when what all philosophers said about good and evil and about all other correlatives. What Isaiah and the Zohar tell us is this. In God were implicit all the correlatives that exist in existence: life and death, good and evil, light and darkness, justice and injustice, peace and war, love and hatred, and so on infinitely. A true monistic philosophy must adequately explain all correlatives, and so also it must explain the correlatives good and evil.

92. Good and evil, as cause and effect, were always regarded by philosophers as well as by mankind generally as two separate, distinct and independent realities or states of existence, and that good could be had without evil. Accordingly, mankind always struggled to attain to the good without the concomitant evil. Even philosophers entertained the illusion that they could enjoy the good without suffering evil. But this is an illusion. In their philosophy, the philosophers convinced themselves that something cannot arise out of nothing; and yet these philosophers never asked themselves the question: out of what can good arise? Can good arise out of nothing? And, if good can arise only out of something, what is that something out of which good can arise? Is it not clear that good, like everything else, can arise only out of its correlative? We saw that life can arise only out of death, light can arise only out of darkness, effect can arise only out of cause; and so on infinitely. It therefore ought to have been clear to the philosophers that good can arise only out of evil. Yet the philosophers never perceived this. Again, the theologians, unable to account for the origin of evil, tried to persuade mankind that evil came from Satan. God is absolutely perfect and infinitely good, and no evil can come from him. But evil does exist. Therefore evil came from Satan. But who is Satan, and how came he into existence? Since throughout the past the evil prevailed over the good, the conclusion must be that Satan is greater and more powerful than

God. If so, what hope is there for mankind? We reject the naive doctrines of the theologians as well as the false doctrines of the philosophers. We start out with the premise: God is the only direct, immediate and immanent cause of all that exists. God, therefore, is the cause of evil as well as of good. It is our task to understand the reason for the existence of evil and good. But, first, we must understand the nature of good and evil.

Good and evil are correlatives, they imply each other; neither can exist without the other, neither can be conceived without the other, and each grows and develops in proportion as the other grows and develops. Evil is a condition to good, and good is a condition to evil. Inherent in evil is good, and inherent in good is evil. Correlatives imply a third reality of which they are correlatives. The third reality is desire. If there was no desire, there would be neither good nor evil. Things are good, when they satisfy desire; things are evil, when they do not satisfy desire. Life is good, death is evil. When one desires to live, life is good; but, when one desires to die, death is good. Again, to him who wants to live poison is evil; but to him who wants to die, poison is good. Some Greek philosophers said that men must be grateful to the gods for providing for them the means by which they can terminate an unbearable life. This is true of all cases. Now, desire is not a thing of air; desire is the essence of man, it is the essence of things, because it is the essence of God. It was God's desire to manifest himself, to be recognized, honored and loved, that determined him to become the world of material realities. Therefore, when desire is satisfied, the thing that satisfies is good; but, when desire is frustrated, the thing that frustrates is evil. But why did God create evil? The answer is: that he might create the good; without evil there could be no good. Existence rests on the eternal and infinite law of equivalents; there must be a quid pro quo; for everything we get from existence we must pay an equivalent. The equivalent must be paid in work, struggle and suffering. Evil is a self-negation, and good is a self-affirmation. We saw in a previous chapter that the law of equivalents works through affirmation and negation.

Whatever preserves us, gives us pleasure, joy or happiness, is good; and whatever destroys us, gives us pain, sorrow and suffering, is evil. But the law of equivalents demands that we pay with pain for pleasure, with sorrow for joy, and with suffering for happiness. Still more, we must pay with death for life. How does existence sustain itself? By feeding on itself. This is the meaning of the circulation, exchange and transformation of matter and energy. The organic beings feed on the inorganic realities, and the latter feed on the former. Man feeds on plants and animals, and the latter feed on man. How does God sustain himself? God is the cause of himself. This means that God is the effect of himself. God feeds on himself. God is life, but he is also death; God eternally and infinitely dies that he may live eternally and infinitely. God is good, but he is also evil. Consider the human body. The human body is full of life, at the same time it is full of death. Every cell, every tissue, every organ, and the whole body live; at the same time they all die. If they did not die, they could not live. Thus we see that good feeds on evil, and evil feeds on good. Perfection feeds on imperfection, and the latter feeds on the former. Light feeds on darkness, and darkness feeds on light. And so it is all through existence.

93. Life is the highest good, death is the highest evil. Yet, as we saw each is a condition to the other. But we must consider another aspect of good and evil. If there was no death, there could not be life. Life is infinite, and therefore life can procreate itself infinitely. But the earth is limited; it can sustain only a limited number of living beings. Professor Huxley tells us that, if a protozoan—a mere microscopic creature—be given the opportunity to increase and multiply according to the capacity of the life in it, and a similar opportunity be given to its progeny, then in the course of six months the aggregate mass of their bodies would be equal to the mass of the earth—so infinitely great is the capacity of the life in the protozoa to increase and to multiply. Again, Professor Owen tells us that

fishes usually throw out a million ova at one time; which, if favored by conditions, would in a short time become millions of fishes. And, if the same opportunity be given to all the fishes in the oceans, seas, lakes and rivers, in one year there would not be room for them in all the waters on the surface of the earth. And the same is true of all forms of life, and the same is true of man. If men did not die, and they increased and multiplied according to the infinite capacity of the life in them, in the course of time there would not be standing room for them on the earth. Every year life throws out infinite seeds of all kinds of vegetation, plants and trees. Suppose that there was no death, then the seeds would in a few years cover the whole surface of the earth, and all vegetation would become extinct. Consider the relation between the herbivors and the carnivors. The carnivors destroy the herbivors. Suppose there were no carnivors, then in the course of time the herbivors would increase and multiply to such extent that they would consume and destroy all vegetation on the surface of the earth, and then all herbivors would perish from hunger. Thus we see that the carnivors actually preserve the herbivors. And so it is in all cases. Living beings feed on one another, they destroy one another; and by this they preserve one another. Good feeds on evil, and evil preserves good. Life feeds on death, and death preserves life. This is true of all forms of good and evil. All this should have been well known and understood; yet even philosophers never perceived this. Is not this strange? All through the past men dreamt of a time when there will be neither death nor evil. What illusion?

Good is that which satisfies desire, evil is that which frustrates desire. But what is desire itself? Spinoza tells us that desire is the essence of man. Desire is not only the essence of man, it is the essence of all existence, because it is the essence of God, it is the essence of the Absolute. If not for desire, there would be no existence. What, then, is desire? Desire is absolute thought. Absolute thought thinks, but to think is to desire; there can be no thinking without desiring, as there can be no desiring without thinking. Absolute thought is thinking desire. Absolute thought is without form, and so the desire of absolute thought is without form. Absolute thinking desire, by self-reflection, forms an idea of itself. This idea is the Infinite Intellect, God. Once the Absolute becomes God, the absolute thinking assumes a definite form. We already saw that an idea is a form of absolute thought, and that an idea is the only force in existence; absolute thought becomes a force when it is channelized through an idea. When absolute thinking desire is comprehended by an idea, the idea becomes a living, conscious and desiring being. The desire inherent in the Absolute is to manifest itself, to be recognized, honored and loved. Whatever is absolute, infinite and eternal is absolute, infinite and eternal in every part thereof. This desire is the essence of the Absolute, it is the essence of God, and it is the essence of all existence. This desire is absolutely egoistic. The Absolute will not tolerate another absolute, God will not tolerate another God, and the desire in every reality and being is egoistic. Even ideas are egoistic. One idea does not tolerate another idea; each idea struggles to be the only idea in existence. And so man is absolutely egoistic. All this is so, because desire is absolutely egoistic.

Egoism and Altruism

94. But egoism implies altruism; they are correlatives, neither can exist without the other, each is a condition to the other, and each grows and develops in proportion as the other grows and develops. Without egoism there can be no altruism, and without altruism there can be no egoism. Let us begin with man. Man in his desire to preserve himself, to be recognized, honored and loved is absolutely egoistic; he is concerned about himself only. He regards all the rest of existence as existing solely for his benefit, to serve him, to recognize him, to honor him and to love him. But he is confronted by the eternal and infinite law of equivalents. There must be a quid pro quo; nothing for nothing. The other individuals and the other realities in exist-

ence are just as absolutely egoistic as he is; they will not serve
him unless he serves them; they will not recognize him unless
he recognizes them; they will not honor him unless he honors
them; and they will not love him unless he loves them. Lord
Bacon said: Non nisi parendo vincitur—nothing can be conquered unless by conforming with it. To affirm oneself, one
must begin by negating himself. As Jesus said: Unless a corn
of wheat fall into the ground and die, it abideth alone; but if it
dieth, it bringeth forth an abundance of fruit. He who saves
his life loses it, but he who loses his life saves it. To realize
one's-desire, to affirm oneself, he must negate his desire and must
negate himself. Again, as Jesus said: Whosoever will be chief
among you, let him be your servant. Whosoever will be great
among you shall be your minister; and whosoever of you will
be the chiefs shall be servant of all. This is true of all relations
of man to existence. To realize any aim or purpose, one must
conform with the nature of things and the order of existence;
and to conform with them is to submit to them, to negate oneself and to affirm them. As the saying is, we must stoop to conquer. Self-preservation is absolutely egoistic; yet, to preserve
itself, a reality or a being must become altruistic. Only in proportion as one is altruistic does he realize his egoism. All this is
so, because the Absolute is absolutely one, and the Absolute is
one in all infinite realities of existence. Men cannot exist all by
himself. To exist, to realize any purpose or aim, men must
cooperate with one another; they must exchange with one
another services, consciousness, life and thought. Thus we see
that egoism and altruism, like good and evil, are correlatives,
neither can be realized without the other, and each realizes
itself in proportion as the other is realized. What is true of
egoism is equally true of altruism. To be altruistic, one must at
the same time be egoistic. If one wants to preserve others, he
must at the same time preserve himself. If one wants to see
others enjoying health and wellbeing, he must at the same time
strive to enjoy health and wellbeing; if one wants to see others
happy, he must at the same time strive to be happy himself.

If one is indifferent to his own health, his own wellbeing and his own happiness, he will necessarily be indifferent to the health, wellbeing and happiness of others. I will have more to say on this subject when I come to speak of man.

CHAPTER XIV

Justice and Injustice

95. Whatever ideas of justice and injustice mankind entertained at different times, they always regarded justice a cardinal virtue, and injustice a cardinal vice. For thousands of years mankind struggled for what they believed to be justice, and revolted and struggled against what they believed to be injustice. Again, from time immemorial, philosophers, jurists and legislators wrote about justice and injustice, defending justice and condemning injustice. And yet, when we examine their definitions of justice and injustice, we find that they did not have an adequate idea either of justice or of injustice. This becomes at once evident from the consideration of the following. First, philosophers, jurists and legislators, as mankind generally, regarded justice and injustice as two separate, distinct and independent states of existence; and therefore believed that they could have justice without injustice. We shall presently see that justice and injustice are correlatives, neither can exist without the other. Second, the philosophers, jurists and legislators believed that justice and injustice exist only in the social relations of men; they never suspected that justice and injustice also exist in existence. We shall presently see that justice and injustice, like cause and effect, good and evil, life and death, are eternal and infinite. Furthermore, we shall see that God is the author of justice and injustice as he is the author of good and evil, life and death, and so on. At the outset, let us consider some of the definitions that came down to us from the past.

According to Plato, justice is this: that every part of the state is doing its own work, and does not interfere with the work of others. The shoemaker should confine himself to shoemaking, the tailor should confine himself to tailoring, the philosopher should confine himself to philosophy, and so on with the rest of society. Now, suppose that each member of society confines himself to his trade or occupation, and does not interfere with the trades and occupations of the other members of society, will this be justice? Must not justice tell us what each one is to receive for his work as an equivalent. Suppose that the shoemaker or the tailor does not get an equivalent for his work, is this justice? Or suppose that the philosopher or the legislator gets more than an equivalent for his work, is this justice? Now, Greek society rested on slavery. Is slavery compatible with justice? The ideal republic which Plato suggested rests on slavery and a caste system. Is this republic compatible with justice? We thus see that Plato had a most naive and primitive idea of justice.

According to Aristotle, justice is the complete virtue with relation to one's neighbors. Each one should behave towards his neighbor according to complete virtue. Now, Aristotle sanctioned slavery, he regarded slaves as not human beings. Next, Aristotle believed that only philosophers and men of leisure, wealth and culture should rule society; but the rest should submit to be ruled. Now, suppose a man treats his horse with complete virtue, this may be justice; but, if one treats his fellowmen as horses, even with complete virtue, is this justice? Is slavery compatible with justice? Here, again, we see that Aristotle had no idea of justice.

According to the Justinian Code, justice is the constant and perpetual wish to render to every one his due. Here we find a more concrete idea of justice, yet it is abstract and inadequate. First, is justice only a wish? Justice must be manifested in deeds; a wish to do justice without realizing that wish in deeds is not justice at all. Here we see the influence of Paul's doctrine, that man is justified, not by deeds, but by faith. Again, justice is the constant and perpetual wish to render to every one his due. What is due to every one? Thus we see that this definition of justice is vague.

An American Court defined justice as the dictate of right

according to the common consent of mankind generally, or that portion of mankind who may be associated in one government, or who may be governed by the same principles of morals. Now, suppose that mankind generally, or a portion of mankind associated in one government, or who are governed by the same principles of morals, agree to be cannibals, slaveholders, exploiters, aggressors and oppressors, is this justice? Does the common consent of mankind, or any part of mankind, constitute the basis of justice? If so, then justice reigned in human society all through the past.

Spencer tells us that justice is this: that every man is free to do what he wills, provided he infringe not upon the like freedom of any other man. Suppose that every man is free to be a cannibal, a slaveholder, an exploiter and an oppressor, and he does not infringe upon the like freedom of all other members of society to be cannibals, slaveholders, exploiters, and oppressors—is this justice? According to this definition, justice reigned in Sodom and Gomorrah, because each one was free to do what his beastly nature dictated, and no one infringed upon the like freedom of the other members of this beastly society.

Finally, the Standard Dictionary tells us that justice is strict uprightness, it is regard for the fulfilment of obligations, it is rectitude, honesty. It is true that justice involves uprightness, rectitude and honesty, but what are they? Suppose that I employ workers and agree to pay them for their work certain wages. I scrupulously keep my obligation, I pay them the wages for their work. But suppose that the wages are not an equivalent for their work, suppose that the wages are only a fraction of the value of the work the workers had done for me, is this justice? Now, capitalism does rest upon the wages system, is capitalism compatible with justice?

We see from the foregoing that neither the philosophers, nor the jurists nor the legislators had an adequate idea of justice. Since they had no adequate idea of justice, they certainly had no adequate idea of injustice. But what is most significant is this. Philosophers, like the rest of mankind, regarded justice and injustice as existing in human society only; no one of them even suspected that justice and injustice, as good and evil, are eternal and infinite. A true monistic philosophy must comprehend the nature of justice and injustice as eternal and infinite attributes of existence. Hence we must leave the philosophers, the jurists and the legislators, and consider justice and injustice in the light of the monistic philosophy.

96. I begin with the Bible. Moses commanded the Jews (Leviticus: 19, 35-36): Ye shall do no unrighteousness in judgment, in miteyard, in weight, or in measure. Just balances, just weights, a just ephah, and a just hin shall ye have. Here we see justice conceived concretely. Justice is conceived as a balance, a pair of scales. If the scales balance each other, this is justice: if the scales do not balance each other, this is injustice. We at once see that the balance involves the law of equivalents. And, first, what is the meaning of the word equivalence? Equivalence means equal powers. When the powers are equal, they balance each other. This is justice. And now we are able to define justice and injustice. Justice is conformity with the law of equivalents; injustice is a violation of the law of equivalents. Existence rests on the eternal and infinite law of equivalents. The Absolute eternally and infinitely goes through transformations, but in all the eternal and infinite transformations the law of equivalents is enforced. This is justice. Thus justice is the foundation of existence. But justice implies injustice, they are correlatives, neither can exist without the other. This raises a question. Justice is conformity with the eternal and infinite law of equivalents, injustice is a violation of this eternal and infinite law of equivalents. The question is: how can they coexist together? The answer is: justice and injustice coexist together as all other correlatives in existence, just as life and death, good and evil, and so on infinitely. We saw that all realities in existence are absolutely egoistic; but to realize their egoism they must be altruistic. Egoism is injustice, altruism is justice. For injustice to realize itself, it must become justice. Injustice is a condition

to justice; without injustice there could not be justice. Just as in the case of two opposing forces, the balance between them arises from the fact that each force is absolutely egoistic, each force asserts itself regardless of the other force. And, just because each force is egoistic, a balance results between them. This is a general idea of justice and injustice. I will consider justice and injustice more closely when I come to speak of man, society and history.

WAR AND PEACE

97. Existence is absolutely one and in perfect harmony with itself in all its eternal aspects, extent and duration; otherwise, existence would be impossible. What in the phenomenal world appear as correlatives are only coexisting aspects of one eternal and infinite process of one existence. It is the same process that in the phenomenal world manifests itself as light and darkness, life and death, good and evil, devolution and evolution, repulsion and attraction, egoism and altruism, justice and injustice, and so on ad infitum. And now we must consider another correlative, namely: war and peace. As in all other cases, philosophers as well as mankind generally regarded war and peace as two separate, distinct and independent states of existence. They believed that peace could be had without war. From time to time idealists initiated movements to abolish war altogether, and prophets and philosophers anticipated a time when mankind will live in perpetual peace and enjoy the good of life without evil. And now the United Nations are planning to establish a world enduring peace. We shall presently see that this is an illusion. Before we can think of abolishing war and establishing an enduring peace, we must first know and understand the nature of war and peace.

What is war, and what is peace? War is defined as a contest or struggle between nations or states, carried on by force and arms. Peace is defined as a state of quiet or tranquility, calm, repose, the absence of war. We shall presently see that these definitions do not reveal the true natures of war and peace.

War is a struggle to overcome resistance. Where there is no resistance there is no war. All realities in existence perpetually struggle to overcome resistance; therefore they are eternally and infinitely at war with one another. What is true of all the elements, forces and processes in existence is also true of living beings. Living beings perpetually struggle against one another, they are perpetually at war with one another. This is well expressed in the struggle for existence. To exist is to struggle; without struggle existence is impossible. The same is true of groups, classes, peoples, nations and races; they are always at war with one another. The same is true of ideas, beliefs, systems of thought, institutions, forms of government and economic orders. Between them there is a perpetual struggle, a perpetual state of war. It is also true of each individual being and reality. Between the different cells and organs of a living body there is a perpetual struggle, a perpetual state of war. Likewise, between the particles of matter there is a perpetual struggle, a perpetual state of war. And the same is true of the faculties of the mind, the different desires, the different aims and purposes; between them there is a perpetual struggle, a perpetual state of war. War is an eternal and infinite state of existence; existence is an eternal and infinite battle-ground. There is war between light and darkness, between life and death, between good and evil, between egoism and altruism, between justice and injustice, and so on infinitely. A struggle to overcome resistance implies a force that struggles. A force that struggles is in motion. Wherever there is motion there is struggle and war. Thus we see that war is the eternal and infinite state of existence. But war implies peace, they are correlatives, neither can exist without the other. Since war is a force in motion, peace must be a force at rest— a state of quiet, tranquility, repose, the absence of war. Peace, then, is rest. But we saw that in existence there is no rest. What, then, is peace?

98. We saw that motion is of two kinds: individual and independent motion, and universal dependent motion. We also saw

that the individual and independent motion is real motion, the universal and dependent motion is rest. Since peace is rest, it would follow that peace is the universal and dependent motion, while war is the individual and independent motion. But we shall presently see that it is just the opposite: the universal and dependent motion is war, the individual and independent motion is peace. We shall presently see that peace is a far more intense struggle than war is, and this just because peace is an individual and independent motion. War is the eternal and infinite state of existence. The individual does not have to struggle to partake of this motion; but the individual has to struggle very hard to attain to individual and independent motion. Let us consider the facts.

The earth consists of infinite particles of matter that are perpetually in motion. This motion is independent of the earth, the earth cannot stop its infinite particles of matter from moving about one another. Again, the earth moves together with the sun and the stars. This motion is also independent of the earth, the earth cannot stop it. Thus the earth is involved in the universal and dependent motion. But, in addition to this universal and dependent motion, the earth has an individual and independent motion, namely, its motion about its axis and around the sun. With relation to the universal and dependent motion, the earth is passive; but with relation to its own individual and independent motion, the earth is active. In this motion, the earth has to struggle. First, it has to struggle against the tendency of its parts to fly apart from one another, and thus destroy the earth. On the other hand, the earth has to struggle against the universal and dependent motion to have its own individual and independent motion. Action and reaction are equal and opposite in direction. The greater the individual and independent motion is the greater is the resistance it meets from the universal dependent motion. For a reality to maintain its integrity, it must struggle against the universal and dependent motion. If a reality did not struggle against the universal and dependent motion, it would be destroyed. This is the deep meaning of self-preservation and the struggle for existence.

Consider the human body. The human body consists of infinite cells that are perpetually in motion. The body cannot stop their motions. Yet that the body may maintain its integrity, it must hold the cells together, it must struggle against their universal dependent motion. If the body did not struggle against the universal and dependent motion of the cells, it could not maintain its integrity. It is the same with the human mind. The mind consists of many faculties, each of which is perpetually in motion. Numerous desires, inclinations, purposes and aims are perpetually struggling with one another. But that the mind is to maintain its integrity it must hold the faculties in check and coordinate them; otherwise the mind would be destroyed. And this is true of existence as a whole. All infinite realities are perpetually in motion. But that existence may maintain its integrity, it must hold in check the infinite realities, it must coordinate them; otherwise existence would be impossible. Existence, then, implies two different kinds of conformity. First, there is conformity with the universal order of existence; second, there is conformity with one's own nature.

99. And now, what is peace and what is war? Peace is an individual and independent motion, war is a universal and dependent motion. Peace, then, is an intenser struggle than war. In other words, peace is a more intense war than war is. Consider the facts. Darkness does not have to struggle; it is the eternal and universal state of existence; but light has to struggle to overcome darkness. Death does not have to struggle; it is the eternal and infinite state of existence; but life has to struggle against death. Evil does not have to struggle for its existence, but good must struggle for its existence against evil. Vice does not have to struggle for its existence, but virtue must struggle for its existence against vice. And so it is in all cases. The reason for this is the following. We saw that devolution brought down absolute thought to the state of diffused matter. Diffused matter is

chaos and darkness, evil and death. Then evolution began to create the world. Evolution had to overcome devolution, light had to overcome darkness, order had to overcome chaos, life had to overcome death, and so all through. Evolution, then, is an eternal and infinite struggle against devolution. We have to struggle to live; but we do not have to struggle to die. Once we give up the struggle to live, and we will surely die. We have to struggle to be virtuous, but we do not have to struggle for vice. Once we give up the struggle for virtue, and vice will overtake us. We have to struggle to be honest and truthful, but we do not have to struggle to be dishonest and false. Once we give up the struggle to be honest and truthful, and we shall certainly become dishonest and false. Slavery does not have to struggle for its existence, but freedom has to struggle for its existence against slavery. If men give up the struggle for freedom, they will surely become slaves. One has to struggle against his passions; otherwise, his passions will destroy him. It is far easier to master external things than to master oneself. It is easier to conquer a city than to conquer one's ambition. And the same is true of peace and war.

It is easier to plunge into a most destructive war than to maintain peace. It is easier for individuals, groups, classes, peoples, nations and races to unite for purposes of war than it is for purposes of peace. War is natural and easy, but peace is rational and very hard. Peace is the highest in existence, and therefore the highest price must be paid for existence. If we want peace, we must struggle against our own passions, vanities and ambitions. In proportion as men will overcome their passions and control their animal natures, in that proportion will they emancipate themselves from war. The United Nations believe that by destroying the military powers of Germany and Japan they will secure peace in the world. But this is an illusion. Even if the United Nations should destroy the Germans and the Japanese, they will not have peace; for the conditions for war reside within the United Nations themselves. So long as they are swayed by their passions and determined by their animal nature, so long as they strive to realize petty aims and vain ambitions, so long they will have wars. To emancipate themselves from war, mankind must realize that they must pay for this a very high price—a perpetual struggle for virtue, honesty and truth. Now, if all this depended upon the will and determination of men, mankind would never emancipate themselves from war. But all this does not depend upon men. Just as their past evolution was not determined by men, so their future evolution will not be determined by men. Inherent in man is his destiny to become rational and morally autonomous. This destiny was implanted in man by God. Races, nations, peoples, classes and individuals will come and go, but mankind will continue to develop and realize the destiny determined by God. The road towards that destiny is not through what is universally regarded as peace, but what it really is a road of hard struggles and wars; struggles and wars, not so much against the external world, as against themselves.

Natural and Rational Dialectics

100. Progress is a movement towards the realization of destiny. What we must be clear about progress is this. Progress is made by ideas, and not by material realities. Progress implies change; that which cannot change cannot make progress. Now the form of a material reality is fixed, inflexible and cannot change; a material reality, therefore, cannot make progress. On the other hand, an idea is fluid, flexible and capable of change. Therefore an idea can make progress. Again, progress implies permanence, for only the permanent can change. Now, a material reality is not permanent; it is brought into existence, it exists for a time, and then is destroyed. But an idea is permanent, and an idea may be eternal. Again, progress is towards destiny, but a material reality has no destiny. For instance, a chair has not the destiny to become a table, a cottage has not the destiny to become a temple; and so it is with all material realities in existence. But an idea has a destiny. A few illustrations will make it clear.

Men were always in need of shelter. The primitive savages built huts, the barbarians built houses, and civilized men build temples, mansions, palaces and skyscrapers. Between the hut of the primitive savage and the modern skyscraper great progress was made in construction, but the progress was not made by the structures. The hut did not become a house, the house did not become a mansion, and the mansion did not become a skyscraper. All these structures came and existed for a time and then passed out of existence just as they were, without making any progress. The progress was made by the idea. The idea brought out the sciences, the arts and the skilled crafts which enable men now to build skyscrapers, bridges, and so on. The idea involved in the construction of a hut is also involved in the construction of a skyscraper, just as the idea of the primitive wheel made by the savage is involved in all the wonderful machines made by men now. The primitive ideas grew and developed and made great progress. Or consider the automobile. Since the first automobile was made great progress was made in the construction of automobiles. Year after year better and more improved automobiles are brought out; but the automobiles did not make any progress. Just as they were made so they remained until they were discarded. But the idea of the automobile made great progress. And so it is with all ideas which realized themselves in material forms. The ideas made infinite progress, but the material realities in which the ideas realized themselves made no progress.

What is true of material realities is equally true of institutions, forms of government, modes of production, and habits of life and thought, because they are the material embodiments of ideas. Consider religion. The primitive savages conceived ideas of religion which manifested themselves in fetish and ancestor worship. The idea of their religion embodied itself in institutions, practices and beliefs—all of which assumed material forms. Since the days of the primitive savages religion made great progress; but this progress was made by the idea of religion, and not by the institutions, practices and ceremonials. The institutions, practices and ceremonials came and went, but the idea of religion made progress. What is true of religion is true of philosophy, politics, science and art. Thus we see that progress is made only by ideas, but not by material realities. But not all ideas make progress; only those ideas make progress that have a destiny, for progress is the realization of destiny. Consider the idea of the triangle. This idea does not make progress, because it has no destiny. Eternally and infinitely the idea of the triangle remains the same. But, on the other hand, an idea which has a destiny makes progress. Consider the acorn. We saw that the soul and essence of the acorn is an idea of God. This idea has a destiny, to become an oak tree, and to reproduce acorns a thousandfold. But the destiny of the acorn is limited. An acorn may realize its destiny, it reproduces itself a thousandfold, but these thousands of acorns are exactly as the first acorn. And may the acorn become an infinite number of acorns, they will all be like the first acorn. And the same is true of all forms of life. Professor Huxley tells us that ninety-five per cent of the living beings on the earth have been so for billions of years. The moneron was the primordial living cell, yet the moneron today is just as it was in the very beginning of life on earth. How, then, is progress possible? To understand the answer, we must again refer to Plato's doctrine of ideas.

101. According to Plato, all material realities are only the realization of the ideas of God. The highest idea is the idea of the good. This idea comprehends all other ideas and subordinates them to itself. This means that the idea of the good is the supreme idea of God, to realize which he created the world. The destiny of existence, then, is to realize this idea of the good. Hence, progress is a movement towards the realization of the good. But ideas can realize themselves only in material forms. This gives rise to the method of dialectics. We saw that creation realizes itself through affirmation, negation and reaffirmation. This is the method of dialectics. The process begins as an affirmation, it then becomes a negation, and then again it becomes

an affirmation. Consider a seed. The seed is an affirmation of life. Put the seed into the ground. The material form of the seed is negated, and the life in it is now free to become a plant. The plant is a negation of the seed. The plant grows and develops until it becomes ripe enough to reproduce seeds. As the seeds come into existence, grow and develop, the plant dies. The new seeds are a negation of the plant. Thus we start out with an affirmation, followed by a negation, and this is followed by a negation of the negation, and the result is an affirmation. The original seed now affirms itself as a hundred or a thousand seeds. This is the method of dialectics.

Dialectics begins as a natural process and becomes a rational process. This gives rise to two kinds of dialectics: natural dialectics and rational dialectics. Natural dialectics pertains to material realities, rational dialectics pertains to ideas. We saw that a material form is fixed, inflexible and cannot change; while an idea is fluid, flexible and does change; a material reality cannot make progress, while an idea does make progress. Natural dialectics gives rise to the following law: Every step in progress becomes a hindrance to further progress. When an idea realizes itself in a material form, that material form becomes a hindrance to further progress. For the idea to make further progress, it must free itself from its material form, it must negate and destroy the material form that it may realize itself in a higher form, and thus make further progress. The acorn must be destroyed that its life may become an oak tree. The cottage must be destroyed that a house may be built. An old body must be destroyed that the life in it may realize itself in a new and better body. Thus every step in material progress becomes a hindrance to further progress. The hindrance arises from the fact that the old material form persists in its being, it persists to occupy space and time. For instance, a ten-story house, when constructed, was a step in progress. Since the ten-story house was constructed, the neighborhood changed so that it now requires an Empire State Building. But the ten-story building occupies the place where an Empire State Building should now be constructed. The ten-story house cannot be converted into an Empire State Building. But the ten-story house brings a good income, and can stand for another fifty years. Hence the ten-story house becomes a hindrance to the construction of an Empire State Building. This is true of all material forms, this is true of institutions, forms of government, modes of production, habits of life and thought, and so on indefinitely. This is the reason why races, nations, peoples, classes and individuals will rather perish than give up their institutions, forms of government, modes of production, and habits of life and thought. But what is true of material forms is not true of ideas. Just because ideas are fluid, flexible and capable of change, without losing their identity, therefore in the case of ideas every step in progress becomes a condition to further progress. We have then the following distinction between natural dialectics and rational dialectics. Natural dialectics which pertains to material forms involves the law: every step in progress becomes a hindrance to further progress. Rational dialectics which pertains to ideas involves the law: every step in progress becomes a condition to further progress.

We have thus considered those aspects of existence which give us an idea of the Absolute, God, and Existence. It is a general idea which must be made more explicit. This idea will become more explicit as we proceed with the consideration of man, society and history. Our next subject is man.

CHAPTER XV

Man

102. The Absolute is absolute thought infinitely extended. By self-reflection, the Absolute forms an idea of itself. This idea is the Infinite Intellect, God. Thus the Absolute becomes a trinity: Infinite Intellect Thought and Extension. God created man in the essence and form of God. This means that, like God, man is a trinity, consisting of a body, a mind and a soul. The body is a form of extension, the mind is a form of thought, and the soul is an idea of God. The soul is the essence of man; the body and the mind are only the means through which the soul functions in the material world. When God conceives the idea of man, God causes a man and a woman to meet, to attract each other, and to conceive the desire to unite as husband and wife. This desire gives birth in them to ideas; the idea in the man assumes the material form of the spermatozoon, and in the woman it assumes the form of the ovum. The real union takes place between these seeds, for they are the embodiment of the soul of the human being that is now conceived. All processes of creation start from the beginning. The spermatozoon and the ovum are destroyed in the process, and they regress to the moneron, the starting point of life. In the moneron is now embodied the soul of the man. The soul is infinite and eternal. The soul now begins the process of creation, it reproduces cells upon cells; and as the cells increase in number they are integrated into groups and groups of groups, and thus they become the organs of the body and the body as a whole. Integration implies differentiation. As the cells become integrated into organs, the organs become differentiated from one another in form and function. Thus comes into existence the human

body. Thought and extension are correlatives, neither can exist without the other. Since the body is a form of extension and the mind is a form of thought, the body and the mind are correlatives, neither can exist without the other. And so, as the cells are integrated into organs of the body, so their corresponding minds integrate into forms of thought. These forms of thought constitute the faculties of the mind. Like the organs of the body, so the faculties of the mind become differentiated in form and function. Between the body and the mind there is a correspondence; whatever takes place in the body the mind is conscious of it. But, at the outset, we must be clear about this. The body does not act, and the mind does not think; it is the soul that acts through the body and thinks through the mind. Since it is the soul that acts and thinks through the body and the mind, it follows that there must be a correspondence between the body and the mind. What takes place in and about the body the soul is conscious of it through the mind. Again, between the body and the mind there is a correspondence, but no causal relation; the body does not determine the mind to think, and the mind does not determine the body to act. The correspondence between the body and the mind arises from this alone, namely, that the soul acts through the body and at the same time thinks through the mind. Since it is one and the same soul that acts and thinks, there is a correspondence between the act and the thought, and this means a correspondence between the body and the mind. Through the body the soul comes into relations with the material forms of the realities of existence, and through the mind the soul comes into relations with the ideal forms of the realities of existence; and thus the soul acquires a knowledge and understanding of the external world.

103. When man is born, the soul begins to function through the body and the mind. It opens up the senses and through them, like through windows, the soul perceives the realities of existence. Through the senses, the soul perceives the realities of

existence, but not the relations among them. The sense-percep-
tions give the soul a vague knowledge of things, but no understanding of them. To understand as well as to know the realities
of existence, the soul must not only perceive the realities of
existence, it must also perceive the relations of them to one
another. For this purpose the soul brings out the understanding.
The understanding and the senses cooperate; the senses perceive
the realities, and the understanding perceives the relations among
the realities. What are the relations among the realities? First,
there is the inner relation in every reality between its form of
extension and its form of thought. Second, there is the organic
relation among all realities in existence; all realities are interdependent and interrelated, because they are all but forms of one
eternal and infinite substance, absolute thought. To know and
understand any reality, we must also know and understand its
relation to all other realities. Third, a reality is only an effect
of the first cause, that is, it is an effect of God. Between an effect
and its cause there is an organic and indissoluble relation. The
knowledge and understanding of an effect depend upon and
involve the knowledge and understanding of its cause. Thus we
see that it is only when the soul brings out the senses and the
understanding that through them it acquires a knowledge and
understanding of the realities of existence.

Now, the senses and the understanding are limited in their
scope; they can function only within the phenomenal world.
But the soul of man is destined to comprehend also the transcendental world. Hence, as the soul grows, develops and makes
progress towards her destiny, she brings out higher faculties.
First, she brings out the faculty of intuition. Intuition is the
faculty through which the soul perceives realities beyond the
visible in time, space and reality. Through intuition the soul
perceives transcendental realities. But notice this. Just as the
senses perceive phenomenal realities, but they do not perceive
the relations among them; so intuition perceives transcendental
realities, but not relations among them. What the senses are in
the phenomenal world, this is intuition in the transcendental

world. But the perception of the transcendental realities, without the perception of the relations among them, gives only a vague knowledge, and no understanding. Hence the soul brings out another faculty to perceive the relations among the transcendental realities, and this is reason. Reason in the transcendental world performs the same function as the understanding performs in the phenomenal world. Reason perceives the relations among the transcendental realities. When intuition and reason cooperate, then the soul also acquires a knowledge and understanding of the transcendental world. But even then the soul has not yet attained to her destiny. No matter how profound intuition may be, and no matter how universal reason may be, through them alone the soul cannot attain to an adequate knowledge and understanding of the totality of existence, that is, of God and the Absolute. For this purpose the soul brings out the intellect— which is the highest faculty. In the intellect all faculties become united, and through the intellect the soul comprehends the absolute, infinite and eternal. I call attention to the following. I use the term intellect, not in the sense in which it is usually used by philosophers, but I use it in the sense in which Spinoza used it. All other philosophers had no adequate idea of the intellect. As we proceed, the nature of the intellect will become manifest.

104. I stated that the soul brings out the senses, the understanding, intuition and reason. This is not accurately speaking correct. The soul does not bring out these faculties, the soul itself becomes these faculties. When man is born, the soul is wholly implicit. As the soul grows and develops, it becomes ever more explicit, and this manifests itself in the successive coming to the fore of the senses, the understanding, intuition and reason. And, when finally, the soul becomes wholly explicit, it becomes the intellect. The intellect is the soul wholly explicit. As I will often use the term, implicit and explicit, it is necessary that I should at this occasion make the meaning of these terms definite and clear.

Suppose we examine a watch. It is a mechanism constructed with great wisdom and skill; it consists of many parts, differentiated in form and function, and yet all together perform a unified function. We look at the watch and marvel at the ingenuity and skill with which it was created, how the parts are made to fit one another, and how all together perform a unified function. We say, it is a wonderful mechanism. Now, if the watch could speak to us, it would tell us the following. I am, indeed, the product of great wisdom and skill, but they are not my wisdom and skill, I am not even conscious of them, and I do not know what I am doing. The consciousness, wisdom and skill which created me, are not mine; they belong to the inventor, they are his. He conceived the idea, and with great wisdom and skill he created me. He is fully conscious of me and of my function, and through me he realizes a purpose of his own. The watch is in a state of implicitness. In the watch are consciousness, wisdom and skill, but the watch is not conscious of them. This unconsciousness constitutes implicitness. But the inventor is in a state of explicitness, because he is conscious of the nature and function of the watch and of the purpose which he realizes through the watch. This consciousness in the inventor constitutes explicitness.

And now, suppose the inventor transferred to the watch the consciousness, wisdom and skill which are in him, so that the watch would become conscious of the wisdom, skill and purpose with which and for the sake of which the inventor created the watch, and the watch would continue to perform its function consciously and, as it were, for its own purpose. Then the watch would pass from a state of implicitness to a state of explicitness; the watch would now become like the inventor explicit. And, whereas before the watch performed its function implicitly, because it was not conscious of what it was doing, now it performs its function explicitly, because now it is conscious of what it is doing.

Know, then, man is the mechanism, and God is the inventor. God created man with infinite knowledge, understanding, wisdom and skill, to realize a purpose of God. But man in the beginning, like the watch, is wholly implicit; he is not conscious of the knowledge, understanding, wisdom and skill with which God created him, and he is not conscious of the purpose for which God created him. In the beginning, man is like the watch; but there is an infinite difference between man and the watch. While the watch has no other destiny than to remain implicit and perform its function implicitly; man is destined to become wholly explicit. This destiny God implanted in the soul of man. Hence, as soon as man is born, the soul passes from the state of implicitness to the state of explicitness; it becomes, in succession, the senses, the understanding, intuition, reason and finally becomes the intellect. When the soul becomes the intellect, it realizes its destiny. It then perceives that it is one with God, it identifies itself with God and attains to what Spinoza calls, the intellectual love of God. By identifying itself with God, the soul identifies itself with all of existence, all realities and processes of existence, and identifies itself with all men. Then man is able to fulfil the two great commandments of Moses: Thou shalt love Jehovah thy God with all thy heart, with all thy mind and with all thy soul; and thou shalt love thy neighbor as thyself. These two commandments are absolutely the highest in eternal and infinite existence, there can be no higher commandments. Even God himself cannot conceive a higher purpose in existence. And may mankind live an eternity, and may they make infinite intellectual and spiritual progress, they will never be able to transcend these two great commandments. This is the destiny of man. This is a general outline of the nature and destiny of man. This outline must be made concrete and definite.

105. Life, as Spencer tells us, is an adjustment of the inner relations to the outer relations. To live in the material world, man must adjust himself to the material realities and the material conditions of existence. Between conduct and consequence there is the causal relation of cause and effect. Whatever man does

consciously, he does to realize a purpose. To realize a purpose, man must choose such conduct as will realize itself in the desired consequences, and thus realize his purpose. Conduct relates to the future, for the consequences of present conduct will realize themselves in the future. The future may be the next moment, the next day, the next year, or any remoter future time. But the future does not yet exist, there is nothing yet of the future which the senses can perceive and the understanding comprehend. How, then, can man determine what present conduct will in the future realize the desired consequences? For this purpose, the soul brings out the faculty of judgment. Judgment is the faculty for the anticipation of the future consequences of present conduct. We may say, judgment is a function of intuition and reason, but limited to the phenomenal world. Judgment may be instructed by past experience, but it does not depend upon past experience. First, one may have an extensive knowledge of past human experiences, yet if his judgment is defective, he will blunder and never realize his purposes. Second, past human experience cannot guide man in life. Consider the facts.

Mankind had infinite experiences. But who can know all the past experiences of mankind? Second, there is no reliable and truthful report of past human experiences. Third, the relations between conduct and consequence are bound up with conditions and circumstances that are infinitely variable. The conduct which can realize a desired consequence under one set of conditions and circumstances will not realize the same purpose under another set of conditions and circumstances. Hence past experiences of mankind are not an adequate guide in life. And human experience itself shows that past experiences are not an adequate guide in life. If indeed, past human experiences were an adequate guide in life, then by this time men would realize all their aims and purposes. And yet the fact is that, even now, men plan, scheme and plot to realize aims and purposes, and invariably are disappointed. Since man is constantly confronted by the problem: what conduct will realize a desired consequence, man must have a faculty to guide him in the choice of conduct. This faculty is judgment. Just as the understanding perceives the relation between cause and effect, so judgment perceives the relations between conduct and consequence. One who possesses a highly developed faculty of judgment will realize aims and purposes which ordinary men, even under the same circumstances, will not realize. The lack of a competent judgment is what Kant calls stupidity. A stupid person may be ever so educated and informed, yet he will blunder in the choice of conduct to realize a desired purpose.

106. But judgment is not an adequate guide in life. Judgment concerns itself about right and wrong, reality and illusion; but judgment does not concern itself about good and evil; judgment is not concerned about morality and the destiny of man. Judgment can anticipate the immediate consequences of present conduct, but judgment cannot anticipate the remote consequences of present conduct. Now, conduct does not exhaust itself in the immediate consequences, just as cause does not exhaust itself in the immediate effect. Now, between conduct and the immediate consequences there may be a direct relation; but between conduct and the remote consequences there is a dialectical relation. This is due to the eternal and infinite law of equivalents. This law demands a quid pro quo; for everything we get from existence we must pay an equivalent; and the equivalent we must pay in coins of work, struggle, suffering and death. We must work for the material things; we must struggle for knowledge and understanding; we must suffer for spiritual growth and development; and we must die to live. Conformity with the law of equivalents is justice and morality; a violation of the law of equivalents is injustice and immorality; the former is good, the latter is evil. When we reflect on the infinite crimes committed by mankind, we perceive that they were nothing else than violations of the law of equivalents. What is stealing? Stealing is taking something without paying for it an equivalent. What is murder? It is taking the life of a person without paying an equivalent for that life with one's own life. What is lying?

It is trying to get something without paying for it an equivalent. What is hypocrisy? It is an endeavor to be recognized, honored and loved without earning them with corresponding merits. And so it is in all cases. The Bible tells us: The joy of the hypocrite is short. This is true of all who try to get something without paying for it an equivalent; their joy is short. Now, judgment can guide men to realize immediate desirable consequences, but judgment cannot guide men with relation to the remote consequences. As said before, judgment is not concerned about morality and the destiny of man.

To guide men with relation to remote consequences, the soul brings out reason. Reason is the faculty that distinguishes between the morally good and the morally evil; reason is concerned about the remote consequences and the destiny of man. The human being becomes a man only when he attains to reason; and he remains a man only so long as he follows the dictates of reason; but, when man disregards reason or he loses his reason, he becomes again an animal. Reason recognizes the law of equivalents. Since we must pay for everything an equivalent, reason dictates that we pay the equivalent at once. The paying of the equivalent means work, struggle, suffering and death. Here, then, we have the rule of reason. Conduct which begins with work, struggle and suffering will realize itself in remote consequences that are good. On the other hand, conduct which begins with leisure, idleness, pleasure and ease will realize itself in remote consequences that are evil. Hence only reason is an adequate guide in life. The subject is important, and therefore it is necessary to illustrate it by a few examples, so that this important subject be adequately understood.

107. In 1917, while the Allied Nations were involved in a life and death struggle with the Central Powers, the Russian Revolution broke out, the Bolsheviki seized power, and they caused the Russian armies to withdraw from the war. The Allied Nations and the reactionary forces in the world determined to destroy the Russian Revolution and the Bolsheviki. They in-

vaded Russia, and with the reactionary forces in Russia they carried on a bitter struggle against the revolutionary Russians. The Russian Revolution asserted itself. It fought off all invaders, and emerged triumphant. The Bolsheviki laid the foundation for a powerful Soviet Russia. Two decades passed, and behold, the same Allied Nations and the same reactionary forces were compelled to come to the help of Soviet Russia, in order to save themselves from destruction by the Axis Powers. Now, the heads of the Allied Nations were men of knowledge and ability, they certainly possessed developed judgments; otherwise, they would not become the heads of the great powers in the world. When they invaded Russia during the Russian Revolution, their judgment showed them that that was the right step for them to take to rid the world of Bolshevism, and to safeguard capitalism and the status quo. And yet, this very invasion of Russia made the triumph of the Revolution possible. If the Russian Revolution did not have to struggle for its life, it would degenerate into a farce, the same as in Germany. And so, by endeavoring to destroy the Russian Revolution, the Allied Nations actually sustained it. At that time, the Allied Nations did not anticipate the remote consequences, that they will be compelled to make peace with Soviet Russia, to save themselves from destruction by the Axis Powers. Thus we see that their judgment, while it guided them with relation to the immediate consequences, did not guide them with relation to the remote consequences.

When Hitler came to power, and announced his determination to destroy Bolshevism and Soviet Russia, most of the European nations that hated and feared Soviet Russia, directly and indirectly, helped the Nazis to create a powerful war machine, convinced that Hitler and the Nazis would use it against Soviet Russia. These reactionary forces believed that a war between Nazi Germany and Soviet Russia will destroy both of them, and then the whole European terrain will be free for the reactionary forces to do what they pleased. Now, Hitler did create a powerful war machine; but he used it, not against

Soviet Russia, but the very nations that helped Hitler create the powerful war machine. Hitler conquered one country after another, enslaved, exploited and oppressed and ruined one nation after another. The heads of the Nations sought to appease Hitler at the expense of Czechoslovakia, Austria and Poland, confident that by this they secured peace for themselves. But, instead of peace, they brought upon themselves a most cruel and destructive war. Thus, again, their judgment failed.

England closed the Burma Road, so that no supplies necessary to the Chinese to carry on their struggle against the Japanese should pass through that road. At the same time the United States sent to the Japanese nine million tons of iron, and large quantities of oil and other necessary means to carry on the war. Why? Because they believed that the Japanese will use these munitions of war against the Chinese and the Russians. But what was the result? The Japanese used these means against the English and the Americans; and now tens of thousands of English and Americans die, and millions of them fight to open again the Burma Road for the Chinese, and to regain the territories which the English and the Americans lost. Thus, again, their judgment failed.

Stalin made a pact with Hitler, in the confident expectation that by this Soviet Russia would be secured against Nazi Germany. Stalin and Hitler united their forces, they conquered and dismembered Poland, and enslaved the Polish people. But what was the result? The result was that the Nazis invaded Soviet Russia, destroyed two-thirds of European Russia, killed, tortured and enslaved more than twenty million Russians. Thus, again, their judgment failed.

Hitler and the Nazis conceived the idea to conquer the world and to enslave the human race. With infinite cunning and keen judgment they created a powerful war machine, and with infinite cruelty and sadism they tortured, enslaved and killed tens of millions of men, women and children. But what was the result? Germany is conquered, the Germans are defeated, the military power is destroyed, the Nazi leaders are all either dead or imprisoned awaiting their doom; and Germany itself is dismembered, ruled by four outside powers, and the Germans are doomed to become an agricultural nation. Thus, again, their judgment failed.

Finally, consider the case of Churchill. During the second world war he occupied a foremost position in the world. He carried on successfully the war against the Germans, and was universally held by enlightened humanity in the greatest esteem. But Churchill was a conservative and reactionary. He hated Soviet Russia, he hated communism and socialism, and he wanted to preserve and to perpetuate the status quo ante. In Italy, in Belgium, in Greece, in Spain, and wherever his influence reached, he used the military and political powers at his command to destroy all liberal and radical movements. The time came for the English to have a national election. Churchill insisted that the elections shall take place in July, 1945, while the war was still on, and while the Potsdam Conference was to take place, to make sure that he would be reelected. He figured that during the war, and while such important post-war matters were to be decided, the English people would not change their prime minister. And yet, what was the result? He was overwhelmingly and decisively defeated, and the Labour Party came into power. Thus, again, a failure of judgment.

Study history, read biographies of great men and women, reflect on the experiences of persons whom you know, and reflect on your own experiences, and you will see that the judgment is not an adequate guide in life. Men invariably failed, because they consulted their judgment, and they did not consult their reason. They did not consult their reason, first, because they were not concerned about the remote consequences of their conduct, they were concerned about the immediate consequences. Second, because they did not attain to reason. They were like infants. Five-year-old Johnnie is not concerned about remote consequences; he wants to be paid at once. How can reason foresee the remote consequences? Reason reveals the truth that there is an eternal and infinite law of equivalents;

that there is an eternal and infinite moral order in existence, that between conduct and consequence there is not only a causal relation, but there is also a moral relation; that morally good conduct must bring good consequences, and morally evil conduct must bring evil consequences. Nothing in creation can change this. If, therefore, one consults his reason, and acts in accordance with the dictates of reason and morality, he need not actually foresee the future consequences, yet he will be absolutely certain that the consequences will be good. Just as one cannot get anything without paying for it an equivalent; so, when one does pay the equivalent, nothing in creation can deprive him from that for which he paid the equivalent. We must pay, and we will be forced to pay, for whatever we get. It is only a question when we should pay. Reason dictates to pay in advance. When we pay in advance, we get an equivalent at a reduced price. But, when we deal with existence on the instalment plan, we get before we pay for it, then we must not only pay a higher price and interest, but we also run the risk of not being able to pay. And then, there is no end of trouble and suffering. Hence, even before we know what reason dictates, even before we know that God determines our existence, our thoughts, feelings and actions, and the consequences of our actions, if only we know that we cannot have anything without paying for it an equivalent, and that prudence will tell us to pay in advance—this alone is already a good guide in life, even though it is not yet an adequate guide. Most men up till now did not yet attain to reason, yet reason was in them. What we call the conscience is nothing else than reason implicit in us, it is the small still voice of God in us. But because it is the small still voice, it is drowned in the shouts and noises of the passions and vain ambitions.

108. We saw that the relations between the understanding and the senses are repeated between reason and intuition. The senses and the understanding function in the phenomenal world, but intuition and reason function in the transcendental world. Just

as not on bread alone can man live, so not in the phenomenal world alone can man live. Man is not an animal; man has a high destiny. But this destiny he can realize only when he rises to the transcendental world. Intuition and reason help him rise to the transcendental world. We must now consider intuition and reason more fundamentally.

Intuition is a transcendental sense whereby we perceive transcendental realities beyond the visible in time, space and reality. Man must perceive beyond the immediate horizon in space to secure the means of life, shelter and security; he must anticipate beyond the immediate in time to prepare himself for the future; and he must penetrate beyond the surface of things to be able to use them in a more effective and adequate manner. For this purpose the soul brings out intuition. Intuition enabled Columbus to discover a new continent; intuition enabled a Moses to perceive the future destiny of mankind; intuition enabled a Newton to perceive the law of gravitation; and so in all cases. Like the diver, intuition plunges into the deep and the unknown, and brings to the surface treasures hidden beyond the visible in time, space and material realities. Intuition enables men to discover what had not been known, to create what had not existed, and to perceive what had not been revealed. Men in whom the faculty of intuition is highly developed are prophets and seers. Prophets are of three classes: retrospective, prospective and introspective. Those who concern themselves about the past are retrospective prophets; those who concern themselves about the future are prospective prophets; and those who concern themselves about the innermost nature of things are introspective prophets. The retrospective prophets of modern times are introspective prophets. The retrospective prophets of modern times brought to light the past evolution of the material world— astronomic, geologic, biologic, psychologic and sociologic. The prospective prophets of modern times, like Marx, revealed the destiny of human society to become one resting on universal communism. The modern introspective prophets, like Einstein, revealed the innermost nature of light, matter, energy, the electron and the proton. But, as stated before, intuition perceives transcendental realities, but it does not perceive the relations among these realities. These relations are perceived by reason.

109. Reason is light. We already saw that absolute thought becomes reason, reason becomes light, and light is the ultimate unit of matter, it becomes matter. Until man attains to reason, he lives in mental and spiritual darkness, and he is shut up in himself like a clam. He neither perceives light from without nor does he have light within himself; he lives in complete darkness and egoism. When he attains to reason, he becomes conscious of reason, and he sees the light of reason, then he opens his eyes, and he sees himself in relation to the rest of the world. He begins to concern himself about the world, he begins to concern himself about his fellowmen, he begins to concern himself about the future, and he begins to identify himself with the rest of existence. And thus he grows and develops and rises ever higher and higher towards his destiny.

Reason is transcendental; it transcends nature and the phenomenal world. Nature is the phenomenal world of material realities, material forms of extension; but reason comprehends the world of ideas, the ideal forms of thought. By perceiving the transcendental world of ideas, man becomes discontented with the material world as he finds it, and begins to change it and to improve it. By changing and improving the external material world, man also changes and improves his own nature. He creates for himself an ever more improved world. From being a mere dependent upon nature, he becomes the master over nature.

Reason is architectonic. Just as the architect makes the plan and guides and directs the workers in the construction of the building according to the plan; so reason makes the plan, and guides and directs the powers of the body and of the mind to realize the plan. When man attains to reason, when he becomes conscious of reason, when reason becomes in him explicit, he becomes also the master over himself. He is no longer swayed by his animal passions, but he controls his passions. He then becomes a morally autonomous person. What moral autonomy is, we shall presently see.

Reason is universal. Reason is not content with anything that is limited in nature, scope and duration; reason wants the totality of existence. Reason is not content with mere pleasure and wellbeing; reason wants happiness. Pleasure and wellbeing, joy, and all other states of gratification are limited in their nature, scope and duration; they satisfy us in part and for a limited time. But happiness comprehends our whole being, it is unlimited in nature, scope and duration. Happiness is an idea of reason, which becomes the aim of all rational human endeavor. This aim urges us to strive after the highest perfection and to enjoy the highest bliss, and that is the intellectual love of God. This, however, man attains when his soul become the intellect.

110. What is moral autonomy? Moral autonomy is self-rule, self-determination. One who attains to moral autonomy, of his own accord and without any external constraint, conforms with the nature, laws and order of existence; that is, he conforms with the will of God. God's will is then his own will; he conforms with the will of God, because it is now his own will. Once man attains to moral autonomy, he conforms with the will of God, even if God did not exist. The nature, laws and order of existence which before imposed themselves upon him from outside and as hostile forces, are now his own nature, laws and order, so that he would now legislate to existence that nature, laws and order. An illustration will make it clear.

When a boy begins to study mathematics, it presents itself to him as something outside of him, something which tyrannizes over him and forces him to think and to reason in accordance with its own nature. The boy hates mathematics, he struggles against it, he tries to evade its rigors and to cheat it in the solution of the problems. And were it not for the insistence of parents and teachers, he would not study mathematics. But he is compelled to study mathematics. He is bright and intelligent and, as he makes progress, he learns to like mathematics. He devotes a number of years on the study of mathematics and, in due time, becomes a great mathematician. Now he is identified with mathematics and its method of reasoning so that, if all books on mathematics were destroyed and all laws of mathematics were expunged from existence, he would legislate to existence the laws of mathematics. He would do this, because now he can think and reason only in the way mathematics requires; the method of thinking and reasoning of mathematics is now the method of his own mind; it cannot think and reason otherwise. This is moral autonomy. Until man attains to explicit reason and moral autonomy, the nature, laws and order of existence appear to him to be outside of him, which tyrannize over him and compel him, against his will and inclinations, to act and think in accordance with their nature. But, when man becomes rational and morally autonomous, he acquires a mode of thinking, reasoning and acting that are in perfect accord with the nature, laws and order of existence. If now existence were to cease to have the same nature, and its laws and order were abrogated, he would legislate to existence its nature, laws and order. But existence is God. Hence a morally autonomous person identifies himself with God and his will; the will of God is now his own will, and he cheerfully conforms with the will of God, because it is now his own will. This is the destiny of mankind. Mankind is destined to attain to explicit reason and become morally autonomous.

111. The senses, the understanding and judgment submit to nature, but reason does not submit to nature. Reason comes with an imperative ought, dictating to nature what it should become. The reason for this is that reason comes to create a world out of chaos and darkness. Now, what should nature become? Nature is the world of material realities; the material realities are the realization of the ideas of God. The ideas are perfect in their forms of thought, but they seldom realize themselves in perfect

material realities. Reason demands of the material realities that they become as perfect as the ideas are. Hence reason endeavors to transform the material realities. But the transformation takes place in accordance with the method of dialectics, and this involves good and evil. Reason is the tree of knowledge of good and evil. The Bible begins the story of man with the tree of knowledge of good and evil. This is very significant. Man is born when he attains to reason, when he knows the difference between good and evil. Until then he is still an animal. And man rises ever higher in proportion as he approaches ever nearer to his true human nature, and that means a knowledge of good and evil. To exist, man must conform with the requirements of existence, and with his own true nature; and this implies a knowledge and understanding of the nature of the realities and processes of existence and also of his own true nature. Knowledge, then, is good. But good implies evil. Good and evil are correlatives, neither can exist without the other, and each grows and develops in proportion as the other grows and develops. The more good man attains the more evil he encounters; and, vice versa, the more evil he accepts the more good he finds in existence. Since knowledge is good, inherent in knowledge is evil. Man becomes conscious of the evil inherent in knowledge because he has reason. What is the evil inherent in knowledge? Things in themselves are neither good nor evil; but things become evil when they negate good. What is it in knowledge which negates knowledge? This is reason itself. Man acquires some knowledge of existence, and he is satisfied. Comes reason and reveals to him that the knowledge which he acquired is inadequate, uncertain and unreliable. By this reason negates the knowledge acquired, and without knowledge man cannot exist. Thus reason destroys the very foundation of human existence. To exist and to preserve himself, man is then constrained to struggle to acquire a knowledge which shall be adequate, certain and reliable. When man attains to a knowledge which he regards as adequate, certain and reliable, reason again reveals to him that even this knowledge is inadequate, uncertain and unreliable; and thus again reason destroys the foundation of man's existence. Man is then again constrained to struggle for a knowledge that shall be adequate, certain and reliable. But no matter how hard and long man may struggle to acquire a knowledge that shall be adequate, certain and reliable, reason will always reveal to him that his knowledge is inadequate, uncertain and unreliable. Thus reason reveals itself to be evil; it is the serpent that brings death upon man. This was the reason why men always hated and feared reason, and they always struggled against it and endeavored to destroy it. Not only the great masses of mankind, but also theologians, philosophers and scientists always struggled against reason. They wrote big books to show that reason is Satan, the devil, the tempter, that it is misleading and brings upon mankind ruin and suffering and death.

Good implies evil, and evil implies good. Since reason is evil, inherent in reason is good. Man came into existence as an animal; and, like all other animals, he would remain an animal. But man was destined to become rational and morally autonomous. For this purpose God implanted in man reason. Reason took hold of the animal, it made him dissatisfied with the conditions of existence as they were and with himself as he was. Reason converted the animal into a savage, the savage into a barbarian, and the barbarian into a civilized man. But reason could raise man ever higher only by destroying him as he was and transforming him into a higher being. This reason could accomplish only by constantly negating the knowledge which he already acquired, and urge him to strive after more adequate, more certain and more reliable knowledge. Reason destroyed old forms of thought, old habits, old institutions, old systems of thought, old social orders, and brought out in their place better and higher forms of thought, and so on. Reason will continue to do this until it raises mankind to moral autonomy. Thus we see that, on the one hand, reason brings evil; on the other hand, reason brings ever greater good. But it is reserved for the intellect to realize the final destiny of man. As the soul passes from the state of implicitness into the state of explicitness it brings out, in succession, one faculty after another, until it brings out the intellect, that is, it becomes the intellect. Then the soul is wholly explicit.

112. And now we must consider the will. What is the will? Much has been said and written about the will; yet thus far, with the exception of Spinoza, no philosopher or psychologists had an idea of what the will is. The will is the soul in its implicit state. The essence of the soul is desire, because desire is the essence of the Absolute, of God and of the whole of existence. Desire is inherent in thought; there can be no thought without desire as there can be no desire without thought. In absolute thought the desire is without form as the absolute thought is without form. We saw that absolute thought becomes a force only when it assumes a form, when it becomes an idea. It is so with desire. Desire becomes a force only when it assumes a form. In the idea is inherent a definite desire. An idea is a living, conscious and thinking being that desires. The soul of man, being an idea of God, desires. It desires to exist and to function in the material world and to satisfy its desires. As the soul is infinite and eternal, its desires are infinite and eternal. The desire of the soul when it is in a state of implicitness is the will. The will is nothing else than a definite desire—a desire for something definite. When man is born, his soul is in a state of complete implicitness. The soul is then will. But in proportion as the soul becomes explicit, in that proportion the will becomes explicit. When the soul becomes wholly explicit the will becomes the intellect. Thus we see that the soul begins as will and becomes intellect. In the will the soul is wholly implicit, in the intellect the soul becomes wholly explicit. Now the soul is fully conscious of itself, of existence and of God. Since the essence of the soul is desire, the soul desires all the time, it continues to desire even when it becomes intellect. But, while in its state of implicitness the will is blind, now in its state of explicitness the will sees. The will is the soul in action, the

intellect is the soul in understanding; but action implies understanding, and understanding implies action. Hence the will implies the intellect, and the intellect implies the will. What the
soul is to desire, to do and to understand are determined by the
nature of the soul, and the nature of the soul is determined by
God. Thus God determines the existence, the nature, the
thought, the feelings and actions of man, and also determines
the consequences of his actions. This brings us to the problem
which we already considered, namely: Is the will free to determine itself or not? In other words, is man free to determine his
existence, his thoughts, his feelings, his actions and the consequences of his actions? I already stated that man is all through
determined by God. But we must consider the matter more
closely.

113. Men naively believe that they are free to determine their
existence, their thoughts, feelings and actions and the consequences of their actions. Let us consider the facts. Are men
free to determine whether they should come into existence or
not? Are they free to determine their sex, their parents, their
stature, their color, the color of their eyes, hair and skin?
Are they free to determine the conditions into which they
should be born, their bringing up and education during their
early years? Are they free to determine the knowledge which
should be imparted to them, what experience they should
have, and what persons they should meet in life? Are they
free to determine the consequences of their actions? Once a
word is uttered, once a deed was done, and the consequences
are absolutely beyond the control of man. Are men free to
determine what kind of mind they should have, the kind of
talent they should possess, or whether they should become
a genius or not? Again, is man free to determine his evolution in life, how long he should live, and what he should
accomplish in life? When we consider human existence soberly,
we then perceive that man is all through determined. Man is
no more free to determine himself than the animal is free to

determine itself, or as any material reality is free to determine itself. Man cannot determine how the external realities should affect him, nor can he determine how facts, ideas and truths should affect him, and therefore man cannot determine his own reactions. All is determined by God, and what God determines man cannot change. Since the soul is an idea of God, when God conceives the soul of man, he already determines the nature of the soul. Since the will is the desire inherent in the soul, the will is already determined by God. God determines what the soul should desire. Thus we see that the will of man is all through determined. Since the will is determined, the whole man is determined. The soul is not free to determine what it should desire and what it should not desire, what it should perceive, feel, think, do and to enjoy or suffer the consequences of its conduct. There is no freedom of will, and therefore man is not free.

But this raises a profound problem. God determines the existence, the thoughts, the feelings and actions of men. Throughout the past mankind, with few exceptions, believed that they were free to determine their existence, their thoughts, feelings, actions and the consequences of their actions. Since God determines everything, God also determined that men should believe that they are free to determine their existence, thoughts, feelings, actions and the consequences of their actions. Therefore this belief must contain a deep truth, it must be a true belief. But this belief is in complete disagreement with the facts of existence. How, then, can this belief be reconciled with the truth we just considered. This we shall presently see.

When considering freedom and necessity, we saw that everything in existence is determined by its nature. But, just because everything is determined by its nature, everything is free to exist and act according to its nature; and nothing in creation can determine a thing to exist and to act contrary to its nature. Thus freedom and necessity are correlatives, both are involved in the nature of things. This is the solution of the problem before us. God determines the existence, the nature, the thoughts, the feelings, the actions and the consequences of the actions of every man. But, just because of this, man is determined to feel free to determine his existence, his thoughts, feelings, actions and the consequences of his action. What does this mean? It means this. As far as God is concerned, and with relation to God, man is absolutely determined by God, and man cannot change this. But, just because man is absolutely determined by God, nothing in existence can determine man, that is, nothing in existence can change or affect the determination of God. This means that with relation to all of existence man is absolutely free. Man comes into existence absolutely determined by God; his nature, his thoughts, feelings, actions and the consequences of his action are all determined by God. Armed with this absolute determination, man faces the world with its infinite conditions, circumstances and events. All these can have no effect on him, because he was already determined by God, the world and its conditions, circumstances and events can have no effect on man, therefore with relation to them he is absolutely free. This is the freedom of which man is conscious, and this is the reason why man feels that he is free to determine his existence, his thoughts, feelings, actions and the consequences of his actions. This is the profound truth which mankind perceived, but which they did not understand. Because they did not understand this truth, they fell into a deep error. The error was this: they naively believed that they are absolutely free, not only with relation to the world, but also with relation to God. But this was a deep error. Men are free with relation to the world, but they are determined with relation to God. They are free with relation to the world, just because they are determined by God. If God did not determine them, they would be determined by the world. This determination by God constitutes man's destiny.

An idea is not merely a form of thought; inherent in an idea is a purpose. This is true of an idea of man as it is of an idea of God. The soul of man is an idea of God. Inherent in the soul is God's purpose. This purpose of God manifests itself in two kinds of destiny. On the one hand, it is the general destiny of mankind, namely, to attain to explicit reason and become morally autonomous. On the other hand, it is the special destiny of the individual: what he is to become, what he shall accomplish, and how he shall fare in his lifetime. And, just as man cannot change his general destiny, so he cannot change his special individual destiny. The special destiny manifests itself early in life in some special inclination, aptitude and talent or genius. A Moses, a Jesus, a Shakespeare, and the like, is born, and not made. And no matter what the conditions and circumstances may be, nothing in existence will prevent them from realizing their special destiny. On the other hand, ordinary men have the special destiny to remain ordinary men; and nothing that they can do will make of them great men. It is vain for you that ye rise early and sit up late, ye that eat the bread of toil and sorrow: So He giveth unto His beloved in sleep. (Psalms: 127.) Ordinary men are not conscious of their special destiny, as they are not conscious of their general destiny. But great men are more or less conscious of their special destiny, as they are of their general destiny. What is true of individuals is true of peoples, nations, races and the whole human race. In every people, nation, race or the human race as a whole there are some individuals who perceive the special destiny of the people, the nation, the race and the whole human race. For instance, the Jews perceived early that they were destined to become a blessing to mankind, to be the means through whom salvation will come. Again, the leading Americans early perceived that the manifest destiny of the American nation is to bring to mankind political freedom. It was and is so with all peoples, nations and races. When I come to history, I will consider this at great length. These perceptions are not idle phantasies; they are the perceptions of the soul. The soul becomes aware of its destinies early in life. The soul speaks a symbolic language, and most men do not understand that language. But great men do understand that language.

CHAPTER XVI

Forms and Order of Knowledge

114. In the first chapter we learned that knowledge comprehends cause and effect. The perception of cause alone or of effect alone is not knowledge; it is the comprehension of both cause and effect that constitutes knowledge. Again, knowledge implies understanding; they are correlatives, neither can exist without the other. Without a knowledge of the realities in existence there can be no understanding of them; and without an understanding of them, it is not a knowledge of them. Knowledge assumes different forms: ordinary knowledge, science, philosophy, art, religion, and so on indefinitely. We shall see later that the forms of knowledge crystallize themselves in the human mind in a definite order. But, at the outset, we must consider a general problem concerning knowledge. How does the soul acquire knowledge? This is an old problem. Profound thinkers wrote much about this problem, but they did not come to agreement. Some thinkers reached the conclusion that all knowledge is learned by the soul from experience; other thinkers reached the conclusion that, while the soul learns from experience, the basis of knowledge resides in the soul itself. Again, Spinoza and the Kabbalists reached the conclusion that all knowledge is directly imparted to the soul by God. In the following I will briefly consider these several theories. I begin with Spencer.

115. According to Spencer, all knowledge begins with experience, arises out of experience, and depends entirely upon experience. Without experience there could be no knowledge. By experience, however, is to be understood, not only the experience of the individual, but also of the whole race of living

beings. Life is a continuous adjustment of the inner relations to the outer relations, through which adjustment resulted the various forms of life and the corresponding forms of consciousness. These forms of life as well as the corresponding consciousness were determined by the outer conditions of existence. Spencer generalizes this by saying: the outer relations produced the inner relations.

This theory of knowledge brought Spencer into conflict with Kant. According to Kant, though all knowledge arises in experience, not all knowledge begins with experience. There is a basis in our consciousness for certain *a priori* intuitions, concepts and ideas, which are anterior to experience, and which make experience possible. Without these *a priori* intuitions, concepts and ideas, experience and knowledge would be impossible.

Now, Spencer fully realized that the individual, on coming into existence, finds himself in possession of certain ultimate intuitions, concepts and ideas, which are anterior to experience, and which in fact make experience possible. But Spencer maintained that, while to the individual these intuitions, concepts and ideas are *a priori*, to the race of living beings they were *a posteriori;* the race of living beings acquired them only through experience. These ultimate intuitions, concepts and ideas have, in the course of evolution, been rendered organic by the immense accumulation of experience, received partly by the individual, but mainly by all ancestral individuals whose nervous system the individual inherits. Just as the individual, on coming into existence, finds himself in possession of a nervous system, which to him is *a priori*, though to the race of living beings it was *a posteriori;* so, also, does the individual find himself in possession of certain intuitions, concepts and ideas, which, though to him are *a priori*, were to the race of living beings *a posteriori*.

Now, Kant was perfectly well aware of this view—for it was the view of the whole empiric school; nevertheless, Kant insisted that these ultimate intuitions, concepts and ideas, such, for instance, as the intuition of space and time, the categories of the understanding, and the ideas of reason, are *a priori*, not only to the individual, but also to the human race; and that without these ultimate intuitions, concepts and ideas, experience and knowledge would be impossible. We shall presently see that Kant was right and Spencer was wrong.

116. Suppose that in front of a looking glass we pass an infinite number of objects, each of which is to reflect itself in the looking glass. Will the looking glass enrich itself in experience and knowledge by the reflections of those objects, so that it will retain them as experience and knowledge? Surely not, because the looking glass does not meet these reflections with a capacity of its own to retain them and to organize them into knowledge. Now, if life, like the looking glass, were devoid of any *a priori* capacity to retain the effects wrought on it by the outer relations and to organize the resulting sensations into knowledge, it could no more enrich itself by experience than the looking glass by the reflections. It is therefore clear that life must bring into the world of experience a capacity of its own to become conscious of any changes wrought in it by the outer relations, retain the resulting sensations, and organize them into knowledge. But life is not like the looking glass; life is conscious of itself and of its experiences. This consciousness is life's own nature; it possesses that consciousness before it comes into the world of experience, and only by virtue of that consciousness can life have experience and acquire knowledge. Life and consciousness are correlatives, neither can exist without the other; just as without life there can be no consciousness, so without consciousness there can be no life. Therefore, the basis of all knowledge is to be sought, not in experience, but in the ultimate nature of consciousness, that is, in the ultimate nature of life itself. Hence, Kant was right when he maintained that, though all knowledge arises in experience, not all knowledge begins with experience. The ultimate intuitions, concepts and ideas are inherent in consciousness itself, and only by means of them can life acquire experience and knowledge. This will be brought to

light by a closer examination of Spencer's own theory of knowledge.

Spencer admits that the ultimate intuitions, concepts and ideas are *a priori* to the individual; but, he insists, that to the race of living beings they were *a posteriori*. The question, then, arises: how did the race of living beings acquire them? Spencer answers by saying, the race of living beings acquired them gradually. At first, the phenomena wrought certain changes in the early living beings, which changes those beings perceived and remembered. In the course of evolution, those changes increased in frequency and definiteness, leaving ever more enduring and more definite impressions in the living beings, until in time those impressions became organic, so that they were transmitted from parent to offspring. And so, in the course of countless generations of living beings, the accumulated impressions crystallized themselves into definite and permanent states of consciousness; which states of consciousness in the case of man assumed the forms of the ultimate intuitions, concepts and ideas. In this manner Spencer sought to reconcile the empiric school with Kant.

Now, suppose we test this theory of Spencer. Spencer starts in the middle of the story and ends in the middle of the story. But suppose we start from the beginning. According to Spencer, we must assume that life comes into the material world a perfect blank, without any consciousness whatever; for, the granting to life any consciousness means to grant to life also a consciousness of some definite form; which practically would mean to grant at once the very position of Kant. Therefore, we must assume that life came into the material world a perfect blank. Now, if life at the beginning was a perfect blank, and had no capacity of its own to become conscious of its own experience, how could life begin to acquire experience? In that case it could no more acquire experience and knowledge than the looking glass could; life then could no more make a beginning than the looking glass could make a beginning. And, not being able to make a beginning, life could not continue. How, then, could life ever acquire experience and knowledge? Again, according to Spencer, knowledge implies organization, classification and differentiation of experience. If life did not bring with itself the capacity to crystallize knowledge from experience by means of a consciousness of its own, how could life ever acquire the capacity to organize, classify and differentiate experience? This capacity must be anterior to all experience; and, indeed, is the capacity that can make experience possible. Without this capacity, experience—if at all—would be but a mass of confusion and chaos. It is perfectly clear that the impressions and the resulting sensations, which come in undetermined, discrete and manifold streams, cannot of their own accord organize themselves into knowledge. That act of organization must be done by something else, and that something else can be nothing else than life itself. Hence, we must grant to life the capacity to organize the impressions and the resulting sensations, experienced in its converse with the material objects, into knowledge; for, if we deny to life this capacity, then the question remains: how and by what means did life acquire this capacity?

It will not do, as Spencer does, to hide oneself behind an Unknowable and say that in some incomprehensible way the Unknowable manifests himself in consciousness and in the material world, and that, somehow, life acquires knowledge from experience. This is a very poor dodge which is entirely inadmissible in philosophy. One that undertakes to formulate a theory of knowledge must go to the root of the matter and tell us in most definite terms how knowledge ever comes. If the Unknowable in some incomprehensible manner manifests itself in consciousness, then the knowledge which man possesses came, not from experience, but from the Unknowable. What becomes of Spencer's theory?

117. Clearly, then, we must grant at the outset that life, on coming into the material world, brings with itself a consciousness and a capacity to become aware of its experiences, organize the impressions received from the external world and the result-

ing sensations into definite states of consciousness, which in time become organized into knowledge. And the consciousness which life brings with itself is not a blank, a chaos, it is a consciousness of the fact that the phenomenal world exists and manifests itself in accordance with a certain order, proceeding in accordance with definite laws, and that life would have to adjust itself to that order and to those laws. Life, therefore, brings with itself a sensibility to perceive objects of experience, an understanding to organize and to interpret those objects of experience, and a reason to organize the interpretations of the understanding. Therefore, the ultimate intuitions, concepts and ideas are *a priori*, not only to the individual, but also to the whole race of living beings, because life possessed them before it entered into the world of experience, and only by virtue of them could life have experience and acquire knowledge. Let us consider the moneron —the primordial living cells, the first form of life on earth. The first moneron had absolutely no previous experience in the material world. The moneron felt hunger, and it moved about to find something to satisfy its hunger. Not every thing the moneron found could satisfy its hunger; the moneron had to choose. Now, the moneron had absolutely no previous experience, it had no hunger, and did not know how to satisfy its hunger. How came the moneron to know that it needed some food, and that it could find the food by searching for it? Hic Rhodus, hic salta! Let Spencer tell how? By his theory he could never explain. It is therefore clear that the moneron possessed *a priori* the necessary consciousness to feel hunger and to know that it could satisfy its hunger by some food which it could find by searching for it. Let us say that the moneron itself acted, as it is called, instinctively—whatever this may mean—but life itself was fully conscious of what it did through the moneron. The moneron procreated itself, it provided food and shelter for its progeny. How did the moneron know about this? The moneron increased and multiplied, the progeny organized themselves, and brought out a higher form of life. How did the monera know to organize themselves in a higher form of life. How did the infinite forms of life come into existence, and, finally, how did man come into existence? Do the cells of the human body know how to create a man? How could living beings bring out ever higher forms of life, could they learn this from experience? Did the animal ancestors of man learn from experience to create man? Can any one rationally entertain this view? The answer is: all this was already implicit in life from the beginning. Hence whatever capacity life possesses, it possessed it *a priori*.

This view will find its rationale and corroboration in the universal manifestation of life. During the intra-uterine existence of a living being, it does not need a mouth to eat, eyes to see, ears to hear, and the other organs to function in later life. Nevertheless, each living being, before it leaves its mother's womb, and before it enters into the material world of independent existence, perfects to some degree and prepares the organs and their appropriate capacities, which it will have to use in the material world outside of the mother's womb. Here, then, we see how life works. Just as each living being comes into existence adequately prepared and equipped with organs and capacities that will become necessary to cope with the outer material conditions of existence; so, also, life as a whole came into the material world prepared and equipped with the capacities that would become necessary to function in the material world. Therefore, consciousness of a definite nature was prior to experience, and made experience and knowledge possible. This is what Kant meant. Knowledge arises out of experience, but not all knowledge begins with experience. That Kant's position is incontestably true will become clear when we reflect on the nature of things. All manifestations of Nature's powers are *a priori* in their nature. A few illustrations will make it clear.

Light possesses a nature and a capacity for motion that are anterior to independent to the objects it reflects. Nevertheless, light must meet with reflecting objects to manifest itself and its nature. In the absence of intercepting and reflecting objects, light could not manifest itself. Likewise it is with life. Life possesses a nature and a capacity to function in the material world that are anterior to and independent of the material conditions and objects of existence. Nevertheless, life must meet the material conditions and the objects to manifest itself. In the absence of the material conditions and objects, life could not manifest itself. But, just as it would be absurd to say that, because without reflecting objects light could not manifest itself, therefore light acquired its nature from the reflecting objects; so, also, it is absurd to say that, because without the material conditions and the objects life cannot manifest itself, therefore the nature of life is the product of the material conditions of existence. And the same is true of consciousness. Consciousness is an activity that follows a nature of its own—a nature that is anterior to and independent of all objects of experience. And, as in the former cases, so in this case it will be absurd to say that, because without the objects of experience consciousness cannot manifest itself, therefore the nature of consciousness is the product of the objects of experience. Hence, we must grant to life an *a priori* nature and *a priori* consciousness. And only by virtue of that *a priori* consciousness life could acquire experience, crystallize knowledge and attain to a multiplicity of forms. And that *a priori* consciousness was a consciousness of the fact, that the phenomenal world presents itself in the forms of space and time, proceeds in accordance with the categories of causation and the like, and that in accordance with that order life would have to function. Therefore the ultimate intuitions, concepts and ideas are *a priori*, not only to the individual, but also to all living beings, to life itself. Kant, therefore, was right, and Spencer was wrong, and with this falls to the ground the whole empirical school of philosophy—a philosophy that vitiated the work of the scientists and philosophers.

118. Again, was Kant entirely right? We shall presently see that he was only partially right. Assuming now, as we must, that consciousness is *a priori* in its nature and capacity, how can consciousness comprehend the objects of experience? Or, in other words, how is truth possible? Spencer and Kant agree

that truth is the accurate correspondence between the inner relations and the outer relations, it is the agreement between cognitions and the objects of cognitions. According to Spencer, life
is impossible unless there is an accurate correspondence between
the inner relations and the outer relations. And there is no doubt
that, without such correspondence, life is impossible. Hence, the
question of truth is to life the most vital question. At its peril
life must find out the truth about the material world, its realities and its conditions. Since this truth is only the perception and
the accurate correspondence between the inner relations and
the outer relations—how and by whom is this correspondence
established?

Spencer tells us, this correspondence is established by the
outer relations. He expresses this by saying: the harmony between the inner relations and the outer relations arises from the
fact that the outer relations produced the inner relations. On
the other hand, Kant tells us that this accurate correspondence,
this harmony between the inner relations and the outer relations,
arises from the fact that the inner relations produced the outer
relations. Spencer agrees with Kant that consciousness comprehends only phenomena, and not the noumenon, that is, the ultimate reality. But, while Spencer assumed that consciousness is
a perfect blank on which the phenomena produced impressions
corresponding with the phenomena, Kant assumed that the phenomena are a perfect blank on which consciousness impressed
certain forms which correspond with consciousness. Their respective views may be compared to a seal and the wax. Spencer
regarded the phenomena as the seal and the consciousness as
the wax, while Kent regarded the consciousness as the seal and
the phenomena as the wax. Since, according to Spencer, the seal
of the phenomena produced the impressions on the wax of con·
sciousness, and since according to Kant, the seal of consciousness
produced the impressions on the phenomena, the seal and its
impressions on the wax must agree. This agreement constitutes
the accurate correspondence between the inner relations and the

outer relations, or the agreement between cognition and the objects of cognition. Let us examine this position more closely.

Both Spencer and Kant assure us that from their philosophy they banished all dogmas and mere assumptions, and that they proceeded in a most thoroughly scientific manner. If so, we have a right to examine their theories most critically. And now the following questions presents itself. What warrant did Spencer have for the assumption that, while the phenomena have a definite nature and possess definite characteristics, consciousness, which is also a phenomenon, is a perfect blank, and can acquire a nature and definite characteristics only from the phenomena? Likewise, what warrant did Kant have for the assumption that, while consciousness, which is a phenomenon, has a nature and possesses definite characteristics, the phenomena are a perfect blank and can receive their nature and forms only from consciousness? Neither of them had any basis in fact and truth for his assumption; both made their respective assumption without the least justification, and without any basis in reality and in reason. That Spencer's assumption was without any warrant we already saw, when we convinced ourselves that consciousness is not a perfect blank, and that it had a nature of its own, independent of and anterior to its converse with the phenomena. Therefore, the correspondence between the inner relations and the outer relations could not arise, as Spencer maintained, from the fact that the outer relations produced the inner relations. Likewise, we shall presently see that Kant's assumption was equally without warrant, and therefore the correspondence between the inner relations and the outer relations could not arise, as Kant maintained, from the fact that the inner relations produced the outer relations. To perceive this, we must re-examine Kant's theory of knowledge.

According to Kant, phenomena are not things by themselves, but only the play of our representations of them, all of which are in the end only determinations of the internal sense; and the understanding is not only a power of making rules by a comparison of phenomena, but is itself the law-giver of nature;

and without the understanding there would be no nature, because phenomena cannot exist without us. Kant tells us: However exaggerated and absurd it may sound, that the understanding is itself the source of the laws of nature and of its formal unity, such a statement is nevertheless true. The whole Critique of Pure Reason is but an elaborate presentation of the view, that our sensibility and understanding determine the phenomena, their laws and their interactions. Now, if nature and the phenomena were perfect blanks, waiting to be created by our consciousness, what basis is there for knowledge? Knowledge implies a consciousness that knows, and objects that are known by consciousness. Consciousness assumes the objects to be what they are, and consciousness endeavors to comprehend the objects. Consciousness itself attests to the fact that the objects are distinct from itself and are distinct from it. Consciousness is the last court of appeal. And if there is a conflict between our consciousness and the philosophers, we must not for a moment hesitate to accept the verdict of our consciousness. Let us grant that the objects in themselves are not what they appear to our consciousness, but the objects themselves must possess a nature of their own, and which in our consciousness assume certain forms. These affections of our consciousness or the representations, as Kant would call them, partake of the nature of the external objects and of our own consciousness. Suppose we look on several objects. Some appear to be green, others appear to be red, others appear to be blue, and so on. Let us grant that the objects in themselves have no color at all. Why, then, do they appear to us in different colors? This must be so, because the objects must differ from one another in structure so that in our consciousness they reflect themselves in different colors. Hence the difference in colors which our consciousness perceives in the objects must reflect differences in the natures of the objects, and these differences are independent of our consciousness. It is the same with taste, and with all other properties of the realities of existence. How, then, can Kant assume that the nature and characteristics of the objects of knowledge are determined by our consciousness?

Kant tells us that the apprehension of the manifold of phenomena is always successive; the presentation of parts follows one upon another. In other words, the states of consciousness, the sensations and the perceptions follow one another in succession. From our states of consciousness, therefore, we could not distinguish between a static and a dynamic object, that is, between a house that stands fixed to the ground and a boat that is gliding down the stream; because, in both cases, the apprehension of the phenomena is always successive. Whether one looks upon a boat as it is gliding down the stream or he examines a house, beginning with the right, going to the left, following from top to the bottom; in both cases the impressions upon the observer are successive. From his own impressions the observer should not be able to tell whether the house is fixed or the boat is gliding down the stream. Kant himself speaks of this, but he tries by subtle sophistries to elude the question. The question is: what enables us to distinguish between a boat gliding down the stream and a house fixed to the ground? If the phenomena are determined by our consciousness, and our consciousness is successive in its states, then we could never distinguish between a moving object and an object that is fixed to the ground. Clearly, then, the distinction must reside in the phenomena themselves, and our consciousness perceive this distinction.

Consider the following. Astronomy reveals the existence of myriads of stars, which are distinct from one another and in different parts of infinite space. If it is consciousness that creates the phenomena, and the stars are only phenomena, how comes it that our consciousness creates myriads of stars that differ from one another in numerous ways and are in different parts of infinite space? What is there in consciousness that determines the infinite matter to divide itself into myriads of stars? And why, again, does the astronomer turn his gaze towards the heaven to study the stars, instead of directing his gaze into his own consciousness and, by introspection, to create within his consciousness the myriads of stars? What is true of the stars is equally true of all infinite realities in existence. How and why does consciousness create infinite different realities, beings and men, each having a nature and characteristics of their own, independently of consciousness? Again, if it is consciousness that creates all infinite realities in existence, then consciousness should have known and understood them all at once. Why, then, does consciousness require infinite time and infinite labor to acquire a knowledge and understanding of the realities of existence?

Again, Kant speaks of the Thing in Itself. What the Thing in Itself is we shall never know. The question is: Are the phenomena in any way related to the Thing in Itself or not? In other words, does the Thing in Itself manifest itself through the phenomena or not? If the Thing in Itself does manifest itself through the phenomena, then the phenomena in some way manifest the nature of the Thing in Itself. On the other hand, if the Thing in Itself does not manifest itself through the phenomena, then the phenomena have an absolutely independent existence. If we are to assume, as Kant does, that the phenomena are only creations of our consciousness, and not manifestations of the Thing in Itself, then we live in a world of our own creation, besides which there is nothing alse. Then we can create a world just as we please. Hic Rhodus, hic Salta! Let Kant show how he could create a world as he pleased? Oh, if only this were true, then we certainly would create for ourselves a world infinitely more beautiful and infinitely more full of delight than any air castles that men ever built!

Kant's theory, like Spencer's theory, when rigorously examined, proves itself to be inherently false; and, when both theories are put into opposition to each other, they cancel and neutralize each other, and we are then left without any theory of knowledge. What, then, is knowledge, and how do we acquire knowledge. For a true theory of knowledge, we must go to Spinoza. This is our next step.

119. Spinoza contemplates existence as the manifestation of God
—a being possessing infinite attributes, each of which manifests
the infinite and eternal nature of God. To us are revealed only
two attributes: Thought and Extension. The attributes are in
themselves, and of their own accord they cannot unite. It is
God by his ideas that unites these attributes in infinite different
combinations. These combinations, which are the attributes
thought and extension comprehended by the ideas of God, are
the realities of existence. God's power is equal in all his attributes, his power of action is equal to his power of thought, and
between his actions and thought there is a correspondence. As
he expressed it: The order and connexion of ideas is the same
as the order and connexion of things. The attribute extension
manifests itself in the material realities, and the attribute thought
manifests itself in our consciousness. Therefore between our
consciousness and the material realities there is a correspondence.
An idea of God comprehends both thought and extension. Since
our soul is an idea of God, it comprehends both thought and
extension; that is, it comprehends the external material realities
and their reflections in the mind. But the soul of man is not separate from and independent of God; the soul of man is an idea
of God, it is in God and part of God. Hence it is God who
through the soul thinks and acts. Thus the soul acquires a knowledge and understanding of the external world and of itself. And,
just as our body conforms with extension, that is, with the nature of the material world, so the mind conforms with thought,
that is, with ideas that realize themselves in the material realities. Man can know and understand only as much as God reveals to him, and no more. Just as God gives him life, so God
gives him knowledge and understanding. And, just as God determines the existence and the nature of man, so he determines
his knowledge and understanding. Without God nothing can
be or conceived. This is the whole truth about knowledge.
There may be infinite errors, but there is only one truth. Once
we know the truth about knowledge, then all erroneous theories
concerning knowledge fall to the ground. A monistic philoso-

phy recognizes only one source of knowledge, and that is God himself. Besides God and independently of him there is no knowledge. And now that we know what knowledge is, the next step is to consider the order of knowledge.

CHAPTER XVII

Order of Knowledge

120. We saw that progress is towards the destiny inherent in existence. The progress in human knowledge is according to this order of progress. But we must now consider this order of progress more closely. The progress of the Absolute is from the centre to the periphery. The Absolute starts within itself, it reflects on itself, and forms of itself an idea. This idea is the Infinite Intellect, God. God conceives the Absolute in infinite aspects or attributes. God himself being an idea of the Absolute conceives infinite ideas. By means of these infinite ideas God comprehends the infinite attributes in infinite modes, and these infinite modes are the infinite realities of existence. This we considered before, but we must now consider this more closely. The Absolute is absolute thought—thought without form, it is the eternal and infinite substance out of which all realities were carved out. Absolute thought moves with infinite velocity. To bring out a world of infinite realities, the velocity of absolute thought must be reduced. Absolute thought is reduced in its velocity, and it becomes reason. Reason is reduced in its velocity and it becomes light. Light is the ultimate unit of matter. Thus the infinite space—which, as we saw, is absolute thought—is now filled with infinite units of matter, which are in a diffused state. This is the darkness and chaos of which the Bible speaks. Thus we see that the Absolute passed from the centre to its periphery, the infinite units of matter scattered through infinite space is the periphery of the Absolute. And now that the Absolute reached its periphery, it moves back to the centre. The infinite units of matter are integrated, and thus come into existence the stars, the planets and all other realities in existence. Thus we

see that the progress of the Absolute is from the centre to the periphery; and, when it reaches the periphery, further progress of the Absolute is back to the centre, and thus a world is created.

But the order of progress of man is just the reverse. Human progress is from the periphery to the centre; and, when the centre is reached, further progress is from the centre back to the periphery. A brief consideration of human progress will make this clear. Men began first to acquaint themselves with external things, and then they began to acquaint themselves with themselves. Men began their acquaintance with themselves at the periphery; they first acquired a knowledge of the surface of their bodies, their forms and functions; then they proceeded to acquaint themselves with their inner bodily organs; and, finally, they reached the cell—the ultimate and central unit of the human body. And now that men acquired a knowledge of the cell, all further progress in biology, psychology, sociology and history begin with the cell. Human progress assumed at first a religious aspect, then a political aspect, then an economic aspect, and finally a human aspect. The religious aspect was accompanied by metaphysical contemplations; the political aspect was accompanied by philosophical speculations; the economic aspect was accompanied by scientific investigations; and, finally, the human aspect now is accompanied by self-consciousness. At first, men bestowed their profoundest thoughts on God, the soul, the immortality of the soul; then they began to bestow their thoughts on the material world, the stars and the earth; then they began to bestow their thoughts on the economic modes of production and distribution; and only now they begin to bestow their thoughts on themselves. Man was the last concern of man himself. Man to himself is the centre of existence. And now that man reached the centre, all further progress will be from man to existence. Man will now begin to reinterpret existence in terms of man. Know thyself, which should have been the beginning, was in the end of human progress thus far. We already saw that anthropomorphism is the only possible and correct view of existence, and anthropomorphism is interpreting existence

from the centre, from man himself. We can now understand
the reason why all human progress was from the periphery to
the centre. The reason is that all creation is from the periphery
of the Absolute to its centre; and therefore man whose destiny is
towards God, therefore his progress had to be from the periphery to the centre.

The progress of the soul is also from the periphery to the
centre. The soul starts out with the senses—the most peripheral
faculty of the soul. By the senses the soul perceives things, but
it does not understand them. Then the soul brings out the understanding. By means of the understanding the soul brings to the
fore concepts by which it is able also to understand the nature
of things. Then, in succession, the soul brings out the faculties
of judgment, intuition, reason, and finally it becomes the intellect. The soul which in the beginning in its complete state of
implicitness was will has now become most explicit in the intellect. Now the soul has attained to self-consciousness, the soul
reached the centre. Once it reached the centre, the soul comprehends itself, existence and God. By means of these different
faculties the soul acquires different categories of knowledge.
The nearer a faculty is to the centre of progress the deeper does
it penetrate into the nature of things and of existence. Philosophers divided human knowledge into different categories. These
different categories of knowledge relate to the different faculties of the soul. Let us consider the different categories of
knowledge.

121. Spencer divides knowledge into three categories: ordinary
knowledge, scientific knowledge and philosophic knowledge.
Ordinary knowledge is ununified; scientific knowledge is partially unified; philosophic knowledge is completely unified
knowledge. The difference between ordinary knowledge and
the other two categories of knowledge is evident; but the difference between scientific knowledge and philosophic knowledge
must be pointed out. Whatever be the attribute, aspect or mode
of existence it is eternal and infinite. Substance, time, space,

matter, motion, force, light, life, thought, and so on—each is eternal and infinite. Geometry concerns itself about the forms of space. Space is infinite and eternal. Now, geometry may become infinite, and yet it will be limited to space only. Again, physics concerns itself about space, time, matter, motion and force. Each of these aspects is infinite and eternal. Physics may become infinite, yet it will be limited to these aspects of existence only, it will not comprehend life, thought, mind, soul, and the like. And so it is with all sciences. Hence, while the knowledge within the scope of a science is unified and may become infinite, yet the knowledge is only of a part of existence. It is only when all knowledge, when all the sciences are unified into one system of thought, which comprehends all aspects of existence, only then is philosophy born. Philosophy, then, is completely unified knowledge.

Again, Spinoza divided knowledge into three categories: ordinary knowledge; scientific knowledge, and intuitive knowledge. Ordinary knowledge is derived from ordinary experience; scientific knowledge is acquired by means of reason; and intuitive knowledge is acquired by means of the intellect. By means of intuitive knowledge we attain to a knowledge of God. By intuitive knowledge Spinoza does not mean what ordinarily is understood by this, as knowledge acquired by means of intuition. Spinoza means the direct knowledge attained by the intellect. It is intuitive, because this knowledge is not acquired by inference, but by direct seeing. Now, while Spencer does not point out the relation of the different kinds of knowledge to the faculties of the soul, Spinoza does relate the different categories of knowledge to the different faculties of the soul. Up till now I spoke of the soul as an idea of God. But we see in men different kinds of soul. We must consider this a little more closely.

According to the Kabbalah, there are five souls: Nephesh, Ruach, Neshomoh, Chioh and Yechidoh. All living beings of all degrees of evolution possess a nephesh. The nephesh is the soul in its most implicit state, it is inherent in the blood of living beings, it is the will and manifests itself in and through the senses and the understanding. By means of the nephesh living beings are able to adjust themselves to the material conditions of existence, and thus acquire a limited knowledge of the material world. The ruach is the soul explicit to a limited extent. The ruach manifests itself in judgment and intuition. This is also to a limited extent true of all living beings. All living beings have to some extent the faculties of judgment and intuition, which in their case it is called instinct. The neshomoh is reason. Only man has a neshomoh. The neshomoh, reason, differentiates man from all other living beings. The Bible tells us that, at first, Elohim created man. Then Jehovah-Elohim breathed into his nostrils a Nishmath Chaim, and he became a rational person. The Nishmath Chaim is the neshomoh, reason; it is the soul that gives life to man. Before man attains to reason, he is only a living animal, the man in him is still dead. The man comes to life only when reason comes to him. Aristotle speaks of active reason and passive reason; passive reason is what Kant calls practical reason. Passive reason brings out the sciences, but active reason brings out philosophy. Next is the Chioh. Finally is the yechidoh. This fifth soul is given to such men as Moses, Jesus and the like. The yechidoh is the intellect. In the yechidoh the soul becomes wholly explicit, self-conscious and conscious of God. Now, whether these are five distinct souls, that is, five distinct ideas of God, or it is one and the same soul that in its evolution becomes, in succession, these several faculties, it is clear that each soul or the soul through each faculty can comprehend existence only to a limited extent; it is only when the soul becomes wholly explicit, or the yechidoh comes to man, that then his soul comprehends the totality of existence. We considered the senses and the understanding, judgment, intuition, reason and the intellect. Now we must reconsider them with relation to the different kinds of knowledge.

122. According to Aristotle, reason is both active and passive. This is also true of intuition. Intuition is both active and passive. Passive intuition perceives transcendental realities, but not the

relations among them. A transcendental reality perceived by passive intuition is what Kant calls the schema. The schema is a perfect form of an idea. Now, religion and art perceive schemas, that is, perfect forms of ideas. An idea of God is perfect, but the material realization of an idea of God in the material world is not always according to the perfection of the idea. For instance, the circle or the sphere, as an idea, is perfect, but the realization of the circle or this sphere in the material world is not always perfect. Now, religion and art perceive the perfect form of an idea. In this respect they agree, being both products of intuition, and for this reason art and religion always cooperated. But because religion is the product of active intuition, and art is the product of passive reason, their effect on men is different. Art pleases and may even elevate the soul; but only religion can stir man and determine him to work, to struggle, to suffer and even to die to realize the perfect form which religion through active intuition reveals. An illustration will make it clear.

God conceived the idea of Man. This idea is the prototype of all human beings that existed and will exist. This idea is perfect, and so also is its form. But, as in the case of the circle, the sphere and all other ideas, so in the case of man, the perfect prototype idea and its perfect form never realized themselves in men. Now, art and religion, by means of intuition, perceived the perfect form of the prototype idea of Man. This form was symbolized as a Moses, a Buddha, a Jesus, and the like. And thus religion and art, through various means, such as statues, paintings, epics, myths, and the like, endeavored to reveal to mankind the perfect form of the prototype idea of Man. Thus far, religion and art cooperated, but their effect on mankind was different. Art pleased and even elevated the soul, but it left mankind passive. But religion stirred and aroused mankind, and determined them to work, to struggle, to suffer and even to die to realize the perfect form of the prototype idea of man. A Moses, a Buddha or a Jesus, seen through the medium of art, leaves the observer passive; but the same symbols seen through the medium of religion arouses the observer to activity. The reason for this difference is this: In art the soul is passive, in religion the soul is active.

Intuition perceives form, reason perceives an idea. A form is individualistic and passive, an idea is universal and active. We saw that an idea is a living, conscious and thinking being. Form is fixed, inflexible and incapable of change, while an idea is fluid, flexible and capable of change. This is the reason why art and religion are fixed, inflexible and incapable of change; while philosophy and science, which are the products of reason are fluid, flexible and constantly change. We saw that progress is a movement towards the realization of destiny, it is a movement, not of form, but of an idea. Intuition cannot perceive the destiny of things, it is reason that can perceive destiny. And now let us consider the different categories of art.

There are five categories of art: architecture, sculpture, painting, music and literature. The lowest of them is architecture, and the highest of them is literature. In these arts we see the evolution of the soul from implicitness to explicitness. Let us consider the distinctive characteristics of these arts.

Architecture is the lowest art, it symbolizes the world of matter. In architecture, matter stands before us in all its massiveness and implicitness. There is an idea in architecture, but it is hidden behind the mass of matter. Architecture is the product of the soul in its implicit state. Whatever idea architecture symbolizes, the idea is not manifest.

Sculpture is higher than architecture. Here matter is reduced to a minimum, and the idea is beginning to manifest itself on the surface. The soul is still at the periphery and is only partially explicit, but to the extent that the soul is explicit it manifests itself in sculpture. The soul in sculpture symbolizes individuality.

Painting is higher than sculpture. Here matter is retired into the background and reduced to two dimensions. Like the spirit of Elohim hovered over the face of the waters, so the soul here hovers over matter; yet it rests on matter, even though it is now two-dimensional. Painting is pure form, it is the schema, disembodied form. In painting the soul is still implicit, it has not yet become conscious of itself.

Music is higher than painting. Here matter is entirely eliminated. The soul here speaks through disembodied sounds and melodies and symphonies. The soul is now free to concern itself about itself, its emotions, sentiments and aspirations. But the soul is still within itself, and therefore speaks an implicit language—the language of music.

Literature is higher than music, it is the highest of the arts produced by passive intuition. Here the soul comes into relations with the external world, comprehends it, and speaks an explicit language, though still an intuitive language.

All these arts are the products of passive intuition.

Religion is the highest product of active intuition. Here the soul comes into relation with the transcendental world; it perceives transcendental realities and truths, but not the relations among them, because intuition does not perceive relations. For this reason religion is, like the monads of Leibnitz, shut up in itself. One religion does not know what is in another religion, and religion is not concerned about the material world. Religion is intolerant, one religion cannot tolerate another religion. So much for the products of intuition.

Philosophy is the product of explicit reason. Reason perceives the relations among transcendental realities and truths. A relation is an idea. For this reason philosophy speaks the language of ideas. While the arts are concerned about forms, philosophy is concerned about ideas. Philosophy comprehends all ideas in one idea. Consider the idea of evolution. Evolution comprehends all aspects of infinite and eternal existence. Evolution is an idea, and not a form. In philosophy the soul comes into relation with the whole of existence. For this reason philosophy speaks a rational and most explicit language.

Since philosophy is the complete unification of all knowledge, it necessarily follows that philosophy comes into relation with all the arts, all sciences and religion. But I will point out here the relation between philosophy and music, and philosophy and religion.

123. Music and philosophy. Spencer tells us that music is the language of the emotions; the emotions express themselves through the implicit language of music. As is usual with Spencer, he begins in the middle of the story. Music is the language of the emotions, but the emotions themselves are the language of the states of the soul. Hence, it would be more correct to say that music is the implicit language of the soul. On the other hand, Schopenhauer tells us that music is the subjective, immediate and implicit language of the will. Philosophy is the objective, mediate and explicit language of the will. While through music the will speaks directly and immediately, through philosophy the will speaks through the medium of ideas. Music is implicit philosophy, and philosophy is explicit music. To understand what Schopenhauer tells us, we must briefly consider his philosophy.

According to Schopenhauer, the world presents itself as will and idea. The will is primordial, it is the substance of existence, it is subjective, implicit and unconscious. To use Spinoza's expression, the will is in itself. The essence of the will is desire, it desires to know itself. The will, therefore, endeavors to come out from its implicitness and unconsciousness; it reflects on itself, and acquires ideas of itself. Through these ideas the will becomes conscious of itself. The will then objectifies itself by clothing the ideas with material forms. These material forms constitute the world of realities. Thus the world consists of will and ideas. The will in its implicit state speaks the language of music, and in its explicit state the will speaks the language of philosophy. Thus music is implicit philosophy, and philosophy is explicit music.

Now, we saw that the will is the soul in its implicit state, and the intellect is the soul in its explicit state. In other words, the soul is both will and intellect. Hence we can say, music is the implicit language of the soul in its implicit state, philosophy is the explicit language of the soul in its explicit state. In music the soul is concerned about itself, its emotions, sentiments and aspirations; in philosophy the soul is concerned about itself and existence, its relation to existence, and the destiny of itself and existence.

Religion and philosophy. In religion intuition attains its highest and most active development; in philosophy reason attains its highest and most active development. When intuition and reason attain their highest and most active development, then they unite and become the intellect. Intuition is the father, reason is the mother, and the intellect is the son. In the son, the father and the mother merge and become one. Hence, when religion and philosophy attain their highest development and most active, then they unite and become the monistic philosophy. Thus the destiny of religion and philosophy is to become the monistic philosophy. The monistic philosophy will unify all knowledge and will comprehend the totality of existence as absolutely one. We must bear this in mind. The different categories of knowledge and the different arts, though distinct from one another, yet they are only differentiations of one eternal and infinite knowledge of existence. All categories of knowledge are organically related to one another, they are interdependent, and cooperate with one another. There can be no science without philosophy, as there can be no philosophy without science; there can be no art without philosophy, as there can be no philosophy without art; and there can be no religion without philosophy, as there can be no philosophy without religion. This must be so, because all knowledge is the knowledge of one and the same soul, and all knowledge of the soul is the knowledge imparted by God to the soul. We saw that all human progress is from the periphery to the centre. And the same is true of the order of knowledge. From architecture, at the periphery, to the monistic philosophy, at the centre, the soul passed from the state of complete implicitness to the state of complete explicitness. Now, man not only thinks, he also feels. Hence, the next subject to be considered are the feelings and emotions.

CHAPTER XVIII

The Feelings and the Emotions

124. The body is a mode of the attribute extension, the mind is a mode of the attribute thought, and the soul is an idea of God. The soul acts through the body and thinks through the mind. Whatever affects the body simultaneously affects the mind, and the soul is conscious of this. As between thought and extension there is a correspondence, so between the mind and the body there is a correspondence. And the soul is conscious of this correspondence. The affections are of two categories: feelings and emotions. Much has been written about the distinction between a feeling and an emotion; yet, when we consider all that has been said and written by philosophers and psychologists about the feelings and the emotions, we perceive that they were not clear about the distinction between them. I simplify the matter as follows. An affection which pertains primarily to the body and the mind gives rise to a feeling; an affection which pertains primarily to the soul gives rise to an emotion. For instance, hunger pertains primarily to the body and the mind; hence hunger gives rise to a feeling of hunger. On the other hand, love pertains primarily to the soul; hence love gives rise to an emotion. Here I will not concern myself about the feelings; here I will concern myself about the emotions. In his Ethics, Spinoza devoted much space to the consideration of the various emotions. What he tells us about the emotions is profound and true, and the reader will do well to refer to the Ethics for an adequate understanding of the various emotions. But here I will give a brief outline of Spinoza's theory of the emotions.

125. Spinoza recognizes only three primary emotions: desire, joy and sorrow. Strictly speaking there is only one primary

emotion, namely, desire; joy and sorrow are only the correlatives of desire. We saw that desire is the essence of existence. It was the desire of the Absolute to manifest itself that brought out the material world. What is absolute, infinite and eternal is absolute, infinite and eternal in every part thereof. Hence desire is the essence of every reality and of every being in existence, and this desire is infinite and eternal. The desire inherent in a living cell to manifest itself is infinite and eternal; one cell can give rise to infinite cells in infinite time; one acorn can give rise to infinite oak trees and infinite acorns; and so it is with every reality and being. Likewise the desire inherent in the human soul is infinite and eternal. The human soul desires infinitely and eternally, it desires to comprehend the whole of infinite and eternal existence, it desires to attain to the highest perfection and eternal happiness. It is this desire that manifests itself in the correlatives, joy and sorrow.

What is joy, and what is sorrow? Joy is the emotion of the soul when it passes to a higher state of perfection; sorrow is an emotion of the soul when it passes to a lower state of perfection. What we must be clear about is this. Joy is not the higher perfection itself, and sorrow is not the lower perfection itself. Joy is the passing to higher perfection, and sorrow is the passing to lower perfection. Spinoza makes this very explicit. He tells us:—

I say passage, for joy is not perfection itself. If a man were born with the perfection to which he passes, he would possess it without the affect of joy; a truth which will appear the more clearly from the affect of sorrow, which is the opposite of joy. For that sorrow consists in the passage to a less perfection, but not in the less perfection itself, no one can deny, since in so far as a man shares in any perfection he cannot be sad. Nor can we say that sorrow consists in the privation of a greater perfection, for privation is nothing. But the affect of sorrow is a reality, and it therefore must be the reality of the passage to a lower perfection, or the reality by which man's power of acting is diminished or limited.

Spinoza bases his whole theory of the emotions upon the

following proposition. If anything increases, diminishes, helps or limits the body's power of action, the idea of that thing increases, diminishes, helps or limits the mind's power of thought. When the body's power of action and the mind's power of thought are increased, the soul passes to higher perfection and feels joy. On the other hand, when the body's power of action and the mind's power of thought are diminished, the soul passes to lower perfection and feels sorrow. The soul starts out in a state of complete implicitness, but inherent in the soul is the desire to become infinitely explicit. For this purpose, the soul opens up the senses and brings out the faculties of the mind, culminating in the intellect, when the soul becomes wholly explicit. Therefore, when anything increases the body's power of action and the mind's power of thought, the soul passes to higher perfection and greater explicitness, and feels joy. On the other hand, when anything diminishes the body's power of action and the mind's power of thought, the soul passes to lower perfection and lesser explicitness, and feels sorrow. Thus we see that joy and sorrow are correlatives, they imply each other, neither can exist without the other, and each increases in proportion as the other increases. It is clear that the soul cannot pass to higher perfection, unless it was in a state of lower perfection; and it cannot pass to a state of lower perfection, unless it was in a state of higher perfection. The greater the state of lower perfection from which the soul passes to the state of higher perfection the greater is the soul's joy; and the greater the state of higher perfection from which the soul passes to lower perfection the greater is the soul's sorrow. What is true of man is also true of God. The essence of God is desire. God desires joy. But God can feel joy only when passing to higher perfection. But that God may pass to higher perfection he must first be in a state of lower perfection. Hence, at first God passes to the lowest perfection, he becomes infinite diffused matter. Thus reaching the state of lowest perfection. Then he begins to integrate the diffused matter and create the world, and thus he passes to higher and ever higher perfection. This gives him the feeling of supreme and eternal joy or happiness. All motion in existence is cyclic, rhythmic, up and down, forward and backward, progressive and regressive, life and death, light and darkness, joy and sorrow, and so on ad infinitum. And this gives us an adequate idea of good and evil. Good is the passing to higher perfection which gives rise to joy, evil is the passing to lower perfection which gives rise to sorrow.

What strikes us here is the fact that the primary emotions are a trinity: desire, joy and sorrow. In all manifestations of the Absolute we meet this trinity. Desire, joy and sorrow are the primary emotions from which are derived all other emotions. No matter what the emotion may be, it is only a form of manifestation of desire, joy and sorrow. To understand any emotion, we must analyze it and reduce it to these three primary emotions. We must do with the emotions as we do in the physical sciences; we analyze and reduce any reality to its elementary constituents. What we must carry out from the foregoing is this: joy and sorrow are correlatives, neither can exist without the other, and each grows and develops in proportion as the other grows and develops. The greater the previous sorrow the greater is the subsequent joy; and the greater the previous joy the greater is the subsequent sorrow. This is in conformity with the eternal and infinite law of equivalents. Joy can arise only out of sorrow, and sorrow can arise only out of joy. This being so, reason dictates that we begin with sorrow that we may attain to joy. And this must be done constantly. Just as God renews the process of creation every day, every moment, constantly; so must we renew our effort to earn joy every day, every moment, constantly. And, just as we cannot get anything from existence without paying for it an equivalent, so, once we paid the equivalent, there is nothing in existence that can deprive us of that for which we paid an equivalent. This truth I presented in an adequate manner in my book: Pain and Pleasure—A Philosophy of Life, published by the Marx Institute in 1919.

LOVE AND HATRED

126. What is love? Spinoza defines love as joy accompanied with the idea of the external cause of the joy. We desire joy, and therefore love that which is the cause of our joy. To love, we must have an idea of the cause of the joy, we must think of it; otherwise, we may feel joy, but we shall not love. But what is the external cause? We convinced ourselves that God is the only cause of all infinite effects in existence. How, then, can we love a person or a thing? The answer is this. We love God in all cases, we love God in the person that we love, we love God in the thing that we love. Most men are not conscious of this, and for this reason their love is really an unconscious love and imperfect. But one who knows that God is the cause of all effects, and that by loving a person or a thing he actually loves God, only he truly loves a person or a thing. We saw that desire is absolutely egoistic. Joy and sorrow are correlative manifestations of desire. Since desire is egoistic, joy is egoistic; and, since love is joy accompanied with the idea of an external cause, love is also egoistic. We love a person or a thing, not for the sake of the person or the thing, but because that person or thing is the apparent cause of our joy. Love, therefore, is egoistic. But egoism implies altruism, they are correlatives, and neither can realize itself without the realization of the other. Love is egoistic, and for this very reason it becomes altruistic to realize itself. In proportion as one wants to realize his love for a person or a thing, in that proportion he must endeavor to preserve that person or thing, and to cause the person to feel joy with the idea of himself as the cause; or he must endeavor to preserve the thing and to enhance its value that it may give him joy. Egoistic love grows and develops in proportion as it becomes altruistic; and, in turn, altruistic love grows and develops in proportion as it becomes egoistic. Thus the most altruistic and sublime love is really the most egoistic. When love comprehends God and the whole of existence, then love is absolutely egoistic; for then love identifies itself with

God and the whole of existence, and thus love loves itself. This is the love with which God loves himself. Now, love implies hatred, just as joy implies sorrow. Hence we must now consider hatred.

127. What is hatred? Spinoza defines hatred as sorrow with the accompanying idea of an external cause. Hatred is just the opposite of love. Just as to love we must have an idea of the object of our love, so to hate we must have an idea of the object that we hate. Since God is the only cause of all infinite effects, God is the cause of our sorrow, and therefore God is also the cause of our hatred. We saw that, in loving a person or a thing, we actually love God. It is the same with hatred. In hating a person or a thing, we actually hate God. The question arises: Does God determine us to hate him? The answer is, yes. God determines us to hate him as he determines us to love him. Love is joy, hatred is sorrow. Joy is the passing to a higher state of perfection, sorrow is the passing to a lower state of perfection. God is eternally and infinitely passing to higher perfection, he feels infinite joy and loves himself with infinite love. This infinite love manifests itself in all of existence, and all of existence loves God. But, in turn, God is eternally and infinitely passing to lower perfection, he feels infinite sorrow, and he hates himself. This hatred manifests itself in all of existence, and all of existence hates God. Thus God determines us to love him and to hate him.

Inherent in love is hatred, and inherent in hatred is love; each is a condition to the other. Without love there can be no hatred, and without hatred there can be no love. If we love one thing, we simultaneously hate its correlative opposite. And we hate the correlative opposite in proportion as we love the thing. If we love truth, we hate falsehood; if we love good, we hate evil. Every virtue hates its correlative opposite vice; and only because every virtue hates its correlative opposite vice that virtue triumphs over vice. Thus good triumphs over evil, love triumphs over hatred, joy triumphs over sorrow, and so in all cases. Love and hatred are each egoistic. We saw that egoism realizes itself in proportion as it is altruistic; and altruism realizes itself in proportion as it is egoistic. It is the same with love and hatred. Love realizes itself in proportion as it is altruistic, and hatred realizes itself in proportion as it is altruistic. Hatred is sorrow, and sorrow is the passing to a state of lower perfection. By hating, one retains himself in the state of sorrow and lower perfection. The more one hates, the more he injures himself. Hence, while one that hates means to do harm to the person or the thing he hates, in fact he harms himself. He harms himself for the sake of the person or thing that he hates. This is a negative altruism. But hatred manifests itself in positive altruism. The positive altruism of hatred is this: it actually does good to the person or thing that it hates. The person hated, to ward off the consequences of the hatred, brings to the fore virtues to combat the hatred, which virtues would otherwise remain dormant. Hatred never destroyed truth or virtue. On the contrary, hatred strengthened truth and virtue. This idea was well expressed by Goethe in Faust. He makes Mephistopheles say: I am part of that power which always wants the evil, and yet always effects the good. I am the spirit that always negates, and this rightly so; for all that arises is worth that it be annihilated. And so all that you call sin, destruction, in short, what you call evil, is my proper element. I am part of that which originally was All; a part of darkness, which gave birth to light.

What Mephistopheles said is a profound truth. Without evil there would be no good, without darkness there would be no light, without death there would be no life, without sorrow there would be no joy, and without hatred there would be no love. Consider war. War is an evil, yet war is a condition to peace; without war there would be no peace. I already considered war and peace. But I call attention to a phase of war which is worth considering. Evolution is a process of integration and differentiation. Human progress in all aspects was the result of integration, and principally the integration of mankind. Individuals were integrated into families, families were integrated into tribes, tribes were integrated into federations of tribes, and federations of tribes were integrated into nations. And now the nations are being integrated into super-nations. All integration of mankind was only through war. History shows no instance in which men united voluntarily; they were forced to unite by war. The American nation was born through war, and through the Civil War the American nation was united permanently. And now the nations are uniting into super-nations. The United States, England, Soviet Russia and China—who would never unite, are now united; the present world war united them. And more than fifty nations of the world came to San Francisco to unite upon a world charter to secure the peace in the world. This could come to pass only because of the present world war. And so, while idealists and philosophers condemn war, they never perceived that war was the condition to peace and union among them.

Virtue and Vice

128. What is virtue, and what is vice? Both terms come from the Latin. Virtue comes from the word, vir, meaning man; vice comes from the term, vitium, meaning fault. Virtue is that which is proper to man; and vice is that which it not proper to man. By man is meant a rational person. Hence virtue means that which is proper to a rational person, and vice is that which is not proper to a rational person. Reason dictates virtue, nature dictates vice. Virtue and vice manifest themselves in conduct. Conduct affects, not only others, it also affects the person himself. Conduct which is in conformity with the dictates of reason helps one to attain the good of life; conduct which is dictated by nature prevents one from attaining the good of life. Virtue and vice are correlatives, neither can exist without the other, and each is a condition to the other. Virtue pertains to reason, vice pertains to nature. Virtue is progress, it increases man's power to think and to act; vice is regress, it decreases man's power to think and to act. Self-preservation is the highest virtue;

all other virtues flow from the virtue of self-preservation. Without self-preservation virtue is inconceivable. If one is not concerned about his own self-preservation, he will not concern himself about the self-preservation of others. If one does not desire good for himself, he will not desire good for others; if one does not seek justice for himself, he will not seek justice for others; and so it is in all cases. Self-preservation is absolutely egoistic; but, just because it is absolutely egoistic, it can realize itself only in proportion as it is altruistic. One can preserve himself, attain to the good of life, enjoy peace, security, justice, and the like, only in proportion as he promotes the self-preservation, the good of life, peace, security and justice for others. Man starts out as an animal with an absolutely egoistic self-preservation. The infant just born is absolutely egoistic; it is not concerned about any one or anything; it is concerned only about itself. But in proportion as the infant grows and develops, in that proportion it finds out that, to satisfy its own egoistic self-preservation it must concern itself about the self-preservation of others. In turn, the infant can concern itself about others only in proportion as it concerns itself about itself. Thus man grows and develops in proportion as the virtue of self-preservation grows and develops both egoistically and altruistically. This is true of all living beings. Whatever be the nature of a living being, it possesses the virtue of self-preservation. But, while this virtue is absolutely egoistic, at the same time it is also altruistic. Every living being procreates itself, it either gives its life for the sake of its progeny, or it provides the means for the preservation of its progeny and takes care of them. Life is not only an egoistic struggle for existence, it is also a mutual aid. Most of the living beings are gregarious, and gregariousness is altruism.

Now, the natural man is virtuous as a natural man. But man is destined to become a rational and morally autonomous person. What helps man to realize his destiny is virtue, and what hinders man from realizing his destiny is vice. The animal nature with which man comes into existence is a virtue as far as he is an animal, but it becomes a vice by hindering man from realizing his destiny. The animal nature manifests itself in the passions. The passions in themselves are good, they are the motive powers which serve man's needs. Without the passions, man could no more struggle for his existence and preserve himself than a mechanism could perform its work without a motive power. To the extent that man is still an animal, the passions are a virtue in him. But to the extent that man is destined to realize moral autonomy and become self-governing, to that extent, if not controlled by reason, the passions become vices. Vice becomes a virtue in the same way that hatred becomes a virtue. Vice arouses our indignation against vice, and thus promotes virtue. Thus we see that, from whatever aspect we contemplate good and evil, we find one and the same story. Existence is absolutely one, it is one substance, one essence, one plan and one destiny.

HONOR AND DISHONOR

129. Spinoza tells us: the desire to join others in friendship to himself with which a man living in accordance with the guidance of reason is possessed, I call honor. I call the thing honorable which men who live according to the guidance of reason praise; that thing, on the contrary, I call base which sets itself against the formation of friendship. This means that a rational person possesses the desire that others should join him in friendship. This desire is honor. On the other hand, the want of such desire in the irrational man is dishonor or base. Only a rational person is honorable and possesses honor; an irrational person is neither honorable nor does he possess honor. Honor implies worthiness. Reason honors that which is worthy. But what is worthy which reason honors? Only one thing is worthy, and that is reason itself. Reason honors itself. Hence only a rational person can honor that which is rational. Honor has its correlative, dishonor; they imply each other, and neither can exist without the other. Honor is opposed to dishonor. This opposi-

tion is indignation. Indignation is the revolt of reason against that which is unworthy of a rational person, against that which shows irrationality. Man is destined to become rational, and who is to strive to become rational and to act rationally. But when men act irrationally, when they act in a manner unbecoming a rational person, then reason is indignant against this irrationality.

And now the question is: in what way are honor and dishonor correlatives, in what way are they conditions to each other? Honor is a desire illumined by reason; reason honors that which is rational. Now, man started as an animal, and an animal is irrational, it exists and acts according to the dictates of nature. Originally and for a long time men existed and acted according to the dictates of nature; but men were destined to become rational persons. To realize this, reason had to negate nature in man, it had to manifest an indignation against the irrational animal nature of man. In proportion as this indignation grew and developed in man, in that proportion man endeavored to become rational. In turn, in proportion as man became rational, in that proportion he became indignant against the irrational in men. Cannibals were not indignant against cannibalism and the other cannibals. Slave-owners were not indignant against slavery and the other slave-owners. Exploiters were not indignant against exploitation and the other exploiters. Oppressors were not indignant against oppression and the other oppressors. But in proportion as men became rational, in that proportion they became indignant against all these anti-social vices. Thus we see that honor is desire illumined by reason, dishonor is desire not illumined by reason. Dishonor gives rise to indignation against dishonor, and thus dishonor is negated, and honor affirmed.

Desire is the essence of God and of existence, and this desire is to be recognized, honored and loved. I already spoke of love, and now I will briefly consider honor with relation to this primordial desire. The soul desires to be honored, as it desires to be recognized and loved. Desire is absolutely egoistic, and so is the desire to be honored absolutely egoistic. But egoism implies altruism. The desire for honor, to realize itself, must become altruistic. The desire for honor is absolutely egoistic in every one. Hence, if one wants to be honored, he must first honor others that the others may honor him. And one is honored in proportion as he honors others. Thus egoistic desire for honor becomes altruistic. There is another aspect of honor which I want to consider. For this purpose, we must refer to the Bible. One of the ten commandments is: Honor thy father and thy mother that thy days may be long upon the land which Jehovah thy God giveth thee. What relation is there between honoring father and mother and long life? This involves a deep truth. To live long, we must honor ourselves, we must honor our body, our mind and our soul. And to honor ourselves, we must begin with honoring our father and our mother. When we honor things which we possess, we will use them rationally and properly, so that they may serve us long. When we honor our body, we will use our body rationally, we will take care of it, so that it may live long. When we honor our mind, we will use it rationally, we will feed it with proper mental food, so that it may serve us through life. Finally, when we honor our soul, we will feed it with spiritual food, so that the soul may rise to ever higher perfection. Thus the soul will preserve our body and our mind. A long life is thus bound up with honor, it is bound up with the desire illumined by reason.

Now, we are only a continuation of our father and mother. To honor ourselves, we must begin with honoring our father and our mother. Now, it is natural for children, who are still in a state of natural dialectics, to negate their parents. We saw that natural dialectics negates the previous steps in progress. On the other hand, rational dialectics preserves the previous steps in progress. Children are a further step in progress, therefore children are prone to negate their parents. Children regard their parents as backnumbers, who are to be retired. Every rising generation starts out with a native vanity and conceit, they believe that they are better and wiser than their parents, and they regard their parents as a hindrance to their own progress. Therefore children are prone to dishonor their parents. Hence the significance of this commandment. Honor thy father and thy mother for thy own sake, that thou mayest prolong thy life.

General Observation on Good and Evil

130. All correlatives in existence are but forms of manifestation of good and evil. I have considered some of the emotions. For the purposes of a monistic philosophy it is not necessary to consider all the emotions. Once we have an idea of the primary emotions, desire, joy and sorrow, we can easily understand all emotions. Besides, Spinoza and other philosophers and psychologists already said much about the various emotions. But I want to conclude the subject which we are now considering with a general observation on good and evil.

When we reflect on all human progress, we perceive that all human progress was conceived in evil, and that all through progress was sustained by evil. If there was no evil, there would be no human progress. Men were deprived by nature of the material means of life. Every other living beings comes into existence with the means by which to struggle for its existence, and nature freely supplies them with food and shelter. But man is coming into existence naked, without the means to struggle for his existence and without food and shelter. This was an evil. But this evil compelled man to enter into social relations with his fellow-men and to cooperate with them. This gave birth to knowledge, industry, science and skill. If men had been provided by nature with the means of life as all other living beings are provided, man would remain an animal. Man suffered from sickness. This was an evil. But this evil compelled man to study his body and life generally. This gave rise to the numerous sciences and arts connected with medicine. Man died. Other living beings also die, but they cannot reflect on death. Man alone reflects on death and suffers. But this evil compelled man to reflect on existence and his own destiny. This gave birth to religion, metaphysics, philosophy and ethics. Man brought with himself into society an animal and anti-social nature, which brought him into conflict with the requirements of social life. This was an evil, but this evil compelled him to reflect on the relation between conduct and consequence, the relations between the members of society to one another and to society itself. This gave birth to the perception of right and wrong, good and evil, reward and punishment, and thus men attained to a knowledge and understanding of themselves and their relation to existence. The worst evil that confronted man was the inhumanity of man to man. It is possible to reconcile oneself with all other evils, but it is impossible to reconcile oneself with the inhumanity of man to man. All other evils are more or less extraneous to man, but this evil resides within man himself. But this evil brought out its correlative sympathy. Sympathy is born from the inhumanity of man to man. If not for this evil, man would not know of sympathy. Let us consider a few cases.

Pharaoh treated the Jews inhumanly. Not only did he enslave, exploit and oppress the Jews, but he also commanded that all the male children born to the Jews should be drowned in the river. What was the result? Moses was born. His mother put him into an ark, and put to float on the river. The daughter of Pharaoh went to bathe, she saw the ark, she sent her maid to fetch the ark, and there she saw the child. She adopted the child, and brought it up. The child grew up and became Moses. Pharaoh was inhuman, but this inhumanity gave birth to sympathy in his own daughter, and brought to the world Moses. If not for the inhumanity of Pharaoh, there would have been no Moses, and the Jews would have become assimilated and lost to the world.

Consider another case. At the time of Jesus, the Jews were oppressed, exploited and slaughtered by the Romans. The roads of Palestine were covered with hundreds of thousands of crosses to which were nailed crucified Jews. The Romans treated the Jews most inhumanly. But this inhumanity gave birth to Jesus.

If not for this inhumanity, there would be no Jesus, and the Gentiles would have remained in darkness and corruption and would perish.

Consider the Russians. For a thousand years the Russians were in darkness, they were oppressed and exploited by their lords and masters, and the Czars treated them most inhumanly. What was the result? The result was the Russian Revolution—a revolution which initiated a great step in human progress. If not for the inhumanity of the ruling classes in Russia, there would have been no Russian Revolution. It was the same with the French Revolution. The French Revolution was also the result of the inhumanity of the ruling classes in France. The result was the Great French Revolution, which brought great light and humanity to the world. It was the same with the American Revolution.

Finally, consider this case. The Zionist movement was born of the inhumanity of the Russian government and other backward governments in the world. These governments treated the Jews most inhumanly. At last came the years of pogroms, beginning in 1881. Out of these pogroms grew the Zionist movement. For nearly two thousand years the Jews submitted to their fate, and bore their suffering with resignation and humility. But these pogroms awoke the spirit of the Jews, it inspired them to face the problem of their existence boldly and soberly; they reacquired their self-respect and dignity, and began to assert themselves. Until then, the Jews depended upon the whims of the Gentiles, but now the Jews determined to depend upon themselves.

What was true of these cases was true of all cases. Existence rests on the law of equivalents; there must be a quid pro quo; for everything good we get from existence we must pay an equivalent; and the equivalent we must pay in coins of work, struggle, suffering and death. We must work for the material means of life, we must struggle for knowledge and understanding, we must suffer for spiritual growth and development, and we must die to live. Evil, is the price we must pay for the good we get from existence. It required infinite wisdom in God to create a world in which by means of evil we can secure the good. Since the means with which to secure the good is given to us, we are to be satisfied. If not for evil there would not be good, and without good existence would not be worth while. Even God could not bear an existence in which there was no good. And even God cannot enjoy the good without suffering the correlative evil. When mankind will attain to explicit reason and they will become morally autonomous, then of their own accord they will decree that there shall be evil in existence that good may abound in it. The law of equivalents manifests itself in reward and punishment. Hence we must next consider reward and punishment.

CHAPTER XIX

Reward and Punishment

131. Inherent in life itself is the postulate that between conduct and consequence there is a causal relation. Just as a cause produces an effect corresponding with the nature of the cause, so conduct brings consequences corresponding with the nature of the conduct. Life, as Spencer tells us, is a continuous adjustment of the inner relations to the outer relations. That a living being may exist, it must adjust itself to the conditions of existence, and this means that it must choose such conduct as will realize itself in consequences that will make it possible for the living being to preserve itself. This is especially true of man. Whatever man does consciously, he does to realize some desirable purpose. To realize that purpose, man must choose such conduct as will necessarily realize the desired purpose.

Now, if the relation between conduct and consequence were direct, simple and immediate, then by this time mankind would have known exactly what conduct to choose to realize desired purposes. But, as we saw before, the relation between conduct and consequence is neither direct, nor simple, nor immediate only. First, conduct does not exhaust itself in the immediate consequences. The immediate consequences are followed by remote consequences, and the remote consequences necessarily are different from the immediate consequencs. Second, the relation between conduct and consequence is not simple. Man is a social being; he can exist and realize purposes only within society. Society is a living organism. The members of society are organically bound up with one another and with society. Each member of the society, directly or indirectly, consciously or unconsciously, partakes of the conduct of the other members

244

of society and of society as a whole, and therefore must share
the consequences of their conduct. Hence, a person may be
rational and moral and be guided by reason, while at the same
time the other members of society are neither rational nor
moral, and will therefore bring upon themselves evil consequences. And the rational and moral person will have to share
with them the evil consequences. Thus, while life postulated
that there is a causal relation between conduct and consequence,
experience showed that there is no such relation. Hence
throughout the past the lament was heard: the righteous suffer
and the wicked prosper. Where is the reward for good conduct,
and where is the punishment for bad conduct? This is an old
problem. Profound thinkers bestowed infinite thought on the
solution of this problem, and thus far failed to solve it. Before
I present the true solution of this problem, it is necessary to
consider the solutions suggested by past profound thinkers.
And, first, we shall consider the law of Karma.

132. The law of karma is the moral law of cause and effect
inherent in the relation between conduct and consequence. Just
as there can be no effect without a cause, and there can be no
cause without an effect; so there can be no consequence without
conduct, and there can be no conduct without consequence.
And, just as every cause produces an effect which corresponds
to the nature of the cause, so every conduct produces a consequence which corresponds to the nature of the conduct. Morally good conduct realizes itself in good consequence, morally
bad conduct realizes itself in bad consequence. But we must
notice a fundamental difference between conduct and consequence, on the one hand, and cause and effect on the other
hand. If I take a hammer and with it I crush a piece of rock, the
effect on the rock is far greater than it is on me; I crush the
rock, but I am not crushed. But far different is the case of
conduct and consequence. If I kill a man, the effect on me is
far greater than on the man killed. The man was killed physi-
cally, and his suffering ended with his death; but I am killed

morally, and my suffering will have no end. The crime tainted my soul, I am a murderer, and all the waters in the world will not wash off the blood of the victim from my being. The crime reacted on me, and it became part of my being. The crime realizes itself in my being, and I must atone for my crime. How great is my crime? By killing the man, I affected not only him, but also his wife, his children, his relatives, his friends and society. The effect will extend itself to the children's children and to many generations thereafter. My crime will disturb the peace and security of the rest of the members of society and the integrity of society itself. All this is the consequence of my crime, all this recoils on me, and for all this I will have to atone with my own suffering. Indeed, "the suffering of my sin is too great to bear." And what is true of evil conduct is equally true of good conduct. The good which I do for others reacts on me, I become a better man, and this will bring me great benefit in life.

As stated before, conduct does not exhaust itself in the immediate consequences, the full realization of conduct requires time. It may take a day, a year, a hundred years, a thousand years, or any longer period of time. Reflect on history, and you will see how true this is. The good and the evil conduct of men a thousand years, ten thousand years ago, are still affecting us today. Now, since life is short, and some conduct may require a long time to realize its consequences, it follows that man must become reincarnated again and again until his conduct is fully realized, until he has fully atoned for his crimes. Hence the law of karma implies reincarnation, and reincarnation implies the immortality of the soul. We saw that the soul thinks through the mind and acts through the body, the mind and the body are the only means in the hands of the soul. It is the soul, and not the body and mind, that commits crimes or does good. Therefore the soul must atone for its crime. Since the soul is immortal, the soul may require any number of reincarnations to atone for its crimes. The law of karma is primarily concerned about evil conduct and its consequences.

The law of karma is a moral law, and a moral law implies reward and punishment—a reward for moral conduct, and punishment for immoral conduct. Reward and punishment imply the freedom of the soul to choose its conduct. If man is not free to choose his conduct, he can deserve neither reward nor punishment. But, while the law of karma postulates that man is free to choose his conduct, at the same time the law of karma postulates that man cannot determine the consequences of his conduct. Man is free only to choose his conduct; but, once he chooses his conduct, he becomes subject to the necessity inherent in the relation between conduct and consequence. Between conduct and consequence there is a necessary relation which nothing in existence can change. Hence, a man may possess infinite cunning, infinite knowledge and infinite skill, yet he will not be able to determine that an immoral act shall not realize itself in evil consequences. But this raises the following question.

Suppose that I committed a crime. The crime made of me a criminal and tainted my whole being. Am I after I had committed the crime free to choose my future conduct? This is impossible. By committing the crime I lost my freedom to choose my conduct; from the moment that I committed the crime I became subject to necessity; my criminal nature will now determine me to continue to commit crimes. The ancient Rabbis tell us that the commission of one crime determines one to commit other crimes. Once I commit a crime, my nature has become changed into a criminal nature, and it will manifest itself in more crimes, and the more crimes I commit the more I will continue to commit. As Spencer tells us: motion set up along any line becomes itself the cause of its further motion along that line. Once I committed a crime, and in an eternity I will not be able to atone for it.

133. When we reflect on the past history of mankind, we find that throughout the past mankind suffered infinitely. The law of karma tells us that mankind suffered because of the crimes they had committed. But was there ever a time or a man when

he did not commit crimes? The Bible tells us that God created man in the essence and form of God. Adam, the first man, was therefore free to choose his conduct. Being free to choose his conduct, he could merit reward for moral conduct, and punishment for immoral conduct. For some incomprehensible reason, Adam chose immoral conduct. This was the original sin. Adam had to expiate for his sin. Adam brought into existence children, grandchildren, and so in the course of time an infinite number of human beings descended from Adam. All of them were conceived in sin and were tainted with the original sin. Before Adam committed the original sin he was free to choose his conduct; but afterwards he was no longer free to choose his conduct. And all his infinite descendants, who were conceived in sin and tainted with the original sin, were no longer free to choose their conduct; they were determined by the original sin to commit more sins and crimes. And so, in the course of time, the infinite human beings committed infinite sins and crimes. By all this they incurred eternal damnation, and not in an eternity of suffering will they be able to purge themselves from the taint of the original sin. The question, then, is: How can mankind free themselves from the consequences of the original sin? For thousands of years profound thinkers reflected on this problem, but thus far they did not solve it.

The Hindu theosophists crystallized the following solution. Man is free to choose his conduct, and by this man is free to determine his destiny. Man is the only one who sets in motion the causes of his suffering or happiness. As he sows, so he reaps. Since man is free to choose his conduct, let him choose conduct that is morally good. In the course of time, the consequences of conduct that was morally bad will come to an end, and thus man will free himself from suffering. Let us consider this solution. First. This solution assumes that, notwithstanding the crimes and sins committed by man, he still retains his freedom to choose conduct. But we saw that this is impossible. Once man committed a crime or a sin, and he lost his freedom to choose his conduct. Second. This solution assumes that man can determine his destiny. This means that, when man comes into existence, he has yet no destiny; and, because he has no destiny, he is free to determine his destiny. But this is an illusion. Destiny is not something which hangs in the air, and every one is at liberty to pick up such destiny as he likes. Destiny is inherent in the very nature of man as it is inherent in the very nature of things. Man can no more determine his destiny than an acorn can determine to become an apple tree and reproduce apples. Not the external condition determine the destiny of things or of man; it is the destiny inherent in the nature of things and of man that determines their evolution. When man comes into existence, already in his nature is his destiny. From the moment of inception to the moment of death man goes through an evolution and experiences numerous changes; but all this is determined by the destiny inherent in his nature, and that nature was already determined by God. Man can no more determine himself to become a saint, a philosopher, a poet or a leader of men than he can determine himself to become a bird, a lion or a serpent. When man comes into existence again and again through reincarnation, the crimes and sins which he had committed in his previous existences are already part of his nature, and determine his future conduct. Therefore man is not free to determine his destiny, and he cannot free himself from the taint of original sin. Thus we see that the Hindu theosophists did not solve the problem.

134. Buddha was well acquainted with the Hindu theosophy and the law of karma. Years of deep reflection convinced him that Hindu theosophy did not solve the problem, and therefore rejected it. More years spent on reflecting on this problem led him to the following solution. The cause of all suffering is inherent in the desire to exist. So long as the desire to exist persists, so long will there be suffering. To free oneself from suffering, one must overcome the desire to exist. Once he ceases to exist as a result of his overcoming the desire to exist, he will not be born again, and thus will put an end to all suffering.

It is clear that, once one ceases to exist, he will cease to suffer. But can man cease to desire to exist? This is impossible. First, the law of karma will not permit him to escape the consequences of his sins and crimes by ceasing to exist. The law of karma demands that all crimes and sins be atoned, and for this purpose man will be called into existence again and again until he fully atone for his crimes and sins. Second, man cannot cease to desire to exist. Desire is the essence of man as it is the essence of God. To desire to cease to exist, man must again desire; and thus in every act of desiring desire is asserted. Man can no more by desire cease to exist than he can raise himself by his own bootstraps. The desire to exist is absolute, and it cannot be overcome. On the contrary, the desire to exist overcomes all suffering. No matter how great the suffering may be, yet man desires to exist. Even when a man commits suicide, even then he does not overcome his desire to exist. He commits suicide to overcome an unbearable life, yet the desire to exist remains in him. Since the desire to exist cannot be extinguished, man may commit thousands of suicides, he will be born again and again to atone for his crimes and sins. Religion perceived this profound truth, and therefore all enlightened religions are against suicide. No matter how unbearable life may be, man must accept all suffering, and leave it to God to terminate his present life. Third, the solution that mankind want is not a cessation of existence; they want a solution that shall free them from the taint of original sin, so that they should cease to suffer. Thus we see that Buddha did not solve the problem.

135. Jesus was well acquainted with Hindu theosophy and Buddhism, and he rejected them. Jesus crystallized the following solution. Adam committed the original sin. This tainted the whole human race. Since then mankind were conceived in sin and were tainted with the original sin, and because of this they are helpless. Mankind cannot save themselves from eternal damnation; only God can save mankind from eternal damnation. But even God cannot overcome the law of karma. The law of

karma demands retribution and atonement, it demands that sin and crime be atoned in suffering. The suffering must be just as great as the sins and the crimes are. But who can assume infinite suffering? Only God can assume infinite suffering. Hence God himself must come down to earth, he must assume the infinite crimes and sins committed by mankind, he must suffer for them, and he must die for them. Only in this manner can mankind be saved.

This solution is contrary to the law of karma. The law of karma does not permit vicarious atonement; he that sinned or committed crimes must suffer and atone for the sins and crimes. Next, the solution of Jesus implies that God himself is subject to the law of karma as a law outside of him and above him; it is like the mysterious fate of the ancient Greeks that ruled over the gods. Is the law of karma outside of and above God? If there is a law of karma, then God himself decreed that law. On the other hand, if God wanted to save mankind from eternal damnation, could he not abrogate the law of karma? Could not his infinite love move him to forgive mankind their sins and crimes? Again, how is the law of karma compatible with God's infinite justice and mercy? Suppose that Adam sinned, let him expiate for his sin. But why should his infinite descendants, who did not commit the original sin, be tainted with the sin and suffer? Would we tolerate such law among men? Finally, by the fruit ye shall know. God in human form came down on earth, assumed the sins and crimes of mankind, suffered and died, and thus atoned for the sins and crimes of mankind. The original sin was wiped out, it is no longer in existence. What should follow? Mankind should have regained their original freedom and perfection, and they should continue to live in peace and enjoy the good of life. Nearly two thousand years passed, and mankind remained as they were before. Even Christians, who accepted Jesus as God in human form who suffered and died for their sake, even Christians remained as they were before; they are still tainted with the original sin, they still commit sins and crimes, and they still suffer. What has God accomplished?

Thus we see that Jesus did not solve the problem. And what is true of these solutions is equally true of all other solutions; none of them solved this problem. The question is: Is this problem absolutely insoluble? We shall presently see that the problem can be solved, and here we shall solve it. But, first, we must consider the original sin.

136. The idea of original sin was perceived by mankind long ago. As soon as the light of reason dawned upon the mind of men, they perceived the idea of original sin. Unable to account for the existence of evil, men of thought reached the conclusion that evil is the result of original sin. But who committed the original sin? The only one that committed the original sin was man himself. Thus man was the author of evil and suffering. But is man the only one that suffers? Even animals suffer; and, according to Paul all existence suffers. Are they all suffering because of the original sin committed by man? The perception that evil and suffering are the consequence of an original sin was a very profound perception, but the question remained: who committed the original sin? We shall presently see that no one else committed the original sin but God: God committed the original sin. This is the reason why evil and suffering are inherent in all existence. Not only man suffers, but all existence suffers. Let us consider what the Bible tells us.

The Bible tells us that in the beginning there was darkness, chaos and death, even before God created man. Next, the Bible tells us that God planted in the Garden of Eden the tree of knowledge of good and evil. Thus God planted the tree of evil that brings death, even before Adam committed the original sin. In a previous chapter I quoted a statement of Isaiah, in which he tells us that Jehovah created evil and darkness, as well as light and peace. And so God created darkness, evil and death even before he created man. Why did God create darkness, evil and death? Foolish theologians tell us that God created all this to test man. Did God expect that feeble and helpless man would be able to stand the test? Mark it well. The Bible tells us that evil presented itself to innocent Eve and Adam in an overpowering attractive form. Indeed, evil is always presenting itself to man in an overpowering attractive manner. Would men commit sins and crimes and suffer, if evil was not so attractive? The Talmud and the Kabbalah tell us that the archangels in heaven succumbed to the attraction of evil. And this, too, is a universal tradition. And Milton, a good Christian, makes of this tradition a great epic, The Paradise Lost. Next, God must have known beforehand that man would succumb to evil. Was not his foreknowledge already the determining cause of man committing the original sin? What, then, is the truth of the matter? This we shall presently see.

137. We saw that God could become the world and manifest himself only by first passing to the lowest state of perfection, become infinite diffused matter. By passing to the lowest state of perfection, God passed to a state of suffering. Why did God pass to the lowest state of perfection to suffer? Because he wanted to manifest himself, to be recognized, honored and loved. God was motivated by desire, and he fell from his absolute perfection. This was the original sin. This original sin tainted the whole of existence. But God committed the original sin, he brought into existence darkness, evil, suffering and death that he might rise to infinite perfection and enjoy supreme happiness. This is true of the whole of existence. The whole of existence, together with God, eternally and infinitely passes to lower perfection, evil, suffering and death that it may eternally and infinitely rise to ever higher perfection, live and enjoy together with God supreme happiness. Thus creation was conceived in original sin, evil and death; but the original sin, evil and death became the condition to virtue, good and life and immortality. Whatever is absolute, infinite and eternal is absolute, infinite and eternal in every part thereof. The soul of man is an idea of God, and has the nature of God, and must go through the same process that God goes through. The soul desires to manifest itself, to be recognized, honored and loved. To satisfy this desire, the

soul passes to the lowest state of perfection, it comes down from God to the earth, it assumes a human form, it starts out in an implicit state, that it may thereafter pass to ever higher perfection, become the intellect, and reidentify itself with God. This desire of the soul, is the original sin of the soul. The soul is, indeed, conceived in sin, for desire is sin; but inherent in sin is salvation. Without sin there could be no salvation. The soul sins, goes down to the state of lowest perfection, but because of this it passes to ever higher perfection. And now we will understand the deep truths involved in the solutions which we considered, but which thus far were not understood. Let us reconsider the solutions which we considered.

138. Theosophy postulates that man is free to choose his conduct, and thus determine his destiny. As the theosophists understood this, it is false. We already saw what the truth is. As far as the world and the conditions of existence are concerned, man is free; but as far as God is concerned, man is absolutely determined. Just because God is absolutely determining man, nothing in existence can change man. Therefore, with relation to existence man is free to exist and act as God determined him to exist and to act. Inherent in man is the destiny which God implanted in his nature; there is nothing in existence which can prevent man from realizing his destiny, because God determined it; and therefore it is correct to say that man is free to determine his destiny, provided we always remember that, with relation to God, man is absolutely determined. But theosophy tells us that man is absolutely free to determine his destiny. Indeed, theosophy does not know of God, it starts in the middle of the story. Somehow a human soul came into existence a perfect blank. The soul was free to determine its destiny, but for some mysterious reason, which theosophy does not know, the soul chose the wrong destiny, and therefore brought upon itself suffering. If, however, we brush aside the illusions which abound in theosophy, we can well perceive the profound truth which is the centre of theosophy. The profound truth is this. Since

God determines the existence, the nature and the destiny of man, he is free with relation to existence.

As I stated in a previous chapter, man has a double destiny. First, every man shares the universal destiny of mankind, to become rational and morally autonomous. Next, every man has his special destiny, what he shall be and accomplish in a given life. Both destinies are determined by God, and nothing in creation can change these destinies. The truth involved in theosophy has a practical value. If man knew what his special destiny is, then nothing could help him. Since, however, man does not know what his special destiny is, it is of great service to him to tell him that he is free to determine his destiny. Let him start with this belief, and let him try to achieve greatness. Life will teach him what he is destined to achieve. In all probabilities he will not accomplish much. But the endeavor to accomplish greatness will accomplish something that will be an adequate compensation for the endeavor. As Emerson said. In every instance, hitch your wagon to a star. Man will never reach the stars, yet it is a wise policy to hitch one's wagon to a star.

What is the truth involved in Buddhism? Buddha reached the conclusion that man's salvation lies in the extinction of the desire to exist. We saw that this cannot be realized. Yet this idea contains a profound truth, it is the truth of dialectics of the law of equivalents. To realize desire, desire must be negated. Unless a corn of wheat fall into the ground and die, it abideth alone; but, if it dieth, it bringeth forth an abundance of fruit. He that loses his life, the same shall save it. Whatever the desire may be, to realize it, it must be negated. Suppose one wants to be recognized. To realize this, he must begin by recognizing others, and thus negate himself. Suppose one wants to be honored, he must begin by honoring others, and thus again he negates himself. Suppose one wants to be loved, he must begin by loving others, and thus again negate himself. We considered this before. The very law of equivalents postulates this. To pay in advance the equivalent for what we desire, means to negate oneself. As Jesus said: Whosoever will come after me, let him deny himself, and take up the cross and follow me. This is the profound truth involved in Buddhism, But Buddha did not understand this truth. Buddha reached the conclusion that we must overcome our desire to exist and thus save ourselves from evil and suffering. This is absolutely false. We are not to overcome our desire to exist and strive to save ourselves from evil and suffering. On the contrary, we must assert our desire to exist and cheerfully accept evil and suffering as the price which we must pay for the good which we may realize. Notice the infinite difference between Jesus and Buddha. Buddha taught that we should completely overcome the desire to exist, so as to save ourselves from suffering. But Jesus taught that, while we must begin with denying ourselves, but this only that we may take up the cross of suffering. We must not run away from suffering. On the contrary, we must embrace it, for only through suffering can we pay the equivalent for whatever is good in existence.

139. And now, what truth is involved in the solution of the problem given by Jesus? First, we must notice this. Theosophy and Buddhism concern themselves about the individual soul of man, as if the soul of the individual man is an absolute entity by itself. But this is not the case. It is true that each human being has a soul of his own—a soul which has a destiny of its own; but the souls of all human beings are but the replicas of the primordial soul of man. Hence no single soul of an individual man can attain to salvation without all other souls of all human beings attaining to salvation. All souls are interrelated and responsible for one another. Hence there is no salvation for any individual human being without salvation for all of mankind. And there is no salvation for mankind without salvation for the whole of existence. Just as the soul of an acorn realizes itself in infinite acorns, so the soul of the primordial man realizes itself in infinite human beings. The original soul sinned—it yielded to the desire to exist in the material world, to be recognized, honored and loved. This original soul tainted the souls of all human beings, because all souls desired to exist in the material

world, to be recognized, honored and loved. As this original sin was only part of the original sin of God, it follows that mankind cannot attain to salvation without God himself attaining to salvation. Hence, God must come down to the earth, just as the human soul comes down to the earth, he must suffer, and he must die. In other words, mankind cannot attain to salvation without God; but, in turn, God cannot attain to salvation without mankind. This is the profound truth in the solution of the problem given by Jesus. I say that this solution was given by Jesus, although Christian scholars maintain that this idea was crystallized by Paul. It is not necessary for our present purpose to go into this question. Since the Christians believe that this was the idea of Jesus, for my present purpose I accept their opinion.

There remain two questions. First, since man is determined by God, man cannot deserve either reward or punishment. Why, then, is he rewarded and punished for his conduct? Second, we saw that sins and crimes cannot be atoned for, because they deprive man of his freedom to choose his conduct; how, then, can man emancipate himself from the law of karma? The answer is: God rewards and punishes according to his purpose. If men knew and understood the purposes of God, they would see the reason for reward and punishment in each case. But, since men do not know the purposes of God, reason dictates to accept from God whatever he determines shall take place, convinced that God has a purpose for this, and man should be grateful that God uses him to realize his own purposes. God gives, God takes, let his name be blessed—this is the deepest wisdom. This profound truth was revealed in the Bible. Let us briefly consider what the Bible tells us in the Book of Job.

Job was whole-hearted, upright, feared God and shunned evil. God blessed him with riches, children and honor. God thought very highly of Job. Satan challenged God, and God permitted Satan to inflict on Job suffering, to prove to Satan that Job would remain steadfast in his loyalty to God. Satan inflicted great suffering on Job, he lost his children and all that he possessed, and he was afflicted with leprosy. His friends

came to console him. Then Job began to curse the day
that he was born, and he began to argue, why did God
inflict on him such great suffering, since he never sinned,
and always feared God? His friends argued with him, and
tried to prove to him that God is just, and he does not pun-
ish unjustly; but Job refused to be convinced. In the end,
God appeared to Job and expressed indignation against his
friends for arguing as they did. And God told Job to pray for
his friends that he may forgive them. God restored Job to his
former state, children and wealth. And now the following question arises. The friends of Job tried hard to defend God and
to justify his ways; while Job refused to be convinced; and yet
God was angry, not at Job, but at his friends? Why? This is the
reason. The friends of Job confidently assumed that they knew
the purposes of God and the way he realizes his purposes.
Therefore, if man suffers, it is because he sinned or committed
crimes. But this is the height of presumptuousness. What can
man know of the purposes of God and the ways he realizes
them? True enough, there is a relation between conduct and
consequence; but, first, the relation is neither direct, nor simple, nor immediate; second, it is God who determines man's
conduct and its consequences. To realize his purposes, God
takes time; some purposes may require a century, some a thousand years, and some even an eternity to be realized. Hence it
is absurd to justly judge of conduct by the immediate consequences. Again, God may inflict suffering, not for past sins
and crimes, but as the price for the good that is to follow. The
friends of Job naively believed that they knew everything
about God and his purposes. For this reason God was angry at
them. Judge not that ye may not be judged.

This being the case, wisdom teaches the following. Let man
endeavor to live an upright life, let him endeavor to be honest,
just and kind, and with an abiding faith in God leave to him
to determine the consequences. In everything that man does
God is a silent partner, and he has the deciding voice. This dis-
poses of the old argument, why do the righteous suffer and

the wicked prosper? As to the question, why should the individual suffer for the sins and crimes committed by the other members of society? The answer is plain. Existence rests on the eternal and infinite law of equivalents. The individual derives infinite benefit from society and for this benefit he must pay an equivalent, and the equivalent he must pay by assuming to share the consequences of the conduct of the other members of society. One animal is not responsible for the acts of the other animals, but man is not an animal; one man is responsible for the acts of his fellowmen. Man is indeed his brother's keeper. If one does not want to share the consequences of the acts of the other members of society, the remedy is plain: let him withdraw from society, live in a state of nature like an animal, and become an animal. God uses men, as he uses all other realities and beings, to realize his purposes. If to realize his purposes, he deem it necessary that man shall suffer, that suffering will not be in vain; the reward will inevitably come in due time. Man must have absolute faith in God, and not worry nor quarrel with God. The reward may not come in the present life, but the termination of the present life does not terminate his existence. He will again and again come to life, and the reward which he earned he will inevitably enjoy.

IMMORTALITY

140. In the past, immortality could not be demonstrated, and therefore men had to believe in immortality. But now it is just the reverse; now death cannot be demonstrated, and one must believe in death. Is there anything in existence that dies? Philosophy and science demonstrated that, just as something cannot arise out of nothing, so something cannot disappear into nothing. Matter is indestructible, motion is indestructible, force is indestructible. In all the infinite transformations that take place in existence, nothing is lost and nothing dies. And what is true of all else is infinitely so of an idea. An idea is a living, conscious and thinking soul. The soul of the electric lamp is an

idea, and this idea is eternal. Lamps may come, and lamps may go, but the idea remains. The soul of an acorn is an idea, and this idea is eternal. Acorns may come, and acorns may go, but the idea remains. It is the same with man. The soul of man is an idea of God, and this idea is eternal. Men may come, and men may go, but the soul of man is eternal. When God summons man into existence, he allots the time of his earthly life. When the time comes to an end, the body returns to its source, extension; the mind returns to its source, thought; and the soul returns to its source, God. But this does not end the career of the soul. Just as God eternally and infinitely realizes himself in the material world, so the soul of man must eternally and infinitely realize itself in the material world. The purpose of an idea is to realize itself in material form and to function in the material world. The soul of the electric lamp realizes itself through infinite reincarnations in infinite generations of electric lamps; the soul of an acorn realizes itself through infinite reincarnations in infinite generations of acorns; it is so with insects, with all forms of life, and it is so with man. The soul of man realizes itself through infinite reincarnations in infinite generations of men. Just as God could not exist without realizing himself in the material world, so the soul cannot exist without realizing itself in the material world.

Reincarnation and immortality take place right here on this earth; there is no other kind of immortality for the soul. And those who believed that, after death, their soul will go up to heaven, and there will enjoy eternal bliss, delude themselves. Can they form an idea of what sort of existence that would be? Would they want such an existence? Let them not be vain and conceited. If it is not below the dignity of God eternally and infinitely to live, move and have his being in the material world, it certainly ought not be below the dignity of man eternally and infinitely live, move and have his being in the material world. And do men know of another planet or a star which they would prefer to our beautiful earth? And would they prefer to live among angels rather than among men? And would they prefer an eternity of idleness to an eternity of active cooperation with God in the procreation and improvement of the world? The Bible tells us that God created the world for work, and not for idleness; and Jesus said, my Father works, and so I work. God eternally and infinitely procreates and improves the world, and by this he perpetuates and perfects himself. And thus God passes to ever higher perfection. It is so with the soul of man. Only by work, by creation, by improving the material world does the soul rise to ever higher perfection. Just as the artists perfects himself through the perfection of his work, so the soul perfects itself through the perfection of its work.

141. And now we come face to face with the problem: How will mankind free themselves from the law of karma. The law of karma, as formulated by the theosophists, does not distinguish between a moral act and an immoral act, both acts require equal time to realize themselves. But, if the law of karma is a moral law, it must distinguish between a moral act and an immoral act, and there must be a vast distinction between them. This distinction was perceived by the Jews and the ancient Greeks. Moses told the Jews that Jehovah visits the iniquities of the fathers upon the children and the grandchildren, unto the third and the fourth generation; but the benefits of good conduct extend unto thousands of generations. Likewise, the Greek poets perceived that a crime exhausts itself in the third generation; but they did not perceive the extent of a moral act. Moses perceived an infinitely profound truth. Reflect on history. Thousands of mighty kings, rulers, conquerors and leaders committed infinite sins and crimes. What became of them, their sins and their crimes? In the course of three or four generations they passed out of existence and were forgotten, and no longer affected mankind. Just as a storm comes, breaks down trees and causes destruction in its path, and then passes away, and the earth heals everything and again dresses itself in beauty and glory; so it is with human life. Cruel, wicked and corrupt rulers and conquerors come, bring destruction upon mankind, then pass away,

and mankind regenerate, bring out new generations, and human life again dresses itself in beauty and glory. On the other hand, the moral acts of a Moses, a Jesus, a Plato, a Euclid, a Newton, a Spinoza, and so on—these deeds live for thousands of generations and continue to enrich human life. Pharoah was forgotten, but Moses will live forever; Nero was forgotten, but Jesus will live forever; Hitler is already forgotten, but Marx will live forever. Mighty nations of ancient times were forgotten, but the Jews will live forever. According to theosophy, the law of karma should have degraded mankind ever more until they would become extinct, because one sin causes other sins, and one crime causes other crimes, and so the sins and the crimes multiply infinitely, until they would destroy the human race. But the facts are just the reverse. Mankind always made progress and so long as they are destined to exist on this earth they will continue to make progress. The anthropoids became savages, the savages became barbarians, the barbarians became civilized men, and the civilized men are destined to become rational and morally autonomous persons, and eventually they will all attain to the intellect and realize the destiny implanted by God in their soul. Mankind will at last fully realize the law of equivalents. What all through they regarded as evil, they will perceive is only the price they have to pay for the good that they get from existence. Men will fully identify themselves with God and will completely submit to his will, for their own will will become identified with the will of God. The law of equivalents is a law of just reward and just punishment.

CHAPTER XX

Man and Woman

142. The Bible tells us that God created man in the essence and form of God. Then the Bible tells us that God created man, male and female. This means that God himself is both male and female. And this also means that man is both male and female, and woman is both female and male. The Kabbalah tells us how the Ain Sof—the Absolute—becomes male and female, father and mother. What the Kabbalah tells us is very profound. Indeed, no other system of thought has penetrated into the mystery of existence and creation as profoundly as the Kabbalah. This is not the place for a presentation of the philosophy of the Kabbalah. But for the purposes of understanding the nature of man and woman, and how they manifest the male and female aspects of the Absolute, we must recall what we learned in the previous chapters.

The Absolute is absolute thought—thought without form. The Absolute reflects on itself and, by self-reflection, forms of itself an idea. This idea comprehends the Absolute. An idea is a form of absolute thought. The idea which comprehends the Absolute gives to absolute thought form. This idea is the Infinite Intellect, God. God perceives the Absolute in two aspects or attributes: extension and thought. Thus the Absolute becomes a trinity; The Infinite Intellect, extension and thought. This trinity manifests itself in all infinite realities and processes in existence. Before God combines the attributes, extension and thought, in infinite combinations, giving rise to the infinite realities in existence, these attributes are given a definite form or nature. Extension becomes will, and thought becomes love. The Infinite Intellect is an idea, and we saw that an idea is a living,

conscious and thinking soul; an idea is life itself. This means
that the Infinite Intellect is life. We have then the following
trinity: life, will and love. What are will and love? We will
begin with the consideration of will and love as we find them
in ourselves.

143. We feel the will to be an urge to externalize ourselves, to
come out from the centre of our being outwardly, to objectify
ourselves, to identify ourselves with the external realities. It is
an urge to alienate ourselves from ourselves, to become something else, to realize ourselves in material form. It is a centrifugal force that tends to fly away from the centre. The will
is an urge to expand, extend, to freedom and action. Love is just
the opposite. Love is an urge to internalize ourselves, to withdraw from the external world into the centre of our being, to
subjectify ourselves, to identify ourselves with the essence of
our own being. It is an urge to affirm ourselves within ourselves,
to become more ourselves. It is a centripetal force that tends
to fly towards the centre of our being. The will is a force of
repulsion, love is a force of attraction; the will is a negation,
love is an affirmation; the will negates our being, love affirms
our being.

If these two opposite forces had been left to themselves, they
would separate from each other forever; the will flying further
away from love, and love withdrawing itself from the will. But
will and love are only aspects and correlatives of life itself. Life
therefore holds them together, reconciles them, and determines
them to cooperate with each other. But, if life held the will and
the love in equilibrium, neither will nor love could function,
they would neutralize each other, and then life itself would be
in a state of death. Hence life allows will and love to function
alternately; life first projects the will outwardly and allows it
to function according to its nature, then life asserts love and
allows it to function according to its nature. At first, the will
externalizes and objectifies itself, then love comprehends the
will, brings it back to the centre to internalize and subjectify

itself. Through this cycle of function, life brings out new forms of itself, and thus perpetuates itself. We must now examine the alternation in function of both the will and the love.

I take a rubber-string and attach it to a rubber-ball; the string and the ball are now forming one reality. While holding in my hand the free end of the string, I throw the ball outwardly in a horizontal direction. By this I impart to the ball a momentum that may carry it twenty or more feet from me. But the ball is attached to the rubber-string. And so, while the ball moves outwardly, the string is being stretched; the further the ball moves away from me the more the string is stretched. This produces in the string a tension. A moment comes when the tension in the string exceeds the momentum of the ball; then the string draws the ball back to my hand, and it comes back to its original position. Let us examine what took place. When the ball moved outwardly, it stretched the string; by this the ball negated the string, compelling it to stretch itself against its own tendency to remain as it was. This is the first negation. But in proportion as the ball negated the string it created in the string the power that will negate the ball itself. When the tension in the string exceeded the momentum of the ball, the string then negated the ball, compelling it to return to its starting point against its own tendency to move further away from the starting point. This was the second negation. The result was that the ball came back to its starting point. This is the method of dialectics. Let us now consider the law of dialectics as it manifests itself in the relation between man and woman.

144. Will is masculine, love is feminine; the masculine is negative, centrifugal; the feminine is positive, centripetal. Man and woman are each life, will and love; but in man will is explicit and love is implicit, in woman love is explicit and will is implicit. Man begins as will, he asserts his will, but ends in love. On the other hand, woman begins as love, she asserts her love, but ends in will. Each goes through two negations, but each starts out from the opposite pole. Man begins as an assertion of will.

He is dominated by an urge to fly away from home, from the environment in which he was born and brought up, from himself, to externalize himself, to identify himself with the external world, there to conquer and to achieve. He conceives aims and purposes, he identifies himself with his duties and his tasks, he negates himself, and now lives for something else than himself. But, while man was asserting his will, the love in him was negated, and was compelled to accompany the will outwardly against its own inclination. But, in proportion as the will carries man outwardly and negates him, in that proportion the tension of his love increases. A time comes when the tension of his love exceeds the momentum of his will, and the process reverses itself; now love begins to negate his will and draws man back to his centre. Until this moment, he did not want to hear of love and marriage. But now he begins to feel that all his aims and ambitions can no longer satisfy him; he now begins to yearn for the opposite sex and to seek his happiness in marriage, home, wife and children. He now seeks to meet the proper woman, wins her as his wife, merges into the centre of her being, and then finds joy, rest and peace. Thus man completes a cycle. And now he begins another cycle. He again asserts his will, but this time his will is accompanied by his love. In all that he now does, he thinks of his wife, his children and his home; and, while he still negates himself for the sake of his duties, aims and ambitions, at the same time he affirms himself in his wife, children and home. And thus he becomes ever more pro-social and more comprehensive in his interests.

And now let us consider the woman. She begins as an assertion of love. She is self-centered, subjective, content to remain with her parents, within her environment, and she has no outside aims and ambitions. She dreams of love, and her all-absorbing ambition is to attract a young man and bring him to herself. And while her love thus asserts itself, her will is negated, it remains dormant and content to remain with love. A time comes when the woman attracts the young man she desires, she brings him to herself and into the centre of her being, and she conceives a child. Now a change takes place in her. Until now her will was negated, but now her will asserts itself and negates her love for herself. Through her child the woman asserts her will; by giving birth to children the woman projects her will outwardly and asserts it in the external world, and through her children she conquers and achieves. Now, she begins to concern herself about the external world, she concerns herself about education, economics and politics, and now negates herself for the sake of her children and her husband. And thus, through these cycles, man and woman become enriched in knowledge and understanding and rise ever higher. What is true of man's will and love, is equally true of God's will and love. Let us now reinterpret the process of creation.

145. The Absolute is absolute thought and infinite light. To bring out the world, the Absolute differentiates itself into life, will and love. He projects his infinite will, which becomes infinite extension. The infinite will, moving from the centre of the Absolute to the periphery of infinite extension, moves from absolute explicitness and supreme perfection to complete implicitness and imperfection—from infinite light to infinite darkness. Then the Absolute projects his infinite love. The infinite love comprehends infinite extension, integrates it, clothes it in infinite forms. Extension comprehended by form becomes a reality. Thus were brought out the stars, the planets, the solar systems, and all other infinite realities in existence.

Life appeared on the earth's surface, at first in the form of primordial cells, then life integrated the cells and brought out infinite series of forms of life, one higher than the other, until man was brought out. Man started as an animal, but his destiny was to become a rational and morally autonomous person. The Infinite Intellect took man in hand, raised him ever higher, and will raise him higher and higher until man will attain to the intellect. When man will attain to the intellect, he will perceive that he and God are absolutely one; he will identify himself with God and the whole of existence, and will partake of the infinite joy with which God contemplates himself and existence. Then man will attain to what Spinoza calls the intellectual love of God. Then man will love God with all his heart, all his mind and all his soul, and he will love his fellowmen as himself.

Creation was not from the centre of the Absolute to the periphery of extension. This was entropy, devolution. Creation was from the periphery of extension to the centre of the Absolute. This was evolution and progress, a return to the starting point. While the will of God moved from infinite light and supreme perfection to darkness and imperfection, the love of God moved back to infinite light and supreme perfection. Viewing creation in this aspect, we see how out of chaos and darkness emerged the world; we see the dawn of light and the appearance of life on the earth; we see the infinite forms of life following one another and rising ever higher, until at last man appeared. The last shall be first. Man was the last in creation, but he is the first to lead existence back to light and perfection. The ladder of creation stands on the periphery of infinite extension, and its top reaches the Absolute. The messengers of God go up by this ladder, they reach God, and receive from him divine light and knowledge, and then descend by this ladder to the rest of mankind, bringing to them divine light and knowledge. These messengers saw God face to face, and thus were able to reveal God to mankind. All progress is a return to the starting point, it is a return to God. The progress in astronomy was a return to diffused matter; the progress in physics was a return to the electron, the proton and the photons; the progress in biology was a return to the moneron; the progress in psychology was a return to the subconsciousness; the progress of religion and philosophy was a return to God.

In a previous chapter we considered the various faculties of the human mind, and now we shall see these faculties in another aspect. Will is mass, love is form; will is masculine, love is feminine; the senses are masculine, they bring to us a mass of perceptions; the understanding is feminine, it comprehends the perceptions in definite forms, and thus a knowledge of the phenomenal world is born. Intuition is masculine, it brings to us a mass of perceptions of the transcendental realities; reason is feminine, it comprehends these perceptions in definite forms, and thus is born a knowledge of the transcendental world. When man and women become mature they unite and give birth to a son; so, when intuition and reason become mature, they unite and give birth to the intellect. Intuition is the father, reason is the mother, and the intellect is the son. Thus the primordial trinity now assumes a human aspect; the human aspect thus returns to the starting point. Creation began with the Infinite Intellect, and it culminates in the intellect of man. Once man attains to the intellect, he perceives that his intellect and the Infinite Intellect are one; that is, he and God are one.

We saw that intuition gives birth to religion, and reason gives birth to philosophy. When religion and philosophy become mature, they unite and give birth to the monistic philosophy. We are now prepared to understand religion, philosophy and the monistic philosophy in their deepest signification. In the next chapter I will present religion, philosophy and the monistic philosophy in their deepest aspect.

CHAPTER XXI

Religion, Philosophy and the Monistic Philosophy

146. Religion and philosophy are correlatives, they imply each other; neither can exist without the other, and each grows and develops in proportion as the other grows and develops. Without religion there can be no philosophy, and without philosophy there can be no religion. This means that one cannot be religious without being a philosopher, and one cannot be a philosopher without being religious. To understand religion and philosophy, they must be comprehended with relation to each other and with relation to existence as a whole. We begin with existence.

Existence is eternal and infinite. Eternity and infinity are correlatives, they imply each other; neither can exist without the other, and each grows and develops in proportion as the other grows and develops. Without eternity there can be no infinity, and without infinity there can be no eternity. Correlatives imply each other, each is a condition to the existence of the other. But at the same time correlatives negate each other; and, just because they negate each other, both exist, grow and develop. Eternity negates infinity, and infinity negates eternity; and, just because they negate each other, both exist, grow and develop. Whatever is absolute, infinite and eternal is absolute, infinite and eternal in every part thereof; for the absolute, infinite and eternal cannot be composed of relative, finite and temporary parts; nor can it resolve itself into relative, finite and temporary parts; but eternally and infinitely it is and remains absolute, infinite and eternal in itself as a whole and in every part thereof. What is true of existence as a whole is true of every part of existence. The whole of existence lives, moves and has its being in every part thereof. This means that every reality in existence is inherently absolute, infinite and eternal. Consider the acorn. It appears to be a finite and temporary thing, yet its soul and essence is eternal and infinite. This one acorn, in infinite time and infinite space can become infinite oak trees and reproduce infinite acorns; that is, this one acorn can become eternal and infinite. It is so with all realities in existence. This we considered many times before. But here we are concerned about the relation between eternity and infinity. Philosophers regarded eternity and infinity as two separate and independent attributes of existence; they did not perceive that they are correlatives of each other, and therefore are interdependent. We must now consider the correlation between eternity and infinity. For this purpose we will consider a living cell. Inherent in the living cell is eternity and infinity, for inherent in the living cell is the whole of existence.

147. A living cell divides itself into two cells, the two cells divide themselves into four cells, the four cells divide themselves into eight cells, and so on ad infinitum. All infinite cells originate in the one cell, the one cell becomes infinite cells. Let us consider what is taking place in this process. Through the successive generations the one cell perpetuates itself to eternity; at the same time it extends to infinity. It starts out as one cell and becomes infinite cells. It starts out as a mortal cell and becomes eternal. Thus we see that eternity and infinity are inherent in the cell. The eternity and the infinity in the cell are correlatives, they imply each other, neither can exist without the other, and each is a condition to the existence of the other, and each grows and develops in proportion as the other grows and develops. In proportion as the one cell perpetuates itself through the successive generation to eternity, it extends through the successive generation to infinity. But, while the eternity and the infinity inherent in the cell are correlatives, each being a condition to the other, at the same time they negate each other; and yet, just because they negate each other, the cell becomes eternal and infinite.

That the cell may perpetuate itself to eternity, it must negate its own infinity and the infinity of the successive generations of cells; each must remain finite in extent. On the other hand, that the one cell may become infinite, it must negate its own eternity and the eternity of all successive generations of cells; all must die. But, just because the eternity and the infinity inherent in the cell negate each other, they both become eternal and infinite. What is true of the living cell is true of all realities in existence, and is true of existence itself. Consider another case, and that is the case of numbers. We start with one. The one becomes an infinite number of ones. As the one becomes an infinite number of ones it also becomes eternal. It started out as one, it became two, three, four, and so on ad infinitum. And what is true of all other realities in existence is also true of the human soul. The human soul is an idea of God. Inherent in the human soul is eternity and infinity; the human soul in infinite time can become infinite human beings. But there is a fundamental difference between the human soul and all other realities in existence. All other realities in existence are not conscious of the eternity and infinity inherent in them, but the human soul is conscious of the eternity and infinity inherent in it. The destiny of the soul is to comprehend its own eternity and infinity, the eternity and infinity of existence, and its identity with God. The soul strives to realize its destiny. The conscious striving to realize its eternity manifests itself as religion, and the conscious striving of the soul to realize its infinity manifests itself as philosophy. In religion the soul is concerned about eternity and the future; in philosophy the soul is concerned about infinity and cause. In religion the soul begins with God and ends with God; in philosophy the soul begins with reality and ends with reality. In religion the soul is concerned about its eternity, that is, its immortality; in philosophy the soul is concerned about present existence.

148. Eternity endures through time, infinity extends through space. In existence there is but one time; all realities exist in one

time, they coexist in one time; but in existence there are infinite spaces, each reality exists in its own space; two realities cannot occupy the same space in the same time. And, though Relativity tells us that there are different times, this is so only with relation to different coordinates; but in itself there is but one time. Time is rightly symbolized by a line; it is one straight line. Infinity is symbolized by extent. Eternity is the attribute thought, infinity is the attribute extension. Thought follows in a line, one after the other. Eternity is one and individualistic; infinity is many and universal. Since religion is manifestation of eternity, it is subjective, internal and individualistic; and, since philosophy is the manifestation of infinity, it is objective, external and universal. Religion develops in man individuality; philosophy develops in man universality. Individuality and universality are correlatives, they imply each other, neither can exist without the other, and each grows and develops in proportion as the other grows and develops. In proportion as one develops his power for thought, in that proportion does he develop his power for the knowledge and understanding of existence; and in proportion as he develops his power for knowledge and understanding of existence, in that proportion does he develop his power for thought. The development of the power of thought develops his subjectivity and individuality; and the development of the power for knowledge and understanding develops his objectivity and universality. But, while individuality and universality are correlatives, each being a condition to the other; at the same time they negate each other. And, just because they negate each other, both grow and develop. In striving to become ever more an individual, he withdraws himself from existence, from the external, objective and universal world; he shuts himself in his own thought, and negates the external world. On the other hand, in striving to become universal, he withdraws himself from his own thought, from his inner, subjective and individualistic self. But, just because of this opposition and negation, man grows and develops internally and externally, subjectively and objectively, individually and universally. Since religion is subjective, internal and individualistic, it concerns itself only about the individual; and, since philosophy is external, objective and univeral, it concerns itself about society and universal existence. This means that in proportion as the soul concerns itself about itself it is religious, and in proportion as it concerns itself about existence it is philosophical.

To comprehend eternity the soul functions through intuition, and to comprehend infinity the soul functions through reason. Intuition is individualistic; it perceives realities, but it does not perceive the relations among the realities. Reason is universal; it perceives the relations among realities, but it does not perceive the realities themselves. To use a statement of Kant, intuition without reason is blind, reason without intuition is empty. It is only when intuition and reason cooperate that man knows and understands the realities of existence. This means that eternity and infinity can be comprehended and understood only when intuition and reason cooperate. And we saw that, when intuition and reason become mature and unite, they give birth to the intellect. In the intellect the soul becomes wholly self-conscious and explicit; it is then fully conscious of itself, of existence and of God. This means that, when religion and philosophy become mature, they unite and become the monistic philosophy. Thus the destiny of the human soul is to attain to a true monistic philosophy—a philosophy which comprehends the Absolute, God, existence, man, society and history.

The conclusion is this. One cannot be religious without being a philosopher, and one cannot be a philosopher without being religious. A truly religious person is a true philosopher; and a true philosopher is a truly religious person. But thus far, neither theologians nor philosophers perceived this truth. Hence most philosophers either disregarded religion or were even opposed to religion. On the other hand, most theologians either disregarded philosophy or were opposed to philosophy. Most philosophers rejected religion, because it originated in ignorance and is superstitution; and most theologians rejected philosophy, because it is a vain speculation. We shall presently see that these philosophers and theologians did not understand philosophy and religion. In this respect, the theologians and the philosophers were no higher than the ordinary men are. Let us consider the facts.

149. Man started out as an animal; he had no knowledge and understanding of the nature of things and the phenomena of existence. But inherent in that animal was the destiny that he should acquire a knowledge and understanding of the nature of things and the phenomena of existence. In the course of time, that animal became, in succession, a savage, a barbarian and a civilized man; he acquired ever more knowledge and understanding of the nature of things and of the phenomena of existence, and created for himself a wonderful world. As men acquired knowledge and understanding, that knowledge and understanding differentiated themselves into different branches of knowledge, the principal categories of which are religion and philosophy. Thus both religion and philosophy originated in ignorance. If we are to reject religion because it originated in ignorance, for the same reason we must also reject philosophy, because it also originated in ignorance. But, if we reject religion and philosophy, we will cease to be rational human beings. The philosophers who reject religion, because it originated in ignorance, betray an ignorance of a very fundamental fact, namely: everything in existence originates in its direct opposite. Existence originated in non-existence; light originated in darkness; life originated in death; good originated in evil, and so on ad infinitum. Man himself originated in a dead and corrupted cell. And what about the philosophers themselves? When they were born, they were ignorant of any knowledge and understanding. And yet, in the course of time, they became philosophers. And what is true of every thing in existence is also true of knowledge. Knowledge can arise only out of ignorance. Hence the fact that religion originated in ignorance is no more reason for rejecting it than the fact that philosophy and science originated in ignorance is a reason for rejecting them. But this is not all.

The philosophers reject religion, because it is superstition. It is true that religion is superstition, but what about philosophy itself, is it not, like religion, superstition? What is superstition? First, superstition is knowledge; without knowledge there can be no superstition. Superstition is a certain kind of knowledge; men must know something to be superstitious. Knowledge involves truth; without truth there can be no knowledge. This means that superstition involves truth; without truth there can be no superstition. But why is this superstition? It is superstition, because it is inadequate knowledge; the truth involved in superstition is inadequately understood. But bear this in mind. Inadequate knowledge in itself is not superstition. If I have an inadequate knowledge of something, and I know it is inadequate, and regard it as inadequate, it is not superstition. It becomes superstition when I believe that the knowledge is adequate and I take it as adequate knowledge. And this is the case of religion and philosophy. Let us consider the facts.

150. Philosophy assumes that it has an adequate knowledge of cause, of substance, of time, of space, of matter, of motion, of force, of life, of thought, of feeling and so on. But what does philosophy know about all these aspects of existence? Philosophy has of all these aspects only vague and inadequate knowledge. And yet philosophy assumes that it has adequate knowledge of all these aspects of existence. The very fact that philosophy begins with an Unknowable and ends with an Unknowable, this alone shows that philosophy has no adequate knowledge of anything in existence. And yet philosophy boasts of possessing an adequate knowledge of existence, and looks with contempt upon religion. Next, what does philosophy know about religion. The philosopher concerned about infinity is entirely ignorant of eternity. Philosophy was not able even to form an idea of eternity. Philosophy may know something of what is, but it has no idea of what is to become. Hegel tells us that philosophy, like the owl of Minerva, takes its flight at the setting of the sun; that is, when the day has already passed.

According to Hegel, philosophy can comprehend the past and the present, but not the future. Since philosophy cannot comprehend the future, it cannot comprehend eternity, and therefore cannot understand religion. Hence, when the philosophers reject religion, they only betray their own ignorance.

And what about religion? Religion assumes to have an adequate knowledge of God, and of his plan and his purpose and of what he desires men should believe and do; religion assumes that it has an adequate knowledge of the human soul, that it is immortal, and that after the death of the body the soul will go up to heaven and there enjoy eternal bliss; or, if man sinned, the soul will go down to hell and there suffer eternal damnation. Religion assumes that it has an adequate knowledge of the freedom of man to determine his existence, his thoughts, his feelings, his actions and the consequences of his actions. But what does religion know about all these things? It has only inadequate and confused knowledge of all these things. And yet it presumes to have an adequate knowledge of these things, and speaks with absolute authority. Is not this superstition? Again, what does religion know about philosophy? What does religion know about the infinity of existence? What does it know about cause, substance, time, space, matter, motion, force, light, life, thought, feeling and so on? Thus we see that both, religion and philosophy, are superstitions. Can religion exist without philosophy; can men live on religion alone? Suppose there was no philosophy, then there would be no science, for philosophy prepared the ground for science. If there was neither philosophy nor science then there would be no men to have religion, then there would be no religion. Thus we see that the philosophers were wrong when they rejected religion, and the religious were wrong when they rejected philosophy.

But there remains this question: Why are ordinary men opposed to philosophy? This is the answer. Whatever is beyond our perception and above our understanding we negate, we declare that it either does not exist or it is not worth considering. We negate this to relieve ourselves of an unbearable consciousness of incompetency and inferiority; this consciousness strikes at the essence of our being and is unbearable. To admit that there is a thing which exists and which is worth knowing, and yet not be able to know and understand it, is to admit that he is incompetent and inferior to other men who do know and understand this thing. Hence, he persuades himself that either the thing does not exist or that it is not worth knowing. Now, ordinary men have not yet developed to such degree of explicit reason to understand philosophy, to reflect philosophically on existence. Philosophy is the language of explicit reason. Since ordinary men cannot understand philosophy, they negate philosophy; they persuade themselves that philosophy is only a vain speculation, and it is not worth bothering about.

Now, it is true that philosophy is speculation; philosophy is not like science. Science deals with matters that can be counted, weighed, measured, tested and experimented. But philosophy deals with matters that cannot be counted, weighed, measured, tested and experimented. Again, science works with concrete tools, but philosophy works with the tool of speculation, it has no other tools. The ordinary man does not realize this. He believes that mankind could get along without philosophy. But this is an illusion. Without philosophy there would be no science, and without science there would be no mankind. Let us consider this more closely.

Primitive men did not speculate. To live, they had to act, they had to produce the means of life—food, shelter and clothing. To produce, they had to know and understand the nature of things. For this purpose they were endowed with faculties for work, knowledge and understanding. To do anything, men had to find out the nature of matter, motion, force, light, heat, and so on. But how could men acquire this knowledge and understanding? They had to speculate on the nature of things; that is, they had to begin with speculation. The result of the speculation was definite knowledge and understanding. Thus philosophy, by speculation, made science, art and industry possible. And all through history, philosophy prepared the ground for science, art and industry. But the ordinary men do not realize this; and, not being able to understand philosophy, they reject philosophy. But, while ordinary men may be excused, theologians cannot be excused; they should have known better. And for theologians to reject philosophy because it is vain speculation is a confession of incompetency.

151. Religion rests on faith and tradition; philosophy rests on knowledge and proof. Faith and knowledge are correlatives, and so are tradition and proof correlatives. What is true of all correlatives is also true of these correlatives. We must now consider these correlatives.

Faith and knowledge are correlatives, they imply each other; neither can exist without the other, and each grows and develops in proportion as the other grows and develops. At the same time they negate each other. And, just because they negate each other, both grow and develop. Whatever man does is to realize some purpose or aim. The purpose or aim will be realized in the future, may that future be the next day, the next year or any remoter future time. Again, to realize any purpose or aim means to overcome difficulties and obstacles. Hence, to realize any purpose or aim, one must first have faith that he will overcome the difficulties and obstacles. Without faith, men cannot undertake to realize any purpose or aim. The higher the purpose or aim and the greater the difficulties and obstacles to be overcome the greater must be the abiding and sustaining faith. But faith alone is not enough. To realize any purpose or aim, men must have a knowledge and understanding of the nature of things and the order of existence. Hence, again, to realize any purpose or aim, men must have both faith and knowledge. Thus faith becomes a condition to knowledge, and knowledge becomes a condition to faith. But, while faith and knowledge are each a condition to the other, at the same time they negate each other; and, just because they negate each

other, both grow and develop. When men conceive a purpose
or an aim, they want to realize it at once; in their imagination
they already see the purpose or aim realized. But as soon as men
begin to realize their purpose or aim, they at once discover that
they do not have sufficient knowledge and understanding of
elements and conditions involved in the realization of the purpose or aim. And here begins a very painful process. The realization of the purpose or aim is constantly postponed ever further, because of the painful discovery that sufficient knowledge
and understanding is lacking. Hence, faith is opposed to knowledge; faith is impatient with the necessity to acquire knowledge.
Faith says: The kingdom of God is at hand; but knowledge says:
The kingdom of God will be realized only "in the end of days,"
when mankind will acquire sufficient knowledge and understanding. Thus faith is opposed to knowledge and negates it.
In turn, knowledge negates faith. Faith is blind; it perceives the
purpose or aim, but it does not see how the purpose or aim
can be realized. For this reason, knowledge is impatient with
faith and negates it. Yet without faith to begin with men
would not endeavor to acquire knowledge. Consider the present
world situation. The nations united for the purpose of establishing an enduring world peace. The nations came together by
faith; they had faith in the possibility of realizing peace on
earth and good will towards men. But as soon as they came
together they at once discovered that they were lacking in
knowledge and understanding of the elements and the conditions involved in the problem. It will take them a long time
before they will solve the problem, and they will acquire much
knowledge and understanding of the problem of war and
peace. But all this knowledge and understanding will result
from the prior faith. If the nations did not have this faith, they
would not come together and they would not struggle to
acquire the knowledge and the understanding required to
establish an enduring peace in the world. Thus we see that
without faith there would be no knowledge, and without
knowledge there would be no faith; and, just because they

negate each other, both grow and develop. The greater the faith the greater will be the resulting knowledge; and the greater the knowledge the greater will be the faith in the possibility of realizing purposes and aims. What is true of faith and knowledge is equally true of tradition and proof.

152. Tradition and proof are correlatives, they imply each other; neither can exist without the other, and each grows and develops in proportion as the other grows and develops. At the same time, they negate each other; and, just because they negate each other, both grow and develop. What is tradition? Tradition is the handing down by one generation to subsequent generations of a fact, event or truth experienced or perceived. The fact, the event or the truth was misunderstood and misinterpreted, yet it was a fact, an event or a truth. The subsequent generations accepted the fact, the event or the truth because in their own experiences the fact, event or truth was confirmed. If they were not confirmed, the subsequent generations would not accept them, and they would not hand them down to their subsequent generations. The subsequent generations also misunderstood and misinterpreted the fact, the event or the truth, yet they remained to be a fact, an event or a truth. Thus in the course of time a tradition was established. How was it established? It was established by proof; the proof was given in the experiences and perceptions of the subsequent generations. Thus we see that tradition rests on proof. In turn, proof rests on tradition; without a tradition there can be no proof. Spinoza tells us that truth, like light, makes itself manifest. Indeed, truth is like light; but, just as light can manifest itself only to him who has eyes to see; so truth can manifest itself only to him who has eyes to see. But not all men possess eyes to see all kinds and degrees of truth. If, indeed, all men had eyes to see all kinds of truths, then mankind would already possess the knowledge of infinite truths of all kinds and degrees. Now, there always were men of exceptional mental and spiritual endowments, who perceived new truths. How

could these men communicate these truths to mankind? Mankind were not able to perceive these truths, and yet they accepted these truths. How was this accomplished?

Let us consider a recent concrete case, and that is the case of relativity. How was relativity accepted by mankind? Einstein perceived the truth of relativity. He communicated it to some of the scientists, who were able to understand it. These scientists had many followers who had confidence in them. These followers could not at once understand the theory of relativity; but because they had confidence in these scientists they accepted the theory of relativity. There was a time, and that not long ago, when it was said that in the world there were no more than a dozen scientists who understood relativity. Once there were a dozen scientists who understood the theory of relativity, then hundreds of thousands of educated men accepted the theory, although they did not adequately understand it. And, once the scientists accepted the theory, then mankind accepted it, although they not even now understand the theory. Thus we see that the theory of relativity was established by tradition. So it was with all theories that enriched human knowledge and understanding. When we reflect on human progress, we perceive that all truths and theories were accepted by mankind on faith and tradition. What about Judaism, Christianity, Evolution, Marxism, Dialectics, Relativity —how many men ever were or are that understood or understand these systems of thought? And yet countless millions of human beings accepted them; they accepted them on faith and tradition. This was true of philosophy, science, art and economics, and it was true of all branches of human knowledge. Thus we see that tradition rests on proof, and proof rests on tradition.

Consider another case. Suppose a book is handed to you. You do not know who the author of the book is. You at once look at the title page to see who the author is. If you find that the author has some title, such as professor, doctor, and the like; you will take the book and read it. And even if you do not at once understand the contents, you will persist to read it, until you begin to understand the book. But, if the author has no such titles, the probabilities are that you will not read the book. What does this mean? When you see that the author has some title, this means that the author has a tradition. Some university, some professors or scholars, attested to the fact that the author is a learned man, he is a thinker, he knows the subject. This tradition is enough to induce you to read the book. But, if the author has no title, this means that he has no tradition to sustain him, then you will not read the book. Consider another fact. Christianity was at first accepted by the ignorant and the poor. They saw and heard Jesus preach sermons to them. They could not understand what Jesus spoke, but they liked Jesus, they had faith in him, and they accepted his sermons, although they did not understand them. Many years passed, and thousands of the ignorant and the poor accepted the doctrines of Jesus, although they did not understand them. Only then, when a tradition was already established, only then did the learned and the thinkers take up the doctrines of Jesus for study and reflection, and only then did they discover that the doctrines of Jesus were profound and true. So it was with Judaism, so it was with Marxism, and so it was with all religious, philosophical and scientific truths. Truth rests on tradition, and tradition supplies the basis for proof.

153. Tradition rests on faith, proof rests on knowledge. That men should accept a truth, they must first have faith in the man who communicated the truth. But between them there is an opposition. Once men accept a truth on faith, they do not want to be disturbed by proof, because they are not capable of understanding the truth. Then their attitude is: *Credo quia absurdum est*—I believe because it is absurd; that is, I believe though it seems to be absurd. Since he has faith in the truth, he does not need any proof of it. But, once the truth is accepted on faith, men grow up to the truth, and then they want also to understand it. Then their attitude becomes: *Credo ut intelligam*

—I believe that I may understand. Thus tradition negates proof, and proof negates tradition; but, just because both negate each other, both grow and develop. Religion rests on faith and tradition, and is therefore opposed to knowledge and proof. On the other hand, philosophy rests on knowledge and proof, and is opposed to faith and tradition. The tree of knowledge of good and evil, that is, the knowledge of affirmation and negation, is the tree that brings death to religion; but this very tree brings life to philosophy. But, because philosophy is a condition to religion, and religion is a condition to philosophy, this very tree of knowledge of good and evil brings life to both religion and philosophy.

The conclusion is this. There can be no religion without philosophy, and there can be no philosophy without religion. The understanding of religion depends upon and involves the understanding of philosophy; and the understanding of philosophy depends upon and involves the understanding of religion. This means that one cannot be religious without being a philosopher, and one cannot be a philosopher without being religious. And, when both religion and philosophy are adequately understood, they become the monistic philosophy. This truth about religion and philosophy was perceived by profound thinkers long ago. But I will conclude with a statement of Professor Huxley. He said:—

True science and true religion are twin-sisters, and the separation of either from the other is sure to prove the death of both. Science prospers exactly in proportion as it is religious; and religion flourishes in exact proportion to the scientific depth and firmness of its basis. The great deeds of the philosophers have been less the fruit of their intellect than of the direction of that intellect by an eminently religious tone of mind. Truth has yielded herself rather to their patience, their love, their single-heatedness, and their self-denial, than to their logical acumen.

CHAPTER XXII

Miracles, Laws of Nature, Prophecy and Prophets

154. Religion rests on miracles, philosophy rests on the laws of nature. A miracle is an event that transcends the laws of nature; by the laws of nature a miracle cannot be explained. Philosophy rejects miracles as being superstition. On the other hand, religion cannot sustain itself on the laws of nature. We shall presently see that religion does not understand the laws of nature, and philosophy does not understand miracles. Miracles and the laws of nature are correlatives, they imply each other; neither can exist without the other, and each grows and develops in proportion as the other grows and develops. Hence, philosophy is superstitious when it rejects miracles, and religion is superstitious when it rejects the laws of nature.

Miracles and the laws of nature imply a cause that determines the existence of things and the events that take place. When in the laws of nature we can see the cause of what exists or takes place, we consider it natural; it is natural for the thing to exist or to take place. But, when in the laws of nature we cannot see the cause of what exists or takes place, we call it a miracle. Philosophy postulates that whatever exists or takes place is determined by a cause according to the laws of nature, and therefore there are no miracles. On the other hand, religion postulates that some things exist or take place not according to the laws of nature, and therefore are miracles. Both views are superstitions. We saw that superstition is inadequate knowledge. Inadequate knowledge in itself is not superstition; it becomes superstition when it is taken as if it were adequate knowledge. And this is exactly what both religion and philosophy do; they take inadequate knowledge as if it were adequate knowledge. Let us first consider religion.

155. Religion postulates that some things exist or take place not according to the laws of nature. How does religion know this? Does religion know all about infinite and eternal existence? When we reflect on the progress of mankind, we see that the progress consisted in this: the more knowledge of existence mankind acquired the more laws of nature they discovered; and so long as mankind will increase their knowledge of existence the more laws of nature they will discover. And when, and if, mankind will acquire an adequate knowledge and understanding of all infinite aspects of existence, then they will discover that all existence in all its infinite and eternal aspects proceed according to the laws of nature. Hence the philosophers are right when they say that everything in existence exists or takes place according to the laws of nature; and therefore there are no miracles in existence. When, therefore, religion speaks of miracles, it confesses that it does not know much about the laws of nature. Religion is therefore superstitious; it regards its inadequate knowledge as if it were adequate.

In turn, philosophy is also superstitious. Philosophers see stars, planets and other heavenly bodies existing and moving in space; they exist and move according to the laws of nature. Again, philosophers see seeds becoming plants reproducing seeds of its own nature, and this takes place according to the laws of nature. Philosophers see a human seed becoming a human being, the human being grows and develops, acquires knowledge and understanding, brings out philosophies, sciences, arts and industries, and creates for himself a wonderful world. All this takes place according to the laws of nature. Hence the philosophers see no miracles in existence. And now, granting that whatever exists or takes place exists or takes place according to the laws of nature, the question is: and what about the laws of nature themselves? Do they exist and take place according to the laws of nature? Did the laws of nature determine themselves to exist, did they determine their nature? The laws of nature are only manifestations of a cause—a cause which determined their existence and nature; what are called laws of nature are only effects of that cause. The so-called laws of nature only show how that cause determines things to exist and to take place, not according to the laws of nature, but according to the determination of that cause. But what is that cause, and how does that cause determine things to exist and to take place? This the philosophers do not know. The philosophers begin with an Unknowable. Since the philosophers do not know that cause, and they do not know how that cause determines things to exist and to take place, and yet tell us that everything exists and takes place according to the laws of nature, they take inadequate knowledge as if it were adequate knowledge, therefore they are superstitious. What do the philosophers know about existence, do they have an adequate knowledge of all infinite and eternal aspects of existence? How can they assert that everything in existence exists or takes place according to the laws of nature, when they know so little about existence? Let us consider the matter more closely.

156. I take a number of different seeds and plant them in the ground. All seeds are planted in the same ground; they are all subjected to the same laws of nature, the same sunshine, the same rains water them, the same winds blow over them, and the same elements feed them; and yet from the different seeds will come out different plants, which will reproduce different seeds. What determined the different results? By the laws of nature this cannot be explained, because the same laws of nature affected them all alike. What, then, determined the different results? The answer is this. The difference was determined by the difference in the forms of life inherent in the different seeds. But it will be said, the difference in the forms of life itself was determined by the laws of nature. Then the following question presents itself. What is life itself? The philosophers do not know what life itself is. Since they do not know what

life itself is, how do they know that the laws of nature determined the difference in the forms of life itself? Perhaps it will be said that the difference in the forms of life was determined by evolution. What, then, is evolution? Evolution is not a cause; evolution is only the way a cause works; evolution itself is only an effect of a cause. What cause determined evolution? Philosophers cannot tell. Since the philosophers do not know the cause that determined evolution and the differences in the forms of life, they do not know whether this takes place according to the laws of nature or as a miracle. Since, however, they assert that this takes place according to the laws of nature, they are superstitious.

Let us now go a step further. Why is a law of nature natural? Who said that a law of nature must exist? Why is it natural that stars, planets and other heavenly bodies should exist and move in space? Why is it natural that a seed should become a plant and reproduce seeds of its own kind? Why is it natural that a human seed should become a human being, acquire knowledge and understanding and create a world for himself? Why is it natural that a world should exist altogether? Why is it natural that matter, motion, force, time, space, light, heat, and all other infinite aspects of existence should exist? Who told the philosophers that it is natural for existence to exist? Neither existence itself nor anything in existence is either natural or necessary; but what is neither necessary nor natural is a miracle. Hence the existence of existence as a whole and the existence of everything in existence are miracles. Existence came into existence before there were any laws in existence, before there were any natural laws. Hence existence did not come into existence according to the laws of nature; it was existence that determined the laws of nature. Likewise, the continued existence of existence is determined, not by the laws of nature, but by existence itself; and, again, the continued existence of anything in existence is determined, not by the laws of nature, but by existence itself. Finally, the nature and existence of the laws of nature are determined, not by the laws of nature, but by existence itself. And that which is determined by existence transcends the laws of nature, and is therefore a miracle.

157. What, then, are the laws of nature? The laws of nature do not exist outside of the realities of existence, and which determines the realities to behave in a certain manner; the laws of nature are immanent in the realities themselves. In what consists the immanence of these laws? It consists in the form of the realities, for form determines function. How do we attain to a perception of a law of nature? Through the observation of the behavior of the realities. When realities behave uniformly in time and space, the uniformity of behavior we call a law of nature. But this uniformity of behavior is determined by the uniformity of the forms of the realities. It is the *uni-formity* of the forms of the realities that determines the uniformity of their behavior. When two or more realities are *uni-form*, that is, when they have the same form, they behave in the same manner. It is this *uni-formity* of the realities that determines the uniformity of their functions, and this constitutes the law of nature. So long as a reality retains its form, so long will it behave in the same manner. When its form is destroyed, then it no longer behaves in the same manner, and then the same law of nature no longer manifests itself through this reality. The laws of nature, therefore, are immanent in the forms of the realities. But the forms of the realities exist only in the phenomenal, material world. Hence the laws of nature pertain only to the phenomenal, material world, the world of material realities. Outside of the phenomenal, material world there are no laws of nature. What is called nature is nothing else than the phenomenal, material world. But the phenomenal, material world is not the only world in existence. Besides the phenomenal, material world there is a transcendental world— the world of ideas. The transcendental world is the original world, and the phenomenal, material world is only the manifestation of the transcendental ideal world. Since an idea belongs to the transcendental world, the nature of an idea is

not determined by the laws of nature. It is the destiny of an idea to realize itself in the phenomenal world in a material form. But to realize itself in the phenomenal world in a material form, the idea must conform with the forms of the material realities. This means that the idea must conform with the laws of nature. But, while the idea must conform with the laws of nature, the nature of the idea is not determined by the laws of nature—the nature of the idea was already determined in the transcendental world. Hence every idea realizes itself in the phenomenal world according to its own nature, although at the same time it conforms with the laws of nature.

The essence of a seed is an idea. Take an acorn, its essence is an idea, which is transcendental. Inherent in that idea is its destiny to become an oak tree and to reproduce acorns a thousandfold. All this is anterior to and independent of the laws of nature. But, when the idea inherent in the acorn begins to realize itself in the phenomenal world in a material form, it becomes subject to the laws of nature. It is so with all realities in existence. Thus the transcendental world is anterior to and independent of the phenomenal, material world. But, when the transcendental world realizes itself in the phenomenal, material world, it becomes subject to the laws of nature. Since what transcends the phenomenal, material world and the laws of nature, the transition of the transcendental world into the phenomenal, material world is a miracle—a miracle which realizes itself in accordance with the laws of nature. Thus we see that the transcendental world is a world of miracles, and the phenomenal, material world is a world of the laws of nature. And thus we also see that miracles and the laws of nature are correlatives, they imply each other, and neither can realize itself without the other. Without an idea there would not be a material reality, and without realizing itself in a material reality the idea cannot realize itself. And now we shall understand why religion believes in miracles, and why philosophy recognizes only laws of nature. Religion deals with ideas pertaining to the transcendental world, therefore it recognizes miracles.

But philosophy deals with material realities pertaining to the phenomenal world, recognizing only the laws of nature. Adequately to understand this, let us consider a few historic cases.

158. I begin with the Russian revolution. The Russians were involved in the first world war that started in 1914. They suffered overwhelming defeats, and the Czar was compelled to abdicate. The government was taken over by the Constitutionalists, who hoped to form a constitutional monarchy. In the meantime the soldiers abandoned the battle-field and began to return home. The economic system collapsed, and great numbers of workers were thrown out of employment. The Constitutionalists could not continue the war, and they could not establish order in Russia. The Constitutionalists were compelled to retire, and their place was taken by the Mensheviki. In the meantime ever larger masses of workers and soldiers found themselves out of employment, and they became revolutionary. The Mensheviki tried to continue the war and to bring order in Russia, but they failed. This prepared for the Bolsheviki to seize power. The Bolsheviki at once withdrew from the war, and proclaimed the revolution. The reactionary forces in Russia combined with the reactionary forces outside of Russia to destroy the revolution and the Bolsheviki. The followers of the Bolsheviki were few, poor and inadequately prepared for the struggle. On the other hand, the reactionary forces in Russia and outside of Russia were rich, numerous and powerful, and were well prepared for the struggle. Against the Bolsheviki were arrayed the powerful nations of the world: Germany, England, France, the United States, Japan, and many other nations. Notwithstanding this, the Russian revolution was victorious, and gave birth to Soviet Russia. Since then Soviet Russia fought successfully against its enemies, against poverty and ruin, and against the backwardness of the Russian people. When, after a long and bloody struggle, Soviet Russia succeeded to establish itself, it became involved in a life and death struggle with the most powerful nations in the world.

The nazi and the fascist nations destroyed more than two-thirds of European Russia, they destroyed infinite property and wealth, and killed out tens of millions of men, women and children. Notwithstanding all this, the Russian people came out of this frightful war victorious, and the powerful nazi and fascist nations were completely defeated. And now Soviet Russia is the most powerful country in the world.

How can this be explained? By the natural laws this cannot be explained, because the natural laws did not determine the course of events. According to the natural laws, the Russian revolution should have been drowned in blood, and yet the Russian revolution came out victorious. Was it natural that there should have been a Russian revolution? There were many other countries which were backward, and where the people were exploited, oppressed and degraded; why were there no revolutions there? Again, if the Russian revolution was inevitable according to the laws of nature, why did not the philosophers foresee it? And even after the Russian revolution broke out, the philosophers did not foresee that the Russian revolution would be victorious. On the contrary, they expected that the Russian revolution would fail. Why did they predict the downfall of the Russian revolution? Again, when Hitler came into power and announced his determination to destroy Soviet Russia, all European powers, directly and indirectly, gave Hitler help to build up a powerful war machine, so that he should be able to destroy Soviet Russia. The ruling powers of the European countries were convinced that Nazi Germany, Fascist Italy and their allies would destroy Soviet Russia. According to the laws of nature this was inevitable. And yet, not Soviet Russia was conquered, but Nazi Germany, Fascist Italy and their allies were conquered. All this cannot be explained by the natural laws. This was why the philosophers and the statesmen pursued a suicidal policy.

159. What, then, is the truth about the Russian revolution? This is the truth. The Russian revolution proceeded according

to the laws of nature, yet it was a miracle. The miracle consisted in this: an idea realized itself in the phenomenal, material world in accordance with the laws of nature. What was this idea? This was Marxism. An idea originates in the transcendental world, the world of ideas. An idea has a nature of its own, which is anterior to and independent of the laws of nature. The destiny of an idea is to realize itself in the phenomenal world in a material form and in accordance with the laws of nature. In realizing itself in the phenomenal world, the idea is not determined by the material world nor by the laws of nature, because the nature of the idea was already determined in the transcendental world before it began to realize itself in the phenomenal, material world. Marxism, Nazism and Fascism are different ideas, and each idea strives to realize itself in the phenomenal, material world according to the nature of the idea, and yet in accordance with the laws of nature, and therefore the results are different, just as the results of different seeds are different. The realization of an idea is a miracle, yet the idea realizes itself in accordance with the laws of nature. By the laws of nature we cannot explain the origin and nature of Marxism; but by the laws of nature we can explain how Marxism realized itself in the phenomenal, material world. Thus we see that miracles and the laws of nature are correlatives, they imply each other; neither can exist without the other, and each grows and develops in proportion as the other grows and develops. Without a transcendental idea, nothing will realize itself in the phenomenal, material world; but without the laws of nature an idea cannot realize itself in material form. Thus every event is both a miracle and a law of nature. Philosophers and historians can show how, in accordance with the laws of nature, Marxism realized itself in the Russian revolution; yet it was a miracle, because the laws of nature did not determine the origin and nature of Marxism, and they did not determine that Marxism should succeed so wonderfully through the Russian revolution. Philosophers and historians begin in the middle of the story, they always begin with the Unknowable.

Somehow, out of a clear sky, Marxism appeared, somehow it
spread, and somehow it accomplished a great revolution, not
only in Russia, but also all over the world. How naive and
childish this is! Is not this superstition? And now let us consider
another historic event.

160. About two thousand years ago, somewhere in a small
country and among a small people, a man appeared by the
name of Jesus. He was a poor carpenter and an ordinary man;
he was not educated at the schools, he did not know of the
philosophies of his time, and he had no connections with influen-
tial people. This poor carpenter took it into his head the idea
that he was called into existence to bring salvation to mankind.
What a pipe dream! What intelligent person would listen to
him! The scholars, the philosophers and the wise men either
ignored him or they ridiculed him with his pipe dreams. And
so he went to the poor, the ignorant, fishermen, beggars, the
unwashed and the unkempt, and preached to them the gospel
of salvation: the kingdom of God is at hand. These poor,
ignorant and derelicts of society, who had nothing to lose,
listened to Jesus. They did not understand what he was talk-
ing to them, but they liked him and they followed him. Suppose
the philosophers and the scholars would listen to him, would
they see anything in his pipe dreams? They would regard him
as crazy and would pay to him and his pipe dreams no attention. Yet what followed? By the fruit ye shall know. Half of
the human race, constituting the Christian world, already follow that poor carpenter; and in due time the rest of mankind
will follow him. And how strange and wonderful it is that,
since Christianity was recognized by Constantine, countless
millions of Christians—philosophers, scholars, poets, as well as
ordinary men, discovered profound, sublime and divine truths
and wisdom in the utterances of Jesus, the poor carpenter—
utterances which the philosophers and the scholars despised and
rejected. Verily, the stone which the builders despised and
rejected became the chief corner stone of modern civilization.

There were and still are many millions of Christians who would throw out all philosophies and all sciences to retain the utterances of Jesus the carpenter; nay more, they would rather give their life to preserve for mankind the utterances of Jesus. How can this be explained? By the laws of nature this cannot be explained, because the laws of nature did not determine this miracle. What was there in the laws of nature that Jesus should have come at all; what was there in the laws of nature that salvation to mankind should come at all? But now that this miracle already happened, now the philosophers and the historians can trace the process and show that it happened in accordance with the laws of nature. True enough, the rise and spread of Christianity proceeded in accordance with the laws of nature, yet it was a miracle, the miracle was that a transcendental idea realized itself in the phenomenal, material world in accordance with the laws of nature. Without conforming with the laws of nature, Christianity could not realize itself; but without the transcendental idea, the laws of nature would be of no avail, there would be neither a Christianity nor a Christian world.

161. And now let us consider another case. About four thousand years ago a man appeared by the name of Abraham. He conceived the idea that he was called into existence that he and his descendants should become a blessing to the human race. What a crazy pipe dream! Suppose the philosophers and the historians were present and heard what Abraham believed concerning himself and his descendants, what would they think of Abraham? And yet, his pipe dream was realized. Four thousand years passed and, behold, Abraham and his descendants became a blessing to more than half of the human race: The Jews, the Christians and the Mohammedans are the ones who are blessed through Abraham. In due time, the whole human race will share in the blessing. How can this be explained? By the laws of nature this cannot be explained, because the laws of nature did not determine this. Not the laws of nature brought out Abraham, not the laws of nature put the idea into the mind

of Abraham that he and his descendants will become a blessing to mankind, and not the laws of nature realized this. All this was a miracle; but this miracle, like all miracles, could realize itself only in accordance with the laws of nature. Now the philosophers and historians can trace the history of the spread of Abraham's idea in accordance with the laws of nature; but the realization and the origin of this idea was a miracle.

And, finally, we come to consider the miracle of miracles. Long, long ago, an animal anthropoid took it into his head to stand up on his legs and walk. What a crazy idea! Who ever heard that an animal should stand up and walk? This animal also took it into his head that he would become a rational human being and create a wonderful world for himself. Suppose that the philosophers and the historians were present when this animal stood up on his legs and declared that he would become a rational human being and create for himself a wonderful world, what would they think of him? They would think that he is not even fit for a lunatic asylum. And yet, this animal made good his idea. This animal, in the course of time, became a savage, a barbarian and a civilized person; he acquired an understanding; he brought out the philosophies, the sciences, the arts and the industries, and created for himself a wonderful world. And he is not yet through with his job; he plans to become a superman, a rational and morally autonomous person, and realize the kingdom of God on earth, where he will live in peace and enjoy the good of life. How can this be explained? By the laws of nature this cannot be explained, because the laws of nature could not determine that this should take place. This miracle had its origin in the transcendental world, and there its nature and destiny were determined. This was a miracle—a transcendental idea realized itself in the phenomenal, material world in accordance with the laws of nature. Without this miracle there would be no human race; and without the laws of nature this miracle could not realize itself.

Thus we see that miracles and laws of nature are correlatives; they imply each other, neither can realize itself without the other; the greater the miracle is the greater is the service which the laws of nature render, and the greater the service which the laws of nature render the greater is the miracle. Thus we see that religion and philosophy perceived truths, but they did not adequately understand them; and, because they did not adequately understand these truths, both of them were superstitious. When, however, we understand both miracles and the laws of nature, then we comprehend religion and philosophy in one monistic philosophy, and then we emancipate ourselves from superstition.

PROPHECY AND THE PROPHETS

162. What is prophecy? Much has been said and written about prophecy, but thus far the true nature of prophecy has not been understood. Maimonides wrote much about prophecy, and the conclusion he reached is this. Prophecy implies philosophy, philosophy is a condition to prophecy, one must first be a philosopher to become a prophet. But Abravanel, Crescas and others disagreed with Maimonides. They asked: If philosophy is a condition to prophecy; if one must first be a philosopher to become a prophet, then Plato, Aristotle and the other great philosophers should have been the greatest prophets, and yet they were not prophets. On the other hand, the great Jewish Prophets were not known to have been philosophers. The critics of Maimonides reached the conclusion that prophecy is a direct gift from God. When God endows one with the gift of prophecy, he will be a prophet, though he is not a philosopher. When we consider the philosophers and the prophets, we see that this is true. Consider the modern philosophers, beginning with Spinoza and ending with Bergson or Dewey. We find that they were not prophets, although they were philosophers. Hegel tells us that philosophy, like the owl of Minerva, takes its flight at the setting of the sun, that is, when the day has already passed away into the past. This means that philosophy

can look backwards but not forwards; philosophy can understand what has already existed, but it cannot foresee what will exist. Thus Hegel explicitly tells us that a philosopher cannot be a prophet. And so, in his Philosophy of History, he tells us wonderful things about the past; but, when he comes to the future, he draws the curtain, and declares: Nihil Ulterius, nothing more. Philosophers usually tell us that they are neither prophets nor the sons of prophets, and that it is foolish to prophesy.

We thus have two opposing views. On the one hand, Maimonides tells us that philosophy is a condition to prophecy; on the other hand, his critics tell us that prophecy is independent of philosophy. Which view is correct? We shall presently see that both views are correct; they are only two aspects of one and the same truth. We shall see that philosophy is a condition to prophecy, and prophecy is a condition to philosophy; to be a prophet, one must be a philosopher; and, to be a philosopher, one must be a prophet. Finally, we shall see that the great Jewish prophets were both great philosophers and great prophets. To understand this, we must again refer to religion and philosophy.

163. Existence is eternal and infinite. What is eternal and infinite is eternal and infinite in every part thereof. The soul is eternal and infinite. Being eternal and infinite, the soul strives to comprehend the eternal and the infinite. The striving of the soul to comprehend the eternal gives rise to religion; and the striving of the soul to comprehend the infinite gives rise to philosophy. We also saw that religion and philosophy are correlatives, each is a condition to the other. In proportion as the soul comprehends the eternal aspect of existence, in that proportion it comprehends the infinite aspect of existence; and, in turn, in proportion as the soul comprehends the infinite aspect of existence, in that proportion it comprehends the eternal aspect of existence. The infinite exists now and it existed through all the eternal past, but the infinite does not yet exist in the future. On the other hand, the eternal existed in the past,

it exists now, and will exist in all eternal future. Hence, when the soul endeavors to comprehend the eternal, it comprehends the future, and the comprehension of the future is prophecy. But the comprehension of the future is in proportion to the comprehension of the past and the present. This means that prophecy is in proportion to philosophy, and this means that philosophy is a condition to prophecy. This justifies the view of Maimonides. But his critics maintained that prophecy is independent of philosophy; prophecy is a direct gift from God, and they were right. Not only the poet is born and not made, but also the philosopher, the prophet, the scientist, the artist, the statesman, the revolutionary and the leader, each is born, and not made. God determines, not only the existence of every one, but also what he shall become. No one can determine himself to become a Moses, a Jesus, a Spinoza, a Shakespeare, a Newton, an Edison, an Einstein, a Marx or a Lenin; nor can society determine all this. Society can determine who shall be a tailor or a carpenter, but not who shall become a genius and create great works. This is determined by God, and it is God who determines whether the philosopher shall also be a prophet or not.

And now the question is: Were the Jewish great Prophets also great philosophers? The answer is, yes. Consider the following. The great Jewish Prophets, from Moses down to the last of the Prophets, spoke in the name of Jehovah; they told us the history of creation from the very beginning to the end, beginning with light and ending with man; they told us of the history of mankind, and they told us of the destiny of mankind; they told us that the destiny of mankind is that all shall attain to the knowledge and understanding of Jehovah, identify themselves with Him, and realize the kingdom of God on earth, live in peace and enjoy the good of life. All this implies the highest and most universal philosophy of existence. No great philosopher ever attained to such high and universal philosophy as the Jewish Prophets attained. The great Jewish Prophets comprehended, not only the past and the present, they also comprehended the eternal future. And how wonderful, that their prophecies concerning the future were, are and will be realized. Put all other philosophers together, and they will not reach the height, extent and depth of the great Jewish Prophets. Thus we see that the Jewish Prophets were, not only great prophets, but also the greatest philosophers. And thus we see that, just as one is religious in proportion as he is a philosopher, so one is a prophet in proportion as he is a philosopher; in turn, just as one is a philosopher in proportion as he is religious, so one is a philosopher in proportion as he is a prophet. And this brings to the question what is the function of the prophet?

164. The function of the prophet is not merely to foretell the future; his function is far more than this. His function is to achieve a revolution in the life of mankind. To achieve a revolution, the prophet must destroy the old and create the new. To destroy the old, he must fully realize that the old has no longer any reason for existence, that it has become an evil, and must be destroyed. To create the new, he must foresee what the new will be and must be. Hence, a prophet must be a revolutionary as well as a philosopher. The Prophet Jeremiah tells us of the nature and function of the prophet. This is what he tells us:—

> And the word of Jehovah came unto me, saying: Before I formed thee in the belly I knew thee; and before thou camest out of the womb I sanctified thee; I have appointed thee a prophet unto the nations.

Thus Jeremiah tells us that he was born to become a prophet; Jehovah brought him into existence to be a prophet. Next, Jeremiah tells us the following:—

> Then said I: Ah, Adonai Jehovah, behold I cannot speak, for I am a child. But Jehovah said unto me: Say not, I am

a child, for to whomsoever I shall send thee thou shalt go; and whatsoever I shall command thee thou shalt speak. Be not afraid of them, for I am with thee to deliver thee.

Here Jeremiah tells us that, once Jehovah brings out a prophet, he must function as a prophet; he cannot refuse to perform the function which Jehovah appointed him to perform, even if that will bring upon him suffering and death. Then Jeremiah tells us further:—

Then Jehovah put forth his hand, and touched my mouth; and Jehovah said unto me: Behold, I have put my words in thy mouth; see I have this day set thee over the nations and over the kingdoms: To root out and to pull down, and to destroy and to overthrow; to build and to plant.

And first, the prophet does not of his own accord conceive the ideas which he is to struggle and realize; they are imparted to him by God. Second, the prophet is called into existence to root out, to pull down and to destroy and to overthrow what is old, useless and a hindrance to the further progress of mankind. Next, he must build and plant, he must build a new world, and plant in it good seeds that good fruit may result. What Jeremiah tells us is true of all prophets. A prophet must be a philosopher and a revolutionary. Consider Marx. Marx, in the first place, was a philosopher, a follower of Hegel and a great student of philosophy. In the second place, he was a prophet, he clearly foresaw the inevitable destiny of mankind —one human society resting on universal communism, living in peace and enjoying the good of life. Finally, he was a revolutionary. And this was the case of the great Jewish Prophets: they were prophets, they were philosophers and they were revolutionaries. And this is the test. If one is only a philosopher, and is neither a prophet nor a revolutionary, then he is not a great philosopher. Consider Plato, Aristotle, Spinoza, Hegel, Kant, and the like; they were neither prophets

nor revolutionaries, and therefore they were not great philosophers. The true prophet cannot reconcile himself with what
exists, when what exists is already useless and an evil; he
struggles to destroy that, so as to clear the terrain for the new
and the good. In the prophet, philosopher and revolutionary—
all in one—man realizes his destiny.

And thus we completed the story of creation. We started
out with the Absolute and ended with the complete man. This
completed man is only an idea in the transcendental world;
this idea has to realize itself in the phenomenal, material world
in accordance with the laws of nature. Our next step is to follow up the process that realizes this transcendental idea in the
phenomenal and material world in accordance with the laws
of nature. The idea of the completed man must become a
human society and go through a process of history and evolution. Hence, our next subject will be society. This I will
consider in the next volume.